Sport and Christianity

Sport and Christianity examines sport and Christianity from a variety of historical perspectives, with the main focus on the period from the nineteenth to the early twenty-first centuries.

The book is not limited to a narrow definition of Christianity, but rather encompasses a wide range of denominations, related philosophies and viewpoints. The contributors are international, and the geographical range of their chapters is equally wide, extending, for example, from China to Argentina, and from Australia to Poland. Some chapters focus on a single sport such as gymnastics, soccer or Australian Rules football, while others look at modern sports more generally. Different methodological and theoretical approaches have been adopted, as contributors enter the debates on topics as varied as cultural imperialism, gender, changing Christian attitudes to leisure, or the intersection between religion, politics and sport.

Demonstrating the many-sided significance of the relationship between Christianity and sport, this book is ideal for scholars of Sport History and Christianity. This book was originally published as a special issue of *The International Journal of the History of Sport*.

Hugh McLeod is Emeritus Professor of Church History at the University of Birmingham, UK.

Nils Martinius Justvik is Associate Professor of History at the University of Agder, Norway.

Rob Hess is Adjunct Associate Professor with the Institute for Sport and Health at Victoria University, Melbourne, Australia.

Sport in the Global Society: Historical Perspectives
Series Editors: Mark Dyreson, Thierry Terret, and Rob Hess

Titles in the Series:

Sport in the Americas
Local, Regional, National, and International Perspectives
Edited by Mark Dyreson

Sport and Protest
Global Perspectives
Edited by Cathal Kilcline

A Half Century of Super Bowls
National and Global Perspectives on America's Grandest Spectacle
Edited by Mark Dyreson and Peter Hopsicker

Sport in Socialist Yugoslavia
Edited by Dario Brentin and Dejan Zec

The Olympic Movement and the Middle East and North African Region
Edited by Mahfoud Amara

Sport Development and Olympic Studies
Past, Present, and Future
Edited by Stephan Wassong, Michael Heine and Rob Hess

Match-Fixing and Sport
Historical Perspectives
Edited by Mike Huggins and Rob Hess

Sport and Christianity
Historical Perspectives
Edited by Hugh McLeod, Nils Martinius Justvik and Rob Hess

For more information about this series, please visit:
https://www.routledge.com/Sport-in-the-Global-Society—Historical-perspectives/book-series/SGSH

Sport and Christianity

Historical Perspectives

Edited by
Hugh McLeod, Nils Martinius Justvik, and Rob Hess

LONDON AND NEW YORK

First published 2020
by Routledge
2 Park Square, Milton Park, Abingdon, Oxon, OX14 4RN

and by Routledge
52 Vanderbilt Avenue, New York, NY 10017

Routledge is an imprint of the Taylor & Francis Group, an informa business

Foreword, Introduction, Chapters 1, 3–6 © 2020 Taylor & Francis

Chapter 2 © 2018 Alexander Maurits and Martin Nykvist. Originally published as Open Access.

With the exception of Chapter 2, no part of this book may be reprinted or reproduced or utilised in any form or by any electronic, mechanical, or other means, now known or hereafter invented, including photocopying and recording, or in any information storage or retrieval system, without permission in writing from the publishers. For details on the rights for Chapter 2, please see the chapter's Open Access footnote.

Trademark notice: Product or corporate names may be trademarks or registered trademarks, and are used only for identification and explanation without intent to infringe.

British Library Cataloguing in Publication Data
A catalogue record for this book is available from the British Library

ISBN13: 978-0-367-36906-4

Typeset in Minion Pro
by Newgen Publishing UK

Publisher's Note
The publisher accepts responsibility for any inconsistencies that may have arisen during the conversion of this book from journal articles to book chapters, namely the inclusion of journal terminology.

Disclaimer
Every effort has been made to contact copyright holders for their permission to reprint material in this book. The publishers would be grateful to hear from any copyright holder who is not here acknowledged and will undertake to rectify any errors or omissions in future editions of this book.

Contents

Citation Information		vi
Notes on Contributors		viii
Series Editors' Foreword		x
Mark Dyreson, Thierry Terret, and Rob Hess		
	Introduction: Sport and Christianity: Historical Perspectives Hugh McLeod, Nils Martinius Justvik and Rob Hess	1
1	Gymnastics, Physical Education, Sport, and Christianity in Germany Michael Krüger	8
2	A Sportful History of Christianity: The Case of Twentieth-Century Sweden Alexander Maurits and Martin Nykvist	26
3	Cultural Imperialism, Nationalism, and the Modernization of Physical Education and Sport in China, 1840–1949 Huijie Zhang, Fan Hong and Fuhua Huang	42
4	Mormon Missionaries and the Emergence of Modern Argentine Sport, 1938–1943 Ryan A. Davis	60
5	'Necessary Cessation from Toil and Work': Young Christian Workers and the Question of Sport on Sundays in Post-War Melbourne Melissa Jean Walsh and Nicholas Thomas Shaw Marshall	86
6	'If God Be for Us, Who Can Be Against Us?': Religion and Religiousness in Polish Football, 2008–2017 Michał Mazurkiewicz	107
	Index	121

Citation Information

The chapters in this book were originally published in *The International Journal of the History of Sport*, volume 35, issue 1 (2018). When citing this material, please use the original page numbering for each article, as follows:

Introduction
Sport and Christianity: Historical Perspectives
Hugh McLeod, Nils Martinius Justvik, and Rob Hess
The International Journal of the History of Sport, volume 35, issue 1 (2018), pp. 1–8

Chapter 1
Gymnastics, Physical Education, Sport, and Christianity in Germany
Michael Krüger
The International Journal of the History of Sport, volume 35, issue 1 (2018), pp. 9–26

Chapter 2
A Sportful History of Christianity: The Case of Twentieth-Century Sweden
Alexander Maurits and Martin Nykvist
The International Journal of the History of Sport, volume 35, issue 1 (2018), pp. 27–42

Chapter 3
Cultural Imperialism, Nationalism, and the Modernization of Physical Education and Sport in China, 1840–1949
Huijie Zhang, Fan Hong and Fuhua Huang
The International Journal of the History of Sport, volume 35, issue 1 (2018), pp. 43–60

Chapter 4
Mormon Missionaries and the Emergence of Modern Argentine Sport, 1938–1943
Ryan A. Davis
The International Journal of the History of Sport, volume 35, issue 1 (2018), pp. 61–86

Chapter 5
'Necessary Cessation from Toil and Work': Young Christian Workers and the Question of Sport on Sundays in Post-War Melbourne
Melissa Jean Walsh and Nicholas Thomas Shaw Marshall
The International Journal of the History of Sport, volume 35, issue 1 (2018), pp. 87–107

Chapter 6
'If God Be for Us, Who Can Be Against Us?': Religion and Religiousness in Polish Football, 2008–2017
Michał Mazurkiewicz
The International Journal of the History of Sport, volume 35, issue 1 (2018), pp. 108–121

For any permission-related enquiries please visit:
www.tandfonline.com/page/help/permissions

Notes on Contributors

Ryan A. Davis is Professor at Illinois State University. The author or co-editor of three books on the cultural history of Spain, his current research explores the place of minority religions (e.g. Mormonism) in Spain and Latin America.

Rob Hess is Adjunct Associate Professor with the Institute for Sport and Health at Victoria University, Melbourne, Australia.

Fan Hong is Professor in Asian Studies at Bangor University, UK. Her main research interests are in the areas of culture, politics, gender and sport, and she has published extensively in these areas.

Fuhua Huang is Professor at the School of Physical Education and Sports, Jinan University, Guangzhou, China. His main research interests are globalization and sport, the professionalization and commercialization of sport, sport history and traditional sports.

Michael Krüger is Professor at the University of Münster in Westfalia, Germany. His main research interests are in sport pedagogy and sport history, especially political, cultural, and ethical impacts of movement, physical education, gymnastics and sport.

Nicholas Thomas Shaw Marshall is a PhD candidate at the Institute for Health and Sport at Victoria University, Melbourne, Australia.

Nils Martinius Justvik is Associate Professor of History at the University of Agder, Norway.

Alexander Maurits is Senior Lecturer in Church History at the Centre for Theology and Religious Studies, Lund University, Sweden. In his research, Maurits has, among other things, written about ideals of masculinity, household ideologies and the use of history.

Michał Mazurkiewicz is Associate Professor at Jan Kochanowski University in Kielce, Poland. He has published widely on sport and religion. His most recent book is *Sport and Religion: Muscular Christianity and the Young Men's Christian Association. Ideology, Activity and Expansion (Great Britain, the United States and Poland, 1857–1939)*, published 2018.

Hugh McLeod is Emeritus Professor of Church History at the University of Birmingham, UK.

Martin Nykvist is a PhD student in Church History at the Centre for Theology and Religious Studies, Lund University, Sweden. He has published on the relations between religion and sport, as well as on gender constructions in the Church of Sweden.

Melissa Jean Walsh, PhD, contributed to the establishment of the Young Christian Workers (YCW) Archive in 2013, coordinating the Archive and YCW Oral History Project until late 2017.

Huijie Zhang is a postdoctoral researcher in the Department of History, Jinan University, Guangzhou, China. Her main research interests are in the areas of sports history, especially Christian involvement in sports in modern China, and traditional sports.

Series Editors' Foreword

Sport in the Global Society: Historical Perspectives explores the role of sport in cultures both around the world and across the timeframes of human history. In the world we currently inhabit, sport spans the globe. It captivates vast audiences. It defines, alters, and reinforces identities for individuals, communities, nations, empires, and the world. Sport organizes memories and perceptions, arouses passions and tensions, and reveals harmonies and cleavages. It builds and blurs social boundaries – animating discourses about class, gender, race, and ethnicity. Sport opens new vistas on the history of human cultures, intersecting with politics and economics, ideologies, and theologies. It reveals aesthetic tastes and energizes consumer markets.

Our challenge is to explain how sport has developed into a global phenomenon. The series continues the tradition established by the original incarnation of *Sport in the Global Society* (and in 2010 divided into *Historical Perspectives* and *Contemporary Perspectives*) by promoting the academic study of one of the most significant and dynamic forces in shaping the historical landscapes of human cultures.

In the twenty-first century, a critical mass of scholars recognizes the importance of sport in their analyses of human experiences. *Sport in the Global Society: Historical Perspectives* provides an international outlet for the leading investigators on these subjects. Building on previous work and excavating new terrain, our series remains a consistent and coherent response to the attention the academic community demands for the serious study of sport.

Mark Dyreson,
Thierry Terret,
and Rob Hess

Sport and Christianity: Historical Perspectives

Hugh McLeod, Nils Martinius Justvik and Rob Hess

ABSTRACT
This paper provides an overview of a collection of works related to sport and Christianity from historical perspectives. After a brief general historiographical introduction, the material connected to the burgeoning field of sport and religion is summarized. In particular, it is noted that the works concentrate on diverse geographic locations and different time periods. The investigations are not limited to a narrow definition of Christianity, but encompass a wide range of denominations, related philosophies, and viewpoints. In terms of variety, it is noted that different methodological and theoretical approaches are adopted, and, given the existing state of play, it is clear that there is still much to be uncovered, documented, and written about when it comes to the enduring topic of sport and Christianity. The conclusion is that any research agenda which emerges from observations on historical perspectives concerning the relationship of sport with aspects of Christianity will continue to resonate and add value to wider understandings of sport, culture, and the human condition.

> ... [W]hile there is a significant amount of scholarship on sports and Christianity, there is a distinct lack of primary empirical research in the area.
>
> Nick J. Watson and Andrew Parker[1]

This collection of papers had its genesis at the 'Inaugural Global Congress on Sports and Christianity', which was hosted by the Faculty of Health and Life Sciences at York St John University, England, 24–28 August 2016. Convened by Nick Watson, the ambitious aims of the Congress, as set out in the programme, were to:

- Encourage global collaboration between academics, practitioners, politicians, clergy, administrators, and athletes
- Produce quality academic and practitioner publications that have societal impact
- Through intentional mentoring and collaboration, develop individuals in their sphere of influence

- Affect a 'culture shift' in modern sport through the sharing of ideas and practices and a 'coming together' of individuals from across the academic disciplines and all streams and denominations of Christianity, culminating in an inclusive and ecumenical event.[2]

The Congress was comprised of 12 'thematic strands', one of which was 'Historical Perspectives on Sports and Christianity'.[3] A relatively small number of papers were presented on the day that this strand was scheduled, and the strand leaders (the authors of this paper and editors of the volume) agreed to elicit additional items by means of a further call for papers on the website of *The International Journal of the History of Sport*. While no specific theme was nominated, the editors encouraged the submission of papers on topics associated with sport, history, and Christianity from a range of temporal, geographic, methodological, and thematic perspectives. As it transpired, the process of peer-review and the final selection of submitted papers has produced a more than suitable palimpsest of material, reflecting a strong diversity of viewpoints, in part helping to address the dearth of 'primary empirical research' identified and bemoaned by Watson and Parker in their systematic, and exhaustive, review of relevant literature published in 2014.[4]

This is not to suggest that the field is barren. In fact, the general intersections between sport and religion have attracted unprecedented academic interest in the last two decades, and readers are directed to the recent works of Watson and Parker for an impressive mapping of the published material as it relates to sport and Christianity.[5] Special issues of sport history journals devoted to sport and religion are also not new, as evidenced, for example, by a hefty multilingual 2009 volume of *Stadion* devoted to ' … a stimulating historiographical debate on the relation between sport and religion'.[6] Indeed, conferences dedicated to investigations of related themes, in some cases tied to the launch and activities of associated research centres (such as the Centre for Sport, Spirituality and Character Development at Neumann College, Philadelphia, in the United States, and the Centre for the Study of Sport and Spirituality at York St John University College, York, in England), pre-date the 2016 Congress at York. And, of course, serious academic analysis (inclusive of philosophical considerations of play and leisure) by trail-blazing historians and sociologists can be traced back at least to the first half of the twentieth century.[7]

With the partial exception of Michael Krüger's paper, the concern here is with the years from the later nineteenth to the early twenty-first centuries. This period saw the emergence of the modern sporting world, including the global diffusion of the world sports of today, commercialization and professionalization, and increasing international competition. Five themes have been prominent in histories of Christianity and sport in this modern sporting world. First, much has been written about the movement known as 'muscular Christianity' which arose in the 1850s and 1860s in Britain and the United States, the countries in which a high proportion of the world sports of today have their origins.[8] Second, historians have examined the role of the churches in relation to the rather different lines of sporting development in many parts of continental Europe. These differed in two major ways from the 'Anglo-Saxon' pattern: gymnastics played a larger role, and for a time were more important than team-sports ('English Sports' as they were sometimes called); and politics shaped sport much more directly in such countries as France or Germany than in Britain or the United States. The politics often had a major religious dimension. In France, for example, in the early twentieth century, sport was mainly organized through three mutually antagonistic federations, Republican, Catholic, and Socialist.[9] Third, an important theme of sports history in recent years has been the part played by Christian missions and schools in the diffusion of European and American sports in Asia, Africa, and Latin America.[10] Fourth, historians have shown how sport offered an arena in which rivalries between different Christian denominations and different religions, or between Christians and Secularists, could be played out, and one which may have exacerbated these antagonisms.[11] And fifth, they have shown how the popularity of sport has been exploited by the churches. Since the later nineteenth century Christian athletes have been favourite role-models, and their faith has been seen as an advertisement for Christianity.[12]

Historians of Christianity and sport have tried to answer one or more of the following three key questions:

1. What were the reasons for the embrace of sport by the Christian churches from the later nineteenth century onwards? The explanations offered have been many, and sometimes contradictory. Among the most common lines of interpretation have been to see it as an aspect of the liberalization of Christian theology,[13] or to see it as a 'masculinist' reaction to the perceived 'feminization' of the churches,[14] or to see it as part of the church's response to anti-clerical politics.[15] Not that these explanations need to be mutually exclusive. The liberalization argument has mainly been advanced with regard to Protestantism, and gains support from the fact that the longest resistance came from the more conservative Protestant churches;[16] but it raises the question of why many conservative Catholics, including a succession of popes, have also been sports enthusiasts.[17] The masculinity argument raises the question of when, how, and why 'muscular Christians' have also championed women's sport.[18] The political interpretation works very well for certain countries, such as France, but is less relevant to places where anti-clericalism was less of a force.

2. Has the role of the Christian churches in the rise of modern sport been proactive and creative, or has it been a defensive damage-limitation exercise? The latter view is strongly argued by Callum Brown, who suggests that muscular Christianity was a 'tactical shift', and that the church remained hostile to games and to the body.[19] Some other historians of sport and leisure have played down the influence of the churches in sport's modern history either by largely ignoring them,[20] or by arguing that this influence was short-lived.[21] On the other hand, local studies in England have tended to highlight the importance of religious organizations in the early development of modern sport,[22] or to show that this role continued for much longer.[23] While the importance of Christianity in the history of European and American sport is at least open to debate, it was unquestionably a major factor in the wider diffusion of sports originating in those countries. In many parts of the world, Christian missionaries and teachers

and officials of the Young Men's Christian Association (YMCA) were among the first to play cricket, football, hockey, volleyball, baseball, or basketball in their locations. There is room for debate about the motives of these Christian sports enthusiasts and the kind of sporting ethos which they tried to inculcate, but nobody could argue that their role was merely defensive or reactive.[24]

3. How far has Christianity been changed by its embrace of sport, and have the changes been on balance good or bad? For some historians, both Christianity and sport are evidently forces for good, and their relationship is seen as entirely beneficial.[25] Many others, while not ignoring potentially darker sides to the relationship, offer a mainly positive view.[26] The contrary view is offered by Dominic Erdozain. He grants that muscular Christianity began as a justifiable reaction against the puritanical excesses of early nineteenth-century Evangelicalism, but he argues that when later nineteenth-century churches and, in particular, the YMCA adopted a 'mission' to promote sport, they were fatally diverted from more important concerns. The result was an internal secularization of Christianity.[27] In the United States, the active involvement of the Evangelical churches in the world of sport, especially since the 1970s, has led to considerable controversy, with some historians and sociologists (as well as theologians) criticizing what they see as an uncritical acceptance of the less savoury aspects of sport.[28]

Each of the papers published here offers answers to some of the questions mentioned above.

The collection begins with Michael Krüger's timely reflections on the 500th jubilee of Martin Luther's propagation of his 95 theses against the Pope, and crucial arguments associated with the Protestant Reformation. As he notes, this event provides an ideal opportunity to consider the relationship between sport and Christianity from the perspective of both German Lutheranism and Protestantism, and the German-specific body-culture of gymnastics and *Turnen*. His conclusion is that both aspects fundamentally influenced the development of modern sports and Christian religiosity worldwide.

Alexander Maurits and Martin Nykvist then move forward in time, changing the focus of attention to Sweden, where a 'sport movement', initially perceived as a rival to the Church of Sweden (the Lutheran state church), was consolidated in the early decades of the twentieth century. However, as they explain, the sport movement grew, and conspicuous representatives within the Church of Sweden and other Christian denominations adopted a more practical view of the movement in order to appeal to people outside the ranks of the church, especially young men. In effect, the sport field soon became a missionary field. Concomitantly, the authors account for collaborative as well as sceptical voices, not only in the Church of Sweden, but also within the substantial Swedish revival movements (namely, the Pentecostal movement and the Mission Covenant Church of Sweden). In addition, and perhaps more poignantly, they analyze these events from a gender perspective, discussing what was simultaneously perceived as the secularization and feminization of Swedish Christianity.

In a completely different setting, Huijie Zhang, Fan Hong, and Fuhua Huang survey how missionary educational institutions and the education and sport programmes of the YMCA, in conjunction with the nation-building project of the

Nationalist government, transformed and modernized physical education and sport in China from 1840 to 1937. The concepts of cultural imperialism and nationalism are central to this study, and the authors argue that the cultural imperialism model is ineffective for an understanding of the impact of missionaries on Chinese society. Instead, they posit that the way in which Chinese nationalism played an active role in resisting, selecting, and reshaping the cultural products (modern physical education and sport) evidences a process that was an active negotiation, rather than a passive acceptance, of Western culture. Nevertheless, as they explain, Christian physical education and sport programmes had long-lasting effects on how physical education and sports became the way to define 'modern' bodies as they were incorporated into the wider education programme of modernizing China under the Nationalist government.

In another location, in a much more confined time period, missionaries of a different ilk were also involved in promoting sport, although perhaps in a more conspicuous way. As Ryan Davis elucidates, in 1938, Mormon missionaries from North America formed an athletic club in Buenos Aires, Argentina. It sponsored professional teams in baseball, softball, and basketball. Their team won three league championships in the four years they played baseball and four championships in the five years they played softball. Two of their basketball players would become national all-stars, one of whom would represent Argentina at the South American Championship in 1940. This story, extending until 1943, is outlined and situated in relation to a range of discourses that, interlaced, constitute important episodes in the cultural context of modern Argentine sport.

The final two papers take a closer look at aspects of Catholicism and sport. In the case study presented by Melissa Walsh and Nicholas Marshall, they examine the philosophies and activities of the Young Christian Workers (YCW), an international movement for young Catholics. From the 1950s through to the 1980s, the Australian YCW became known for running campaigns on a range of social issues and the provision of services – including sporting events and competitions. In their paper, Walsh and Marshall focus attention on the development of the Australian YCW (Australian Rules) Football Association during the 1950s, and trace the history of YCW members' participation in public debates about the morality of Sunday sport, which climaxed with a local referendum in the Melbourne suburb of Camberwell in 1959. Drawing on archival materials and interviews conducted with former young workers, their paper deftly explores tensions within Christianity around the meaning of 'leisure', 'idleness', and Sunday as a day of observance and rest, showing how religious strains around Sunday sport were shaped by class, youth, and masculine identities.

Finally, Michał Mazurkiewicz brings the volume up to the present day by returning to Europe and looking at more topical historical developments regarding the religious side of Polish football. His paper features several aspects, including discussion on the policy of the Catholic Church towards sport in recent decades, the rise of sports chaplaincy, and public manifestations of the religious beliefs of football players, managers, and fans. The main focus of interest is, however, on the increasingly popular religious pilgrimages organized since 2008 by fans across a number of Polish football clubs.

To conclude, it is worth noting that the investigations in this volume are not limited to a narrow definition of Christianity, but encompass a wide range of denominations, related philosophies and viewpoints. In terms of variety, it is also noted that different methodological and theoretical approaches are adopted, and, given the existing state of play, it is clear that there is still much to be uncovered, documented, and written about when it comes to the enduring topic of sport and Christianity. The inference is that any research agenda which emerges from observations on historical perspectives concerning the relationship of sport with aspects of Christianity will continue to resonate and add value to wider understandings of sport, culture, and the human condition.

Notes

1. Nick J. Watson and Andrew Parker, *Sport and the Christian Religion: A Systematic Review of Literature* (Newcastle Upon Tyne: Cambridge Scholars Publishing, 2014), 119.
2. *Inaugural Global Congress on Sports and Christianity Handbook* (York: Faculty of Health and Life Sciences, York St John University, United Kingdom, 24–28 August 2016), 1.
3. The authors of this paper wish to thank Nick Watson for his key role in conceptualizing and arranging the Congress, and for his willingness to include a specific strand devoted to 'Historical Perspectives on Sports and Christianity'. His published works (often in collaboration with Andrew Parker) and his encouragement of relevant academic networks have also had a defining and beneficial influence on the development of the field.
4. Watson and Parker, *Sport and the Christian Religion*, 119.
5. Apart from Watson and Parker's bibliographical compilation, *Sport and the Christian Religion*, see also the oft-cited Nick J. Watson and Andrew Parker, 'Sports and Christianity: Mapping the Field', in Nick J. Watson and Andrew Parker (eds), *Sports and Christianity: Historical and Contemporary Perspectives* (New York: Routledge, 2013), 9–88. For an appraisal of the latter work, see Rob Hess, 'Review of N.J. Watson and Andrew Parker (eds), *Sports and Christianity: Historical and Contemporary Perspectives*', *Sporting Traditions* 30, no. 2 (2013), 119–21. Also especially relevant is Part III ('Western Perspectives on Sport and Christianity') of the recently published collection, Afe Adogame, Nick J. Watson, and Andrew Parker (eds), *Global Perspectives on Sports and Christianity* (London: Routledge, 2018).
6. Manfred Lammer, Maureen Smith, and Thierry Terret, 'Introduction', *Stadion* 35 (2009), 2.
7. See, for example, Johan Huizinga, *Homo Ludens: A Study of the Play Element in Culture* (London: Routledge and Kegan Paul, 1949 [Originally published in 1938]), and Josef Pieper, *Leisure: The Basis of Culture* (London: Pantheon Books, 1952 [Originally published in 1947]).
8. For two examples from the large array of literature, see Clifford Putney, *Muscular Christianity* (Cambridge, MA: Harvard University Press, 2001), and Malcolm Tozer, *The Ideal of Manliness* (Truro: Sunnyrest Books, 2015).
9. Richard Holt, *Sport and Society in Modern France* (London: Macmillan, 1981); Hugh McLeod, 'Muscular Christianity, European and American', in David Hempton and Hugh McLeod (eds), *Secularization and Religious Innovation in the North Atlantic World* (Oxford: Oxford University Press, 2017), 203.
10. See, for example, Nam-Gil Ha and J.A. Mangan, 'A Curious Conjunction – Sport, Religion and Nationalism: Christianity and the Modern History of Korea', *The International Journal of the History of Sport* 11, no. 3 (1994), 329–54; Markku Hokkanen, '"Christ and the Imperial Games Fields" in South-Central Africa – Sport and the Scottish

Missionaries in Malawi, 1880-1914: Utilitarian Compromise', *The International Journal of the History of Sport* 22, no. 4 (2005), 745–69.
11. Hugh McLeod, 'Religion, Politics and Sport in Western Europe, c.1870-1939', in Stewart J. Brown, Frances Knight, and John Morgan-Guy (eds), *Religion, Identity and Conflict in Britain* (Farnham: Ashgate, 2013), 195–212; for cricket and conflict in a multi-religious context, see Ramachandra Guha, *A Corner of a Foreign Field: The Indian History of a British Sport* (London: Picador, 2002).
12. See, for example, Stefano Pivato, 'Italian Cycling and the Creation of a Catholic Hero: The Bartali Myth', *The International Journal of the History of Sport* 13, no. 1 (1996), 128–38.
13. Norman Vance, *Sinews of the Spirit* (Cambridge: Cambridge University Press, 1985).
14. Putney, *Muscular Christianity*, 2–3.
15. Laurence Munoz, *Une histoire du sport catholique* (Paris: L'Harmattan, 2003).
16. Andrew Doyle, 'Foolish and Useless Sport: The Southern Evangelical Crusade Against Intercollegiate Football', *Journal of Sport History* 24, no. 3 (1997), 320–3, 337; Dominic Erdozain, *The Problem of Pleasure* (Woodbridge: Boydell & Brewer, 2010), 240–7.
17. Kevin Lixey, 'The Vatican's Game Plan for Maximizing Sport's Educational Potential', in Nick J. Watson and Andrew Parker (eds), *Sports and Christianity: Historical and Contemporary Perspectives* (London: Routledge, 2013), 250–68.
18. Putney, *Muscular Christianity*, 148, notes the importance of the Young Women's Christian Association in the development of women's sport in the United States – a theme neglected alike by historians of sport, of women and of religion.
19. Callum Brown, 'God and Games – Yin and Yang', paper delivered at a conference on 'Historians on Sport', Leicester, 29 October 2005; see also Callum Brown, *The Death of Christian Britain* (London: Routledge, 2001), 97–, 107–8.
20. Mike Huggins, *The Victorians and Sport* (London: Hambledon and London, 2004); Wolfgang Behringer, *Kulturgeschichte des Sports: Vom antiken Olympia bis ins 21. Jahrhundert* (Munich: C.H. Beck, 2012).
21. Peter Bailey, *Leisure and Class in Victorian England: Rational Recreation and the Contest for Control, 1830-1885* (London: Routledge and Kegan Paul, 1978).
22. Douglas Reid, 'Labour, Leisure and Politics in Birmingham, ca. 1800-1875' (PhD diss., University of Birmingham, 1985); Jeremy Crump, 'Amusements of the People: Leicester, 1850-1914' (PhD diss., University of Warwick, 1985).
23. Jack Williams, 'Churches, Identities and Sport in the North, 1900-1939', in Jeff Hill and Jack Williams (eds), *Sport and Identity in the North of England* (Keele: Keele University Press, 1996), 113–36.
24. David Goldblatt, *The Ball is Round: A Global History of Football* (London: Viking, 2006), 479, 484–5; Gerald R. Gems, 'The Athletic Crusade: Sport and Colonialism in the Philippines', *The International Journal of the History of Sport* 21, no. 1 (2004), 1–15; A.D. Downes, '"From Boys to Men": Colonial Education, Cricket and Masculinity in the Caribbean, 1870-c. 1920', *The International Journal of the History of Sport* 22, no. 1 (2005), 3–21.
25. Peter Lupson, *Thank God for Football!* (London: SPCK, 2006).
26. See, for example, William J. Baker, *Playing with God: Religion and Modern Sport* (Cambridge, MA: Harvard University Press, 2007).
27. Erdozain, *The Problem of Pleasure*.
28. Tony Ladd and James A. Mathiesen, *Evangelical Protestants and the Development of Modern Sport* (Grand Rapids, MI: Baker, 1999); more frankly hostile is Robert J. Higgs, *God and the Stadium* (Lexington, KY: University Press of Kentucky, 1995).

Disclosure Statement

No potential conflict of interest was reported by the authors.

Gymnastics, Physical Education, Sport, and Christianity in Germany

Michael Krüger

ABSTRACT
Germany is both the country of origin of Protestantism and of *Turnerism*, which has led to a specific concept of national gymnastics. In 2017, the 500th anniversary of Martin Luther's act of nailing his theses to the door of the Church of Wittenberg (on 31 October 1517) was celebrated. About 300 hundred years later, Ludwig Jahn, son of a Protestant minister, started to run a gymnastics ground at a park in Berlin, where young boys and students were educated in 'body and mind' according to Jahn's slogan (which later became the brand of the German *Turner* movement) *frisch, fromm, fröhlich, frei* ('fresh, pious, cheerful, free'). The notion of piety has been widely discussed by contemporary gymnasts, because even then, some regarded piety as old-fashioned and in fact incompatible with a free and enlightened world. The purpose of this paper is to consider the Christian impact on German gymnastics and sport since the beginning of a civil movement of body culture in clubs and societies in the nineteenth century. The paper is based on a wide range of academic research and other selected sources.

Modern sports are closely associated with the Christian religion. As a consequence, this association has been discussed intensively by scholars of the Christian world. Notably, the collection edited by Nick Watson and Andrew Parker, published in 2013, provides an elaborate and distinctive overview of this discourse, paying particular attention to the Anglo-Saxon aspect of Christian culture.[1] In 2017, the 500th jubilee of Martin Luther's propagation of his 95 theses against the Pope in Rome, including crucial arguments of the Protestant Reformation, was celebrated in Germany. This event provides an excellent opportunity to consider the relationship between sport and Christianity from the perspective of both German Lutherism and Protestantism, and the German-specific body-culture of gymnastics and *Turnen*. Both aspects fundamentally influenced the development of modern sports and Christian religiosity worldwide.

The paper will first reflect on the state of the art of the scholarly discourse on sports and religiosity in the German-speaking world. Second, there will be reflections on the fundamental change of Christian somatism provoked by Luther's interpretation of the gospel and his reforms of the church. Third, there will be a description and interpretation of the consequences of these spiritual and societal reforms for the genesis of the German gymnastics and *Turner* Movement, dating from the age of Enlightenment at the end of the eighteenth century. Luther's new respect for the body had a lengthy incubation until its reception and transformation through German gymnastics and *Turnen*, finally flowing into the sports movement including their organizations and institutions as a civil religion, compensating for the loss of Christian religiosity since the nineteenth century. These processes are considered in a separate section, before concluding remarks are made.

German Studies in Sport, Ethics, and Christianity

The thesis that sport functions as a world religion is by no means recent. In 1932, the German journal *Der Querschnitt* published a special issue on sports. The introduction from the journalist Hanns Seiffert was entitled 'Weltreligion des 21. Jahrhunderts' and ironically subtitled 'cited by a work of the 120th century'. As a fictional work, a scientist of the future 120th century reports on the archeological research of the twentieth century and the mysterious cult of a ball representing the major object of that strange religion. The journal was contributed to and read by intellectuals of the roaring twenties in Berlin, such as the poets Bertolt Brecht, Robert Musil, Alfred Polgar, and others.[2] The new fashion of sport was both admired and criticized, or commented on ironically, by the avant-garde of German modern art, literature, and culture.

Three years later, in 1935, Pierre de Coubertin himself argued in his famous radio speech, broadcast worldwide before the Berlin Olympics of 1936, that the primary aim of Olympism ought to be that of constituting a religion.[3] He created the term *religio athletae* and argued for transferring the spirit of Olympic sports to the world by means of both the Olympic Games and elite Olympic athletes. These athletes do not talk in words, but act through athletic sports and their best practice behavior. They are idols for the mass of young athletes who strive for better performance and fair play. The religious claim of Coubertin corresponded, whether consciously or not, to the claim of Nazi ideology and propaganda that it would replace the Christian religion with new forms of cults and rituals for the masses.[4]

Numerous scholars in Germany and abroad discussed academically the question of what *religio athletae* really means, and whether sport could or should be compared with true religions. For the German-speaking world, the *Lexikon der Ethik im Sport* should be mentioned and particularly appreciated.[5] The compendium was published in 1998 by the physical educator and outstanding scholar of sport, Ommo Grupe, and the Catholic scholar of ethics, Dietmar Mieth. The book contains a preface by the then highest representatives of both churches in Germany, the Catholic cardinal Lehmann, and the speaker of the Protestant (*Evangelische*) churches, bishop Kock. In addition, prefaces from the then umbrella organizations of German sport organizations, the German Sports Federation (DSB), and the National Olympic Committee (*NOK für Deutschland*), as well as a foreword by the German Minister of the Interior who is responsible for sport, were included. These prefaces and the voluminous compendium itself make clear that ethical questions or challenges of sport, and its context, were and still are of common interest and relevance to sports organizations, churches, and the state. Furthermore, the crucial interest of the churches and contributions of theologians in the compendium, especially of Eilert Herms,[6] emphasize their concept that sports are by no means a religion at the same level of true religions like Christianity, but at most, religious surrogates. Quite explicitly, this is the opinion of both Christian confessions in Germany, the Catholics and the Protestants.[7]

Sports are fascinating elements of modern life and can even lead to a genuinely better life, but they cannot deliver answers to the fundamental questions of life and death. Contrary to true religion, sport lacks transcendence. However, the obligation of the churches, as well as of the state and the sports organizations, include ethical issues in the first instance. Sport, as a phenomenon of modern societies, used to be a means of ethical orientation in society generally, a mechanism for fair play, mutual respect and understanding, health and well-being, discipline, self-control and so on. These ethical or moral issues correspond to the pedagogical or ethical perspectives of Olympism and Olympic Education as generated by Pierre de Coubertin and other Olympic philosophers, as ultimately contained in the Olympic Charter.[8] The quotation from Coubertin is still valid in the concept of Olympic education that the effects of sport and athletics — Coubertin preferred to speak of athletics rather than sport — 'can be healthy or harmful, depending how and in which spirit we use it'.[9]

The current version of the Olympic charter does not repeat the initial claim of Olympism to be a religion, but states that it is just a 'philosophy of life, exalting and combining in a balanced whole the qualities of body, will and mind. Blending sport with culture and education, Olympism seeks to create a way of life based on the joy of effort, the educational value of good example, social responsibility and respect for universal fundamental ethical principles'.[10] In other words, Olympism, as the philosophy of global sports, is obliged to adhere to 'universal fundamental ethical principles' which are essential to most religions. One example is the so-called 'golden rule', including all world religions and even atheists: 'Do not act against others as you would not want them to act against you'.[11] Etzioni considers the golden rule as a common denominator of ethics and moral norms in multi-religious and mostly secular modern societies.[12]

The paradigmatic change of the Olympic charter from the claim of Olympism constituting a religion to the concept of representing a 'philosophy of life' (among others) reveals another, qualitative step in the process of both the secularization of sports and of modern society. From a historical perspective, the correlation (and its development) between the genesis of sport on the one hand, and Christian religion and its institutions on the other, are of particular interest. Which figurations of society and politics favoured the rise of sport and athletics as an Ersatz-Religion? The connections between the Catholic and protestant churches on the one hand, and the new Ersatz-Religion of sport, physical education, and gymnastics, represented in the various organizations of German gymnastics on the other, developed and improved since the nineteenth century, at first in the *Turner* movement, and later, in the twentieth century, in the organized sports clubs' movement.

In fact, both Christianity and sports are processes and products emerging from the occident, both conquering the world, the first before and the latter after the age of Enlightenment. In England, the mother country of Western sport, the connection (or metaphorically speaking, the symbiosis) between sport and Christianity in the version of the Anglican Church became apparent in the concept of 'muscular Christianity'.[13] In the USA, the Christian organization of the Young Men's Christian Association (YMCA), initially established in nineteenth England and Europe, from associations or clubs of young Christian men, became a powerful and influential organization of sport for all, especially young men, and firmly based on Christian faith and morality.[14] Some major sports games had been developed at first in the context of the YMCA. Basketball is such a game, invented by James Naismith, claiming educational purposes like mutual respect, prevention of bodily contact and aggression, in short, fair play.[15] It seems noteworthy that the concept of muscular Christianity was specifically popular in Protestant and Anglican spaces, but less so in Catholic regions of the world.

Spiritual and Somatic Basics of Gymnastics and Sport

At first glance, the fundamentals of sport are body and movement. By contrast, Christianity is grounded on spirit and faith. Therefore, especially German historians have claimed a so-called *Leibfeindlichkeit* ('somatophobia') of Christianity, legitimizing the critical attitude of the Christian churches towards sports.[16] This *Leibfeindlichkeit* has its roots in the asceticism and monasticism of the European Middle Ages. The orders of monks considered the body as the place or birthplace of sins, and consequently as an obstacle on the path to God.[17]

As Lyndal Roper analyzed in her brilliant biography of Martin Luther (1483–1546), a crucial issue in his reform of Catholicism was a new approach to the human body.[18] Luther himself was an Augustinian monk since 1506, but then he harshly criticized the sort of asceticism practiced by his monastic order. Throughout his life, Luther was fighting against the *Teufel* ('devil') and afraid of damnation in hell (in his words, *Höllenschlund*). In the monastery, the ideology was preached that an ascetic life and pious performances could contribute to salvation of the soul and free people of their sins. Schilling calls this the Catholic concept of *Leistungsfrömmigkeit* ('piety of performance').[19] The initial step in Luther's revolt against the Pope, whom he later called the 'Antichrist', was his criticism of the Pope's concept of *Leistungsfrömmigkeit* articulated in the commerce (literally a business practice) of selling indulgences. Luther's new and indeed paradigmatic knowledge or, theologically speaking, gnosis, was that neither performance nor paid-for indulgence, nor a pious life can guarantee salvation of the soul after death, but only faith and God's grace, and respecting the Bible — *sola fide, sola gratia, sola scriptura* — which were the three basic components of Lutherism.

Accordingly, Luther denied and polemicized against the monks' view that the body is the shelter of the sin and that, in consequence, ascetic life, fasting and sexual abstinence could help to free humans from their sins. His reformatory concept of the body was also a result of his basic studies of original Bible texts, which he translated into German for the common people. However, his actions were probably as relevant for the reformation process as his academic and exegetic studies. The contemporaries of Luther regarded his leaving the Augustinian order and even more his marriage to Katharina von Bora, an Augustinian nun, who had fled her order, as true revolutionary acts. Katharina bore Martin Luther six children. Luther did not, in fact, condemn sexuality and bodily lust (*Fleischeslust*) in his work, neither with respect to sexual needs nor to eating and drinking. He also loved music and dance as natural and holy behavior. He even used rather drastic words to express basic human needs. His quotations in this context became legendary for the new Protestant use of the body, bodily needs, and the Protestant body image and the way one should act and behave bodily, for example: *Warum rülpset und furzet ihr nicht, hat es euch nicht geschmacket?* ('Why do you not burp and fart, did you not enjoy the meal?').[20] Roper also demonstrates this new Protestant body concept by interpreting various portraits of Luther himself, changing from the ascetic monk to the 'fat doctor', as painted by Lukas Cranach.[21]

The new, Protestant body concept was part of the Protestant shift towards the real world, by contrast to the retreat of Catholic monasticism from the world. Referring to Luther, the Christian individual is existentially free, but imprisoned by God's will and grace. Therefore, he is expected to commit to public affairs and politics, so that the message of the gospel can be spread, put into action and the devil banned.[22] He is obliged to follow his conscience, and he is only dependent on God and his grace. The human is close to Jesus Christ, without any person or institution (like the church) between. Conscience is a crucial term in the theology of Luther. It also became fundamental to a new way of ethical thinking. Indeed, it is not possible to erase one's sins either by praying or by confessing or doing good work or even by paying indulgence. However, the will of God is to act as free humans according to one's conscience and according to the norms and rules as told by Jesus Christ, written down by the prophets and evangelists in the Bible, and, finally, translated for all by its new prophet, Martin Luther.[23]

This idea was crucial for the legitimation of Protestant rulers, and later, nation states like Prussia. Additionally, the idea of Protestantism, or, referring to the sociologist Max Weber (1864–1920), the 'ethics of Protestantism', was fundamental for the emerging 'spirit of capitalism'.[24] Luther's father was a more or less a successful coal-mining entrepreneur in the county of Mansfield, the hometown of Martin Luther in Saxonia. Martin Luther himself and his wife were also business-minded and economically successful. However, he declined certain interests as 'Jewish'. Roper is right when she assesses Luther's actions, his habitus and lifestyle propagated by himself, the paintings of Lukas Cranach and his followers as being as influential as his writings.[25] He encouraged people regarding their commitment in society, politics, and economy, not because of the absolution of sins, but because activity and progress are in accordance with the words and will of God and even part of a godly lifestyle. By contrast, the absolution of sins and a sanctuary life in the other world are only dependent on the grace of God.

Apparently, Luther's body concept was still far removed from the concept of an ascetic, athletic, and powerful body in modern sports, reminding one much more of the ideal of *kalokagathia* in Greek antiquity than of the Bible. *Kalokagathia* means the ideal of beauty and goodness in Greek antiquity. However, the Lutheran reforms paved the way for a new perspective on, and interpretation of, Bible texts. The most quoted paragraphs in the Bible respecting the Christian body and self-concept, are the epistles of Paul to the community of Corinth, one passage being 1 Corinthians 6: 19–20 (and translated into German by Luther):

> *Oder wisst ihr nicht, dass euer Leib ein Tempel des Heiligen Geistes ist, der in euch ist und den ihr von Gott habt, und dass ihr nicht euch selbst gehört? Denn ihr seid teuer erkauft; darum preist Gott mit eurem Leibe.* ('Or don't you know that your body is a temple of the Holy Spirit, who lives inside you, and you got your body from God, and that you are not your own? Because you are bought expensively; therefore, praise God by your body').[26]

Another passage is 1 Corinthians 3: 16–17:

> *Wisst ihr nicht, dass ihr Gottes Tempel seid und der Geist Gottes in euch wohnt? Wenn jemand den Tempel Gottes zerstört, den wird Gott zerstören, denn der Tempel Gottes ist heilig — der seid ihr.* ('Don't you know that you are the temple of God and that the Holy Spirit (the Spirit of God) lives inside you? If anyone destroys the temple of God, he will be destroyed by God because the temple of God is holy — you are the temple').[27]

Paul refers to the human and his body as the 'temple of God' and the home of the Holy Spirit. In consequence, every human is asked to care for the body, one's own and those of others. The *Lutherian* exegesis of these paragraphs were incompatible with the monkish asceticism and ideology of abstinence. The *Lutherian* and Protestant, and finally the Catholic perspective on physical education, including exercises and sports, relates to this quotation in Paul's epistle. For Luther, care of the body as the temple of God meant eating, drinking and expressing bodily needs including singing and dancing, instead of mortification of the body and self, as he had experienced with his own body during his lifespan as a monk. However, the care for the body need does not mean intemperance, crapulence and excessive sexuality, but a tempered, controlled, and reflected need for the body as a useful instrument of both the human mind and the temple of the Holy Spirit. Therefore, Luther polemized harshly against heretics in the reformatory movement, such as the *Wiedertäufer* ('Anabaptists') in Münster/Westfalia who misunderstood his marriage to an 'escaped' nun as a legitimation of polygamy. By contrast, Luther condemned polygamy as a work of the devil, as indeed practiced by the Islamic 'Turks'.

As Schilling pointed out in his biography of Luther, the basic ideas of Luther and other protestant theologians, like Johannes Calvin (1509–1564) and Huldrych Zwingli (1484–1531), were also respected by Catholic reformers, especially Ignatius von Loyola (1491–1556) and his Jesuit order. One major point is the idea of public education including education of the body.[28]

Considering the various contemporary papers, comments, and moratoria from both churches referring to sports, physical exercises and physical education, the request for a modest use and care of the body remains their common denominator. This concept legitimizes the perennial church criticism of the excesses of sports on various levels. These included top level sports as a new way of radical mortification of body and self, contrasting to the freedom of a Christian person; towards the de-sacrification of Sunday through sports activities; towards the exploitation of the body for the needs of politics, the economy or the military; and finally, the excessive and exclusive care of the body as an end in itself, for an attractive and sexually appealing body.[29]

The protestant theologian Eilert Herms argued in his article on 'sport and religion' in the 'Lexikon der Ethik im Sport' that the body culture of sport should be assessed positively, when or insofar as sports and physical education contribute to a modest handling of both the body of the sporting person and that of partners and opponents in play and competitions.[30] Unacceptable from a Christian perspective, however, is an understanding of sport legitimizing sports and sporting competitions in themselves. The theological reason for this criticism is that sport without God implies that the power of sport and of the athlete derive from the human body but not from God. Herms regards the main difference between Christianity as true religion on the one hand, and sport as an Ersatz-Religion on the other, as just this point. The last is a cult of the 'Here and Now' (*Diesseitigkeit*) leading in consequence to human hubris, whereas the Christian concept supports a kind of sport in abjection of God and the limits of human power, performance and suffering. Following this interpretation, Wolfgang Huber, head of the Protestant churches in Germany from 2003 until 2009, made this difference clear when he distinguished between an 'Olympic image' of the human on the one hand, and a 'Jesuanic image' of the human on the other 'Christian hand', including his suffering and helplessness.[31]

The Protestant perspective of the human body was compatible with the (new-) humanistic perception of antiquity including gymnastics, athletics, and agonistics, as promoted by the European and especially the German educated classes. The antique idea of *kalokagathia*, as interpreted in the period of New Humanism, combining a sound mind in a sound body, conformed to the Protestant version of the epistles of Paul as cited in the Bible. Paul even requested his readers to fight and compete like athletes for their faith and against the devil.[32] Therefore, Uta Poplutz referred to Jesus Christ as an 'athlete of the gospel'. Like an athlete at Olympia, Jesus Christ was fighting and competing for his faith, living a life in harmony of body and mind. She could show, in her detailed study on the metaphors of *agon* in the biblical texts of Paul, that there are numerous impacts in the Bible of ancient athletics and agonistics.[33] They were part of the contemporary life and experience of the Evangelists in their time and space.

The German *Turner* and Sports Movement and Their Relationship to Christianity

Prussia was the Protestant core of Germany, before and after the foundation of the German Empire, as a crucial benchmark in the process of German nation building. German scholars, teachers, educators, and Protestant priests did not see any difference and certainly no conflict between the Protestant care of the body as an instrument of the mind and Holy Spirit through useful, modest forms of ascetic physical education on the one hand, and the ideal of the body concept as perceived in Greek antiquity. Philosophers and poets, ranging from Johann Wolfgang Goethe (1749–1832) and Friedrich Schiller (1759–1805), both national poets and heroes, and other representatives of German *Klassik* ('classicism') and idealism like Friedrich Hölderlin (1770–1843) and Johann Joachim Winckelmann (1717–1768), to Friedrich Nietzsche (1844–1900), Jacob Burckhardt (1818–1897) and Ernst Curtius (1814–1896), supported this concept. Curtius initiated the Prussian, and since 1871 the German, archeological excavation of ancient Olympia. To be sure, he was a Protestant scholar, just as the audience in the Sing Academy in Berlin, where he presented his famous speech in 1852. He asked for research and excavation of the antique venue of Olympia, which were the 'life of our life' as he stated.[34] The most famous listener to his request and finally supporter of the idea was the Protestant Prince of Prussia.

A characteristic of the German and Scandinavian approach to the sports movement is the substantial impact of physical education and exercises. Both nation-states are mainly Protestant. In Germany, the philanthropist Johann Christoph Friedrich GutsMuths (1759–1839), and in Sweden the *Gymnasiarch* ('teacher of gymnasts') Per Henrik Ling (1776–1839) created systems of gymnastics, physical education and exercises for health and well-being which were sustainable ideals for further concepts of physical education around the world. Ling was the son, and GutsMuths the son-in-law of a preacher. The father of German gymnastics, Friedrich Ludwig Jahn (1778–1852), was the son of a Protestant minister as well.[35]

Although bodily or physical education had primarily been an element of general education since the period of European Enlightenment and subsequently part of secular national education in the process of nation building, its impact on Lutherism and Prostestantism, including their body concepts, seems all too clear. By contrast, neither GutsMuths nor Jahn mention any Christian or religious motives for their concepts of physical and national education. For GutsMuths, rationality and utility are relevant arguments for physical exercises and bodily education, but not spiritual and religious ones, according to the secular idea of the Enlightenment, which he feels obliged to follow in the field of physical education.[36] However, he does not reflect on any contradiction with his Protestant education and faith.

For Jahn, the German *Volk* ('people' or 'folk') and the German *Volksthum* ('the idea of the people') were the new Ersatz-Religion. He regarded *Turnen* as part of this new *volksthümliche Erziehung* ('people's education'). Jahn combined Protestantism, nationalism, and *Turnerism* when he wrote that German gymnastics were 'a holy work and nature'.[37] *Gott verlässt keinen Deutschen* ('God does not abandon any Germans') is a famous quotation from Jahn's *Deutsche Turnkunst*, which he mentioned in the context of the so-called *Befreiungskriege* against Napoleon and the so-called *Völkerschlacht* near Leipzig in 1813, when Napoleon was beaten by European allies including Prussia and a small group of German *Turners* led by Jahn himself.[38] A teacher of German gymnastics performs a highly relevant work, as Jahn argues in the chapter on the job of a *Turnlehrer* ('physical educator'): *Werdende Männer sind seiner Obhut anvertraut, die künftigen Säulen des Staates, die Leuchten der Kirche, und die Zierden des Vaterlands* ('He must educate young men, the pillars of the future state, the lights of the church, and the ornaments of the fatherland').[39] Physical educators, as future 'lights of the church', underline Jahn's approach to the concept of the future nation state included these three issues of state formation, a national church, and 'we-feelings' for the Fatherland. Young men, educated by physical educators, should play leading roles in these three fields of German nation building. In his rules of gymnastics (*'Turngesetze'*), Jahn mentioned the slogan of the *Turner* movement: *Frisch, frei, fröhlich und fromm — ist des Turners Reichthum* ('Fresh, free, cheerful, and pious — this is the richness of a gymnast')[40] which is still used today. The first three words expressing the dynamic feeling of the young gymnasts in the early nineteenth century remained unchallenged. However, the last word — *fromm* ('pious') — was somewhat controversial.[41] The revolutionary *Turner* Movement of the late 1840s rejected the word *fromm*. At the pre-revolutionary *Turnfest* in Heilbronn in 1846, the logo of the German *Turner* Movement, the '4Fs' designed as a cross, was interpreted as follows: *Das Kreuz ist ein Christen-Zeichen, ein allgemeines, es ist aber auch das spezielle deutsche Zeichen* ('The cross is a Christian symbol. However, it is a specific German one too').[42] Christianity and German nationalism were united in *turnerism*, or in the German *Turner* movement.

Jahn derived the word *fromm* from the old German adverb *voran* which means to go ahead, and it was intended to express the dynamic, progressive perspective of German *turnerism*.[43] Jahn felt like he was standing in a line of national reformers since Luther. Like Luther, Jahn regarded himself as reinventing German national and popular culture and language by means of both a new popular body culture named *turnen* and through reforming the German language. He propagated purging the German language of borrowed words, especially French, and he used a similar rather drastic vocabulary to counter his opponents, as Luther had done 300 years ago.

Without doubt, Jahn and the early *Turner* and student's movement related to Luther and Protestantism. The *Wartburgfest* was celebrated on 31 October 1817, in remembrance of the day when Luther had nailed his 95 theses onto the door of the church in Wittenberg 300 years before.[44] This event became famous, because the students not only did gymnastics at the same place where Luther had lived and worked. Additionally, they protested against the old powers in Germany and Europe by burning books and symbols of (in their opinion) political reactionism in a public action. The public burning of writings was in memory of Luther's public burning of the Papal bull, the Pope's edict excluding and excommunicating Luther from the Catholic church. Later, not only edicts and books, but also heretics and witches, were burnt. Historians like Wolfgang Benz considered the book burning at the Wartburg by students and *Turners* (in fact, the books were fakes) as a prelude to the far uglier book burnings of the Nazis in 1933.[45]

Lutherism and Protestantism characterized the German *Turner* movement of the nineteenth century. This is true for both, the clubs-movement and the system of body or physical education at schools that were formally introduced by the German states since the middle of the nineteenth century, first in Protestant Prussia, and then step-by-step in other German states. *Turnen*, or in general physical education at schools, were intended to contribute to the education of discipline and bodily health.[46] That is indeed what Paul implied in his epistles on caring for the body as a temple of the mind and Holy Spirit. The body concept of the so-called *Turnphilologen* in Germany, Austria, and Switzerland included a clear hierarchy between body and mind. They dealt with training the body in order to enhance the superior mind of the individual. Adolf Spieß (1810–1858), one of the founders of a systematic theory and methodology of physical education and gymnastics at schools, was the main representative of this educational body concept at schools and in *Turner* clubs.[47] The Protestant perspective includes the belief that the individual acts divinely when he respects both his own body as a temple of the Holy Spirit, as well as others and their bodies.

Not by chance, Spieß was also the son of a Protestant minister, just as numerous other academic teachers of gymnastics, for example Otto Heinrich Jäger (1828–1912) from Stuttgart, an influential physical educator, who combined German *Turnerism* with Greek athletics and Protestantism in a version of pietism in Württemberg/Southern Germany.[48] Another fine example is Theodor Georgii (1826–1892), the first speaker of the united German *Turnerschaft* from 1860 until 1887 who was the son of a Protestant minister from a village in Württemberg and pupil at Philip Wackernagel's school, a former student and fan of Jahn.[49]

Free gymnastics clubs that spread throughout Germany since the middle of the nineteenth century were a branch of the secular club movements of the middle classes. Anyone could become a member, independent of religious or confessional affiliations or social class. The *Deutsche Turnerschaft*, the umbrella organization of gymnastics clubs in Germany, founded in 1860, included both Jewish and Christian members of both confessions, and of all classes and professions, mainly from the middle of German society. The *Turnerschaft* felt like the core of the German people, nation and nation state. Indeed, the *Turners* initialized a popular movement of the masses, based on body and movement and backed by the spirit of nationalism and the ethics of Protestantism. Since 1871, the German empire was the German nation state led by Protestant Prussia.[50]

The statistics kept by the *Turner* organizations did not register the religion or confession of its members nor their political orientation, just their age and profession. Until the end of the nineteenth century, children, youths, girls, and women were not registered as regular members. *Turner* clubs were certainly 'national' or patriotic, but not political in the sense of a political party, regarding the charter of the *Turnerschaft*. Furthermore, they were not religious or confessional, but neutral and secular. The German people and the nation-state became their new Ersatz-Religion, similar to most of the other nations during the age of nationalism. Citing Norbert Elias, nationalism 'is one of the most powerful, if not the most powerful social systems of faith of the nineteenth and twentieth century'.[51]

There were various reasons for the success of nationalism and patriotism as an Ersatz-Religion in Germany. One included the function of building bridges between the different Christian confessions. The confessional 'divorce' since Luther and the age of reformation was an obstacle to the process of nation building. During the German Empire, Reichskanzler *Bismarck* fought the so-called *Kulturkampf* in the

1870s, which was in effect a disempowerment of the Catholic Church and a victory of the secular German nation state, including its ruling Prussian (and Protestant) elites.[52]

However, nationalism and patriotism could not prevent the splitting of German society to various classes, confessions and other religious groups, especially the Jews. Consequently, the most united *Turner* club-movement fragmented in the early twentieth century in various groups of interest and ideology. There were gymnasts and sportsmen of diverse sports, in politically neutral gymnasts and sports, nationalists and socialists, and even Protestant, Catholic and Jewish *Turners*. With respect to religion, in the 1920s special clubs for Protestants and Catholics were founded in close connection to their churches, the so-called *Eichenkreuz* Clubs as part of the YMCA of the Protestant churches, and the clubs of so-called *Deutsche Jugendkraft* (DJK), the youth organization of the Catholic Church in Germany, and in addition, Jewish nationalists founded Makkabi clubs. Numerous gymnasts and sportsmen who were until then organized in clubs of the *Deutsche Turnerschaft* left the *Turnerschaft* and joined these religious or confessional clubs including the Makkabi. In 1927, about one million members were organized in confessional sports clubs in Germany, compared to 1.6 million in the *Deutsche Turnerschaft*, 1.37 million in sports clubs, and one million worker's sport organizations.[53]

A simple reason for establishing these new religious clubs was the growing attraction of sports and games for youth, combined with the fear of churches that they would lose youth to the sports clubs. The famous movie *Chariots of Fire* ('*Die Stunde des Siegers*') illustrates this fundamental conflict and crisis in England. The situation in Germany and on the continent was similar. However, not everybody behaved like the stars of the movie, the athletes Eric Lidell and Harold Abrahams, who were finally able to combine their faith with their love and passion for sports.[54] In reality, the churches lost members and fought a desperate and hopeless struggle for the holy Sunday, freedom of work, sports, and games.[55] In fact, the churches even found some allies in the sports organizations and the trade unions for a work-free Sunday for sports, recreation, and sometimes even contemplation, without the stress and rush of the everyday work life.[56]

Christian Perspectives in German Sports

The sportization of modern societies, including Germany, did not stop at the Christian churches. The Third Reich and World War II contributed both to the process of secularization and sportization. In the period of National Socialism (1933–1945), the Nazis oppressed the Christian churches just like other opponents. Consequently, this oppression included the DJK and *Eichenkreuz* Clubs. But in the long run and beyond the dark years of atheist and anti-clerical Hitlerism, the concept of confessional sports clubs with a close connection to the churches could not gain sustainable recognition in Germany.

After the lost war and the 'unconditional surrender' of the Third Reich in 1945, the Germans, in common with, or rather controlled by, the Allies, re-organized their state and society, including new institutions and new ideologies. This was also true for the sports organizations. In 1950, representatives of former civil and workers sports and gymnastics clubs, supported by representatives of the former confessional sports clubs, founded the *Deutsche Sportbund* (DSB) in West Germany as a free and independent umbrella organization of associations of sport clubs, actually based on their own volition, by contrast to the period of Nazism. The former confessional sports organizations joined the DSB. Actually, the names of the DJK clubs still remind one of the 1920s and the 1930s, as culmination points of the confessional sports and *Turner* movement.[57]

The first statute of the DSB in 1950 includes the sentence in §3.5 that the DSB 'respects the cultural and religious norms of the German people'.[58] However, the new sports movement was by no means indifferent towards these ethical and religious norms. By contrast, the German sports movement was in a sorry state, particularly regarding its moral status during the Nazi period, so that, citing Willi Daume, first president of the DSB, it had to work hard to achieve new moral integrity.[59] One step along this path for a new and fair ethical fundament of the sports movement in Germany was the close cooperation with churches and confessions. According to the Charter of the German Sports movement of 1966, cooperation with both churches was explicitly requested.[60] Consequently, so-called *Arbeitskreise Kirche und Sport* ('Workshops on church and sport') were established and discussed mainly ethical issues on sport. These workshops organized numerous events mostly in academies of the churches like *Bad Boll* or *Bad Tutzing* — both Protestant academies, serving as a sort of ethical think-tank of the churches and as bridges between churches and society. Additionally, both churches in Germany nominated official *Sportpfarrer* ('preachers for sport') to undertake the counselling of athletes at the Olympic Games, among other obligations.[61]

In the other German state under control of the communist USSR, the German Democratic Republic (GDR), the influence of churches on society and politics was dramatically undermined. However, the GDR was situated in the territory of the former core of German Protestantism, parts of Prussia (which no longer existed after 1945), Saxonia and Thuringia, where Luther came from. During the authoritarian leadership of the Sozialistische Einheitspartei Deutschlands (SED), the ruling communist party in the GDR, the churches could only exist and work under strict control by the party, the state, and the secret service. Confessional sport organizations were simply put of the question. The GDR was a secular, even atheist, state, dominated by its Ersatz-Religion and state ideology of socialism and Marxism. Body culture and sport were squeezed into this ideological bed of Procrustes.

However, on the occasion of the 500th anniversary of Luther's birthday in 1983, the GDR ideologists claimed the reformer as a forerunner of the German tradition of socialism realized in the GDR.[62] In fact, the Protestant church of the GDR grew as a cell of resistance against the dictatorship of the SED and its Marxist elites. Ironically, the spirit of Luther and his opinion on the freedom of a Christian human underpinned the ultimate fall of the regime.

When the wall fell, and the Iron curtain collapsed, both German states united in one German nation state in 1990. This revolutionary act happened without any notable acts of violence. Although the current members of the churches in East Germany are few in number, the influence of Protestant thinking and working in united Germany is again substantial. This phenomenon becomes apparent less in the permanently decreasing number of members of both churches in Germany, but rather — among other examples — in the fact that leading positions in politics and society are officiated by Protestants.

In fact, Lutheran Protestantism was secularized. During the period of the GDR, socialism, achievement, and sport replaced the former role of Protestantism. From this perspective, Prussian Protestantism was sportizised, but remained an essential part of the habitus of Germans in both the East and West. Chancellor Merkel is the daughter of a Protestant minister, and the last president of the Republic, Joachim Gauck, was both a Protestant minister in the former GDR and a representative of the opposition against the SED dictatorship. In addition, and in some way as a legacy of Luther, he was a father and grandfather, but lived officially unmarried with his second longtime partner. Merkel's and Gauck's welcome policy of refugees in 2015 is not comprehensible without their Protestant habitus and background.

In May and June 2017, both the so-called *Evangelischer Kirchentag* ('Protestant Church-Convention') and the *Internationales Deutsches Turnfest* ('International German Gymnastics Festival') took place in Berlin, the latter shortly after the former. Both are mass events lasting for several days including tens of thousands of participants and visitors. Both events represent mass movements of body and mind, the one focused on the body, the other on spirit and faith. According to Martin Luther, these are two sides of the same coin.[63] The atmosphere at and impressions from the *Kirchentag* and the *Turnfest* were similar in a sense. They comprise happy and mostly young people (or at least people who felt young), looking for and mostly successfully experiencing we-feelings by praying and singing at the *Kirchentag* and doing gymnastics at the *Turnfest*. The former seems to be clerical and the latter secular. However, both are *fromm* ('pious') in the sense of the *Turner* movement; committed to ethical norms popularized since the age of Luther and obligated to a modest and disciplined culture of body and mind for all, which was established by Luther and developed in the German *Turner* and Gymnastics Movement since the early nineteenth century. 'Sport for all' today is by no means a contrast to the message of the gospel, but rather a current objectivation. In the words of Uta Poplutz, in Berlin, at these festivals you could also meet 'athletes of the gospel'.[64] The practice of sports for all, as realized at such a *Turnfest*, represents more than commercialized top-level sport, but in fact the visions of a sports movement based on Christian ethics and morality.

The starting point of this paper on German sports, gymnastics, physical education, and Christianity is Martin Luther and his new body concept, in contrast to the former notion of the body as the origin and seat of the devil. Luther's exegesis of the gospel respected the body, according to St Paul, as the temple of God and the Holy Spirit, dedicated to humans to care for this gift. It took several centuries and the period of the European Enlightenment for this new body concept of the age of reformation to flow into the concept of ascetic gymnastics and physical education. Apparently, there is substantial evidence of the link between Protestantism, German gymnastics, and even modern sports. The basis for this connection was the Lutheran body concept. But in consequence, the relationship between Christianity and sports in a broader sense of the concepts developed in many fields: with respect to didactical and methodological concepts of physical and health education by means of physical exercises, play and games; regarding the ascetic ethics of gymnastics and fair competition; and not least, the development of institutions of gymnastics and sports at schools and in clubs, duly appreciated by the Protestant Prussian state, and later by the secular and even atheistic German states.

Today, there is no real contrast between the secular messages of the Christian religion, independent of whether Catholic or Protestant, on the one hand, and the spirits of various sports on the other. Both are more or less accepted and called 'philosophies of life', as cited in the preamble of the Olympic charter. Most people in the modern world have no problem following various, and even radically different philosophies of life simultaneously, a Christian life and 'lifestyle' among them. Physical education, health education through a healthy movement, sports, exercises, and play are just one of the fields in modern western societies in which Christian values and concepts of body and appearance are present latently in everyday life, mostly without God and the Christian faith.

Notes

1. Nick Watson and Andrew Parker (eds), *Sports and Christianity: Historical and Contemporary Perspectives* (New York: Routledge, 2013).
2. Hans Seiffert, '*Weltreligion des 20. Jahrhunderts: Aus einem Werk des 120. Jahrhunderts*', *Der Querschnitt* 12, no. 6 (1932), 385–7.
3. Pierre de Coubertin and Organisationskomitee für die XI. Olympiade Berlin 1936 e.V., *Pax Olympica: Weltsendung des Reichssenders Berlin am Sonntag, dem 4. August 1935 mittags*.
4. Nicholas Goodrick-Clarke, *The Occult Roots of Nazism: Secret Aryan Cults and their Influence on Nazi Ideology; The Ariosophists of Austria and Germany, 1890-1935* (New York: New York University Press, 1992).
5. Ommo Grupe and Dietmar Mieth (eds), *Lexikon der Ethik im Sport*, 2nd ed. (Schorndorf: K. Hofmann, 1998).
6. Eilert Herms, '*Sport und Religion*', in Ommo Grupe and Dietmar Mieth (eds), *Lexikon der Ethik im Sport*, 2nd ed. (Schorndorf: K. Hofmann, 1998), 486–98.
7. From a Protestant respectively Lutheran perspective see especially the contributions in the distinctive work of Ommo Grupe and Wolfgang Huber (eds), *Zwischen Kirchturm und Arena: Evangelische Kirche und Sport* (Stuttgart: Kreuz, 2000).
8. See especially the writings of Coubertin in Norbert Müller (ed.), *Pierre de Coubertin, 1863-1937: Olympism* (Lausanne: International Olympic Committee, 2000); Pierre de Coubertin, *Die gegenseitige Achtung*, 1st ed. Hildegard Müller (ed.) (St Augustin: Academia-Verl. Richartz, 1988); and Pierre de Coubertin and O. Andersen, *Der Olympische Gedanke: Reden und Aufsätze* (Schorndorf: Karl Hofmann, 1967).
9. Pierre de Coubertin, Erhard Höhne, and Volker Kluge, *Olympische Erinnerungen*, 1st ed. (Berlin, Germany: Sportverl, 1987), 24–5. Initially, Coubertin wrote these words in the second edition of the '*Bulletin du Comité International des Jeux Olympiques*' (1894).
10. Olympic Charter in the version of 2014: https://stillmed.olympic.org/Documents/olympic_charter_en.pdf (accessed 17 May 2017).
11. https://en.wikipedia.org/wiki/Golden_Rule (accessed 13 June 2017).
12. Amitai Etzioni, *Die Verantwortungsgesellschaft: Individualismus und Moral in der heutigen Demokratie* (Frankfurt: Campus-Verl., 1997).

13. William J. Baker, 'Religion', in Steven W. Pope and John Nauright (eds), *Routledge Companion to Sports History* (London: Routledge, 2012), 217; see also in general Nick J. Watson and Andrew Parker, 'Sports and Christianity: Mapping the Field', in Nick Watson and Andrew Parker (eds), *Sports and Christianity: Historical and Contemporary Perspectives* (New York: Routledge, 2013), 9–88; and Hugh McLeod, 'Sport and Religion in England, c. 1790-1914', in Nick Watson and Andrew Parker (eds), *Sports and Christianity: Historical and Contemporary Perspectives* (New York: Routledge, 2013), specifically 112–30.
14. John J. MacAloon (ed.), *Muscular Christianity in Colonial and Post-Colonial Worlds* (Abingdon: Routledge, 2006); Clifford Putney, *Muscular Christianity: Manhood and Sports in Protestant America, 1880-1920* (Cambridge, MA: Harvard University Press, 2003).
15. Springfield College, AAHPERD Biography – Naismith.
16. See the compendium of articles on sport science and studies for the preparation of the Olympic Congress of Munich 1972 - Ommo Grupe and Helmut Baitsch (eds), *The Scientific View of Sport: Perspectives, Aspects, Issues* (Berlin: Springer, 1972), especially 43–83 regarding sport in the view of Catholic and Protestant theology of the twentieth century, and 84–88 on 'Sport and Non-Christian Religions'. Armin Ader, '*Zu den Ursachen der Leibes- und Sportfeindlichkeit*', *Leibesübungen und Leibeserziehung* 25 (1971), 30–2, considers the reasons of '*Leibfeindlichkeit*' and '*Sportfeindlichkeit*' in Christianity. The Christian criticism of agonistic sport is also grounded in the persecution of the early Christian communities in Rome when they became victims in Roman *munera*. See also generally the work of Franz Walter, *Der Leib und sein Recht im Christentum: Eine Untersuchung des Verhältnisses moderner Körperkultur zur christlichen Ethik und Askese* (Donauwörth: Auer, 1910).
17. Arnold Angenendt, *Geschichte der Religiosität im Mittelalter*, 2, überarb, Aufl (Darmstadt: Primus-Verl., 2000), is fundamental for the analysis and understanding of the religiosity in the Middle Ages including the *Leibfeindlichkeit*, here especially 560–6.
18. Following Lyndal Roper, *Luther. Der Mensch Martin Luther* (Frankfurt: Fischer, 2016), in English: Lyndal Roper, *Martin Luther. Renegade and Prophet* (New York: Random, 2016); Lyndal Roper, *Der feiste Doktor: Luther, sein Körper und seine Biographen*, Historische Geisteswissenschaften 3 (Göttingen: Wallstein-Verl., 2012).
19. The biography of Heinz Schilling, *Martin Luther: Rebell in einer Zeit des Umbruchs*, 2. Auflage der Sonderausgabe, 2017, Kindle Edition (14661 Positionen) (München: C.H. Beck, 2017) gives an excellent overview of the historical context of Luther's theology and reformation. See here Pos. 1301 ff.
20. http://www.mitteldeutsche-kirchenzeitungen.de/2016/01/21/%C2%BBwarum-rulpset-und-furzet-ihr-nicht%C2%AB/ (accessed 19 May 2017). Another saying which is, however, not established as having been stated by Martin Luther himself is: '*Wer nicht liebt Wein, Weib und Gesang, bleibt ein Narr sein Leben lang*' ('He who does not love wine, women and song remains a fool all lifelong'). Ultimately, it is not relevant whether the saying is from Luther or not, but that people did relate the saying to Luther's Protestant message. See https://www.aphorismen.de/suche?text=wein+weib+gesang&autor_quelle=&thema= (accessed 20 May 2017).
21. Following Roper, *Der feiste Doktor*.
22. His writing Martin Luther, *Von der Freiheit eines Christenmenschen*, edited by Dietrich Korsch, Grosze Texte der Christenheit 1 (Leipzig: Evangelische Verlagsanstalt, 2016 [first published in 1520]) was the most important contribution to this concept of the free human in the face of God.
23. Schilling, *Martin Luther*.
24. Max Weber, *Die protestantische Ethik und der Geist des Kapitalismus*, Beck'sche Reihe 1614 (München: Beck, 2010 [*erstmals erschienen* 1904/1905]).
25. Roper, *Martin Luther*.
26. https://www.bibleserver.com/text/LUT/1.Korinther (accessed 22 May 2017), *Die Bibel nach Martin Luther's Übersetzung, revidiert 2017.*

27. Translation by the author. Victor C. Pfitzner, 'Was St. Paul a Sports Enthusiast? Realism and Rhetoric in Pauline Athletic Metaphors', in Nick Watson and Andrew Parker (eds), *Sports and Christianity: Historical and Contemporary Perspectives* (New York: Routledge, 2013), 89–111, discusses another crucial quotation from Corinthians (9: 24–27) on the contest metaphors in St Paul's letters. See also Uta Poplutz, *Athlet des Evangeliums: Eine motivgeschichtliche Studie zur Wettkampfmetaphorik bei Paulus*, Herder's Biblical Studies Book 43 (Freiburg im Breisgau: Herder, 2004) and Alois Koch, '*Paulus und die Wettkampfmetaphorik*', *Trierer Theologische Zeitschrift* 1 (2008), 39–55. My focus is on the body concept based on quotations from Corinthians.
28. Heinz Schilling, '*Luther, Loyola, Calvin und die europäische Neuzeit*', *Archiv für Reformationsgeschichte* 85 (1994), 5–31; Heinz Schilling, *Martin Luther: Rebell in einer Zeit des Umbruchs* (German Edition) (Kindle-Positionen 11681–2); Theodor Ballauff and Klaus Schaller, *Pädagogik: Eine Geschichte der Bildung und Erziehung*, Orbis academicus 1, 12 (Freiburg: Alber, 1970), 87–100.
29. In the view of the Protestant churches in Germany, Grupe and Huber, *Zwischen Kirchturm und Arena*, from a Catholic perspective in Germany, Günther de Hrabe Angelis and Manfred Paas, *Partnerschaft: Spurensicherung beim Arbeitskreis, Kirche und Sport'in der Katholischen Kirche Deutschlands* (Neuss: Neusser Druckerei und Verlags GmbH, 1991), among others. The Second Vatican Council was a benchmark in the changing attitude of the Catholic Church to sports. See Grupe and Mieth, *Lexikon der Ethik im Sport*, 289–92.
30. Herms, 'Sport und Religion', especially 496.
31. Wolfgang Huber, '*Die Würde des Menschen ist antastbar*', in Ommo Grupe and Wolfgang Huber (eds), *Zwischen Kirchturm und Arena: Evangelische Kirche und Sport* (Stuttgart: Kreuz, 2000), 133–50. It is debatable whether the term 'Jesuanic' is really appropriate for clarifying the difference, because the life and death of Jesus Christ was indeed a kind of mortification or sacrifice similar to that of fanatical athletes mortifying and sacrificing themselves for sports and victories.
32. See Koch, '*Paulus und die Wettkampfmetaphorik*' and Pfitzner, 'Was St. Paul a Sports Enthusiast?'.
33. The title of the dissertation of Uta Poplutz, *Athlet des Evangeliums: Eine motivgeschichtliche Studie zur Wettkampfmetaphorik bei Paulus*, Herders biblische Studien ('Herder's Biblical studies'), Bd. 43 (Freiburg im Breisgau: Herder, 2004) refers to the combination of Christian asceticism with Olympic athleticism and agonistics.
34. Ernst Curtius, 'Olympia', in Avery Brundage et al. (eds), *Die Olympischen Spiele: Mit einem Vorwort von Rudolf Hagelstange*, Reclams Universal-Bibliothek 9330 (Stuttgart: Reclam, 1971), 39. The full quotation in German is: 'Was dort in der dunklen Tiefe liegt, ist Leben von unserem Leben'.
35. Carl Euler, *Friedrich Ludwig Jahn: Sein Leben und Wirken* (Stuttgart: Krabbe, 1881).
36. Guts Muths and Johann Christoph Friedrich, *Gymnastik für die Jugend: Enthaltend eine praktische Anweisung zu Leibesübungen; ein Beytrag zur nöthigsten Verbesserung der körperlichen Erziehung* (Schnepfenthal: Buchhandlung der Erziehungsanstalt, 1793).
37. Friedrich Ludwig Jahn and Ernst Wilhelm Bernhard Eiselen, *Die deutsche Turnkunst* (Berlin, 1816), 216.
38. Ibid., 235.
39. Ibid., 215.
40. Ibid., 233.
41. Carl Wassmannsdorff, 'Noch einmal das Wort "fromm" des Wahlspruches der Turner', *Monatsschrift für das Turnwesen* 6 (1892).
42. Quoted by Michael Krüger, 'Das Heilbronner Turnfest: Festkultur und Turnpraxis in der frühen Turnbewegung', in Peter Wanner and Peter Wieser (eds), *Adolf Cluss und die Turnbewegung: Vom Heilbronner Turnfest ins amerikanische Exil*, Kleine Schriftenreihe des Archivs der Stadt Heilbronn 54 (Heilbronn: Stadtarchiv Heilbronn, 2007), 48.

43. Wassmannsdorff, 'Noch einmal das Wort "fromm" des Wahlspruches der Turner', 173–5; Rudolf Gasch (ed.), *Handbuch des gesamten Turnwesens und der verwandten Leibesübungen* (Wien: Pichler, 1920), 811.
44. Eduard Dürre, 'Jahn und das Wartburgfest' *Deutsche Turnzeitung* 23, no. 16 (1878), 117–19.
45. Wolfgang Benz, *10. Mai 1933: Bücherverbrennung in Deutschland und ihre Folgen* (Frankfurt am Main: Fischer-Taschenbuch-Verl., 1983).
46. The writing of Carl Ignatius Lorinser, *Zum Schutze der Gesundheit in den Schulen* ['For the prevention of health at schools'] (Berlin: Enslin, 1836), initiated and supported the introduction of physical education at schools in Prussia.
47. See his work 'Lehre der Turnkunst' in Adolph Spieß, *Die Lehre der Turnkunst* (4 Thle. Basel, 1840–1846), first published in four volumes from 1840 to 1846.
48. Michael Krüger, 'Otto Heinrich Jaeger - der Rothstein des Südens. Zur Debatte um das Jaegersche Wehrturnen in Württemberg', *Sportwissenschaft* 19, no. 2 (1989), 172–93.
49. Hermann Bausinger, *Sportkultur: Sport in der heutigen Zeit* (Tübingen: Attempto-Verl., 2006), 148–58, wrote a biographical draft on Georgii as a leading light of the democratic and national *Turner* movement.
50. This and following according to Michael Krüger, *Körperkultur und Nationsbildung: Die Geschichte des Turnens in der Reichsgründungsära - eine Detailstudie über die Deutschen*, Reihe Sportwissenschaft 24 (Schorndorf: Hofmann, 1996).
51. Norbert Elias, *Studien über die Deutschen: Machtkämpfe und Habitusentwicklung im 19. und 20. Jahrhundert* (Frankfurt: Suhrkamp, 1990), 194, translated by Michael Krüger.
52. Erich Schmidt-Volkmar, *Der Kulturkampf in Deutschland: 1871-1890* (Göttingen: Musterschmidt-Verl., 1962).
53. Michael Krüger, *Einführung in die Geschichte der Leibeserziehung und des Sports* (Schorndorf: Hofmann, 2005), 103-4; Edmund Neuendorff, *Geschichte der neueren deutschen Leibesübung vom Beginn des 18. [achtzehnten] Jahrhunderts bis zur Gegenwart: Band IV: Die Zeit von 1860-1932*, four volumes (Dresden: Limpert, 1930-1936), 642–3; See also Baker, 'Religion', regarding the role of the YMCA for the ideology of muscular Christianity in the sports movement of Britain and the United States. Steven Huebner, *Pan-Asian Sports and the Emergence of Modern Asia, 1913-1974* (Singapore: NUS Press, 2016), refers to the role of the YMCA in the promotion of Asian sports and games.
54. The movie was released in 1980 and won an Oscar for the best film in 1982. See Hugh Hudson, Colin Welland, and Ben Cross, *Die Stunde des Siegers* (Twentieth Century Fox Home Entertainment Deutschland, 2009).
55. Ibid. Michael Krüger, 'Begegnungen: Themen und Entwicklungen von Turnen und Sport bei den Akademietagungen in Bad Boll', in Ommo Grupe and Wolfgang Huber (eds), *Zwischen Kirchturm und Arena: Evangelische Kirche und Sport* (Stuttgart: Kreuz, 2000), 251–67, shows in his documentary of workshops at the academy of Bad Boll/ Germany, organized by both churches and sports federations, how highly relevant the issue of a sports-free Sundays was to the churches after the Second World War.
56. See the public debate on this issue of a work and shopping-free Sunday in the radio feature: http://www1.wdr.de/nachrichten/verkaufsoffener-sonntag-streit-100.html (accessed 24 May 2017).
57. The early years of the DSB, including the process of re-establishing sports clubs and sports associations in Germany, are described and analyzed in detail by Deutscher Sportbund (ed.), *Die Gründerjahre des Deutschen Sportbundes: Wege aus der Not zur Einheit* (Schorndorf: Hofmann, 1990).
58. Ibid., 71.
59. Willi Daume, *Deutscher Sport 1952 - 1972* (München: ProSport, 1973), especially, 17–21.
60. Herbert Haag, August Kirsch, and Wilfried Kindermann (eds), 'Grundlagen der Zusammenarbeit zwischen Kirche und Sport (1976)', in *Dokumente zu Sport, Sporterziehung und Sportwissenschaft* (Schorndorf: Hofmann, 1991), 14–19.
61. The cooperation between the churches and sport organizations is described in detail by Rüdiger Schloz, 'Zwischen Unverhältnis, und Partnerschaft: Fünfzig Jahre Kirche und

Sport', in Ommo Grupe and Wolfgang Huber (eds), *Zwischen Kirchturm und Arena: Evangelische Kirche und Sport* (Stuttgart: Kreuz, 2000), 53–71, and Norbert Wolf, 'Zeittafel: Kirche und Sport: Entwicklung der Zusammenarbeit von 1945 bis 2000 aus evangelischer Sicht', in Ommo Grupe and Wolfgang Huber (eds), *Zwischen Kirchturm und Arena: Evangelische Kirche und Sport* (Stuttgart: Kreuz, 2000), 318–26.
62. http://www.zeit.de/1983/03/die-schwierigkeit-luther-zu-feiern (accessed 24 May 2017). However, Luther's opponent, Thomas Müntzer, one of the leaders of the peasants' war (in 1525, was even more glorified than Luther.
63. Lyndal Roper, *Der Mensch Martin Luther: Die Biographie*, with the assistance of Holger Fock and Sabine Müller (Frankfurt: S. Fischer, 2016), emphasizes that Luther's body concept included mental, emotional, and spiritual impacts which was in opposition to concepts of other radical reformers like the Swiss Johannes Calvin (1509–1564) and Huldrych Zwingli (1484–1531).
64. Poplutz, *Athlet des Evangeliums*. The vision of 'sport for all' from a theological perspective is considered by Peter Noss, 'Sport für alle - eine Vision theologisch betrachtet,' in Dieter H. Jütting and Michael Krüger (eds), *Sport für alle: Idee und Wirklichkeit* (Münster: Waxmann, 2017), 395–404.

Disclosure Statement

No potential conflict of interest was reported by the author.

ⓐ OPEN ACCESS

A Sportful History of Christianity: The Case of Twentieth-Century Sweden

Alexander Maurits and Martin Nykvist

ABSTRACT
The sport movement was consolidated in Sweden during the first years of the twentieth century and grew rapidly from the 1920s and onward. Preceding and during these events, the Church of Sweden – the Lutheran state church – was losing its axiomatic position within Swedish society and church attendance was decreasing. In this situation, many perceived the sports movement as a rival to the church or even saw sport as a new religion. However, as the sport movement grew, prominent representatives within the Church of Sweden and other Christian denominations adopted a more pragmatic view of the sports movement in order to appeal to people outside the ranks of the church, especially male youth. The sport field soon became a missionary field. The aim of the current essay is to account for the collaborative as well as the sceptical voices not only in the Church of Sweden, but also within the substantial Swedish revival movements, i.e. the Pentecostal movement and the Mission Covenant Church of Sweden. Further, these events will be analyzed from a gender perspective, discussing what was simultaneously perceived as a secularization and feminization of Swedish Christianity.

The sports movement means more and more to the male youth. That is joyful in itself. However, it is disheartening that the male youth is becoming less visible during Sunday service, without anything being done to spread the gospel to the youth where it gathers. (Manfred Björkquist, 1929)[1]

In his appeal to create closer ties between the Church of Sweden and the sports movement, Manfred Björkquist (1884–1985), later the first bishop of the diocese of Stockholm, expressed that the goal of such a collaboration was to reach people with the gospel. In two regards, his statement is indicative of how similar initiatives were discussed throughout the twentieth century. First, the focus on male youth indicates that there was a certain group of people that were to be reached. Second, addressing the issue of Sunday sport illustrates the importance of sabbatarianism during the twentieth century.

The aim of this paper is to establish which attitudes towards the sports movement were expressed within a few major Christian denominations in Sweden during the twentieth

This is an Open Access article distributed under the terms of the Creative Commons Attribution-NonCommercial-NoDerivatives License (http://creativecommons.org/licenses/by-nc-nd/4.0/), which permits non-commercial re-use, distribution, and reproduction in any medium, provided the original work is properly cited, and is not altered, transformed, or built upon in any way.

century. The prime focus will be the Church of Sweden, while also taking perspectives from the extensive revival movements into consideration. The account will be largely chronological in nature, thus revealing when and why the attitudes have changed. This, however, does not ignore the fact that, at times, parallel opinions have been asserted in different confessions and traditions. The tensions, but also the assimilation that occurs between the different Christian denominations and the advocators of sports stands at the centre of this essay.

Modernity and Religious Life in Sweden around 1900

Since the Reformation of the sixteenth century Sweden was a mono-confessional Lutheran state. This fact was, for example, expressed in the Civil Code of 1734, according to which apostasy from the 'true evangelical creed' was to be punished with expatriation and loss of inheritance right. However, this was to change during the course of the nineteenth and the beginning of the twentieth centuries.

As with other Northern and Western European societies, the situation in Sweden during this period was marked by increasing religious diversity and pluralization. As a consequence the law of 1734 was reformed with the introduction of the Dissenter Acts, decreed in 1860 and 1873 respectively. It was now possible to leave the Church of Sweden, provided that you instead joined another denomination which was officially approved by the Royal Majesty, and that you did not practice your religion in public. Notwithstanding the fact that only a couple of denominations chose to seek approval from the Royal Majesty as legitimate Christian communities, the Dissenter Acts are indicative of the religious pluralism that marked Sweden in the latter half of the nineteenth, and especially, during the twentieth centuries.

The Lutheran, state-sanctioned form, of Christianity certainly lost its position as the foundational ideology of Swedish society, but religion continued to play an important part, both socially and culturally. As has been argued elsewhere, the Established Church of Sweden, but also other denominations, roused itself to work against these attritional tendencies in various ways. One way to counteract the perceived societal challenges was to engage in different associational activities, thus working parallel to or together with the evolving social movements and associations that were established during the latter half of the nineteenth century, i.e. the Labour movement, the temperance movement, and the sports movement.[2]

In this paper, the main focus is on the connection between the Church of Sweden and the emerging sports movement. But the account of the Swedish situation would be insufficient if the attitudes to sports within and the activities initiated by the Mission Covenant Church (founded 1878) and the Pentecostal movement (established in Sweden 1906–1907) were not mentioned. Therefore, this paper will also include examples from these denominations.

Sabbatarianism and Feminization

In an article in the conservative daily paper *Nya Dagligt Allehanda* dated 6 February 1900, six teachers of religion from elementary and secondary grammar schools in Stockholm, a majority of which were clergymen, gave voice to their disapproval of sport events taking place on Sundays. This is one of the earliest public reactions from representatives of the

Church of Sweden to the growing sports movement. They claimed that the sporting activities of youth, 'laudable in themselves', were too often arranged during the hours of divine service.³ Ten years later, a conservative Christian weekly magazine claimed that sport was 'one of our time's most vigorous means of dechristianizing the Swedish youth'.⁴ It was not the sporting activities as such that were deemed problematic, but the fact that they took place on Sunday. Unlike Britain, where factories and shops had been closed during one afternoon of the week since the 1870s and 1880s,⁵ Sunday remained the only day available for participating in, or spectating, sport in Sweden until the work-free Saturday was introduced in the 1960s.

The late nineteenth and early twentieth centuries saw an increasing concern from Christians about work and leisure – not least the latter – during the Sabbath. A crucial reason behind this concern was the fact that Sweden at this time went through a period of urbanization. In the growing cities, factory workers, shopkeepers, and clerks were not able to include religious practices in their workdays. Religion became, to a larger extent than had been the case in agricultural society, associated with Sunday exclusively. From the point of view of the church, it was thus considered important that Sunday remained a day dedicated to religious devotion.⁶

At the same time, new arenas emerged in society, of which the sports movement was only one. In particular, men were getting involved in mass politics, not least in the rapidly growing Labour movement, which had its strongest foundation in the Swedish Social Democratic Workers Party, established in 1889. The sports movement as well as the Labour movement, which were both seen as rivals to the church, were to a very large extent male-dominated. As an example, one can mention that in 1942, the youth associations of the major Christian denominations in Sweden were female dominated, with 62% of the members being girls, while 73% of the members of the youth sporting associations were boys.⁷ Thus, clergy and other representatives of the church expressed anxiety over what they experienced as a 'feminization' of the church and of Christian religion, due to the fact that men chose to get involved in the recently established social movements rather than going to church.

The fear of a 'feminization' of religion is crucial for understanding how and why members of both the clergy and the laity approached the sports movement throughout the twentieth century. In the 1960s and 1970s, the historian Barbara Welter introduced what later came to be known as the 'feminization thesis'. Welter argues that Western Christianity went through a process of 'feminization' during the nineteenth century, claiming that it became domesticized, soft, and amenable.⁸ This thesis has later been the subject of due criticism by historians and theologians.⁹ Interesting to note, however, is the fact that the narrative of the feminization thesis palpably coincides with the narrative of the perceived feminization in the early twentieth century. In Sweden, as well as in other parts of Europe, means were taken in order to make the church appealing to men. By and large, this was done by reinforcing gender differentiations and discursively presenting Christianity as something stereotypically 'manly'.¹⁰

It can be called into question whether or not a feminization actually took place, both in church and in society at large. Historians are in general agreement that gender constructions were quite tenacious. For example, women did only in part make their way into the public domain and the ideal of the man as the sole breadwinner remained important in the rising welfare state.¹¹

Sports and Physical Education in Modern Sweden

From the 1920s, sport became an essential part of Swedish popular culture and the youth – mainly the male youth – used it in an ever-increasing amount as a cultural tool to reach emancipation and in their quest to find social belonging. The sports movement's involvement in raising the youth was for a long time met with suspicion, since it was claimed to have clear connections to dubious public entertainment.

The debates in the 1930s and 1940s were to a large extent based on ethics and expressed that the (male) youth must be led on the right track. It was not uncommon to see clergy in the front rows of these debates, but they were far from alone. Many columnists, politicians, and others concurred with the agitated priests. In the same way as the Labour movement and other social movements of the time, the church wanted to prevent the coming into being of a generation of youth that was independent and uncontrolled. In other words, representatives of the church were not concerned about sporting activities, they were concerned about the youth.

Physical activities were considered important throughout the twentieth century, even though the place of sport was often debated. As early as 1820, Physical Education (PE) was introduced as a mandatory feature in the secondary grammar school, and it remained mandatory with the introduction of *Volksschule* in 1842.[12] During the nineteenth and early twentieth centuries, PE followed the ideals of Ling gymnastics, which was introduced by Per Henrik Ling (1776–1839) who was influenced by the German philosopher F.W.J. Schelling (1775–1854). Ling used exercises as a tool to develop both body and mind. As concluded by the Swedish historian Jens Ljunggren, the purpose of Ling gymnastics was 'to form the harmonious body as a worthy temple of the spirit'. The goal was to foster a balanced physical development, good posture, character, strength, and health, while the proponents of Ling gymnastics expressed 'a distaste for specialisation, quantified physical performances and movements that were adapted to practical working life'.[13] In light of this, it is not surprising that the Lingians were, to say the least, sceptical towards modern sport.

Throughout the nineteenth and twentieth centuries, schools had two to three hours of mandatory PE per week. By the end of the twentieth century, the ideals of Ling gymnastics were still prevalent, but had been complemented with learning outcomes connected to recreation, fellowship, and development of a creative ability.[14] Criticism of PE was scarce, also from representatives of the church. The latter were instead occupied with defending the role of Christian instruction in schools.[15] The lack of scepticism towards PE can be interpreted as a result of the fact that it did not have any connections to the sports movement and competitive sport per se. The focus was rather to develop a sound physique, an aim which advocates of the church, too, considered important.

Towards Closer Relations

After it had its first boom in Sweden during the 1920s, a shift can be observed in how the Church of Sweden valued the sports movement. In the first decades of the twentieth century, only a few individual endeavours had been made to establish a connection between the Church of Sweden and the sports movement. The most prominent of these was the founding in 1899 of an athletic association called The Reverend's Lads by Ernst Klefbeck (1866–1950), who served as a minister in one of the parishes in Stockholm. The association, which initially consisted of Klefbeck's former confirmands, changed its name to Hellas in connection with the 1912 Stockholm Olympics.[16] In contrast to Britain, however, there was never any Christian or church-based sport leagues in Sweden.[17]

The years 1929–1930 can be seen as a turning point in the historical relation between the Church of Sweden and the sports movement. During this short period a number of initiatives were started by representatives from the Church of Sweden in order to strengthen the ties with the fast-growing sports movement. The men behind these initiatives had in common a connection to the Young Church Movement (*ungkyrkorörelsen*). The latter's aim was to counter the 'dechristianization' of Swedish society as well as the increasingly popular Free Church movement. Based on the Folk Church theology of Einar Billing (1871–1939), the Young Church Movement's motto was 'The people of Sweden – a people of God'. This signalled that the grace of God was offered to all citizens of Sweden and that the Swedish people were chosen. To reach people with the gospel and the ideals of the movement, members were from 1909 and a few years onwards sent on 'crusades' throughout the country. During these crusades the proponents of the Young Church Movement, mostly young men from the laity, travelled in pairs to give talks and take part in discussions with members of the working class. In order to be a Folk Church, the church had to reach people where they gathered, as Manfred Björkquist stated in the initial quotation above.[18] Doing so required a more sympathetic attitude towards the sports movement than had been expressed in the early twentieth century.[19]

In February 1929, the Archbishop of the Church of Sweden and also an originator of the Young Church Movement, Nathan Söderblom (1866–1931), held an opening speech in connection to one of the most popular sporting events in Sweden at the time, the Swedish Ski Championships. The speech, which was entitled 'The Virtues and Dangers of Sport', shows how the earlier condemning approach to the sports movement was becoming more nuanced and even appreciative.

According to Söderblom, there were five virtues inherent to sport. First, he claimed that sport always involved a quest for perfection. Söderblom evidently saw sport as competitive by nature and he claimed that competing equals strove for perfection. In order to strengthen his argument, Söderblom cited St Paul's letter to the Corinthians, where the author uses athletic imagery: 'Do you not know that in a race all the runners run, but only one receives the prize? So run that you may obtain it.'[20] Second, Söderblom saw the physical exercise that sport entailed as a virtue. This, he proceeded, should also remind us of the importance of spiritual exercise – which in order to be successful had to be regular and well planned in the same way as its physical counterpart. The third virtue of sport was discipline, which again was supported with references to the epistles of St Paul. When referring to 1 Corinthians, the key aspect was restraint: 'Every athlete exercises self-control in all things. They do it to receive a perishable wreath, but we an imperishable.' And in 2 Timothy the corresponding ideal was submission: 'An athlete is not crowned unless he competes according to the rules.'[21] The ideal of self-restraint was also visible in what Söderblom saw as the fourth virtue of sport, viz. the ability it fosters to bear hardships, pain, and disappointment. The Biblical analogy of dealing with setbacks in sport was Christ's exhortation in the Sermon on the Mount that one should not look gloomy when fasting (Matthew 6:16–18). Söderblom stressed that instead of showing self-pity, one should seek 'the manly virtue to be your own master, and not a slave under opinions, feelings, and occurrences'. The fifth virtue, the uniting nature of sport, was different from the previous virtues, since it stressed sport's potential for society rather than the individual. Söderblom claimed that sport contributed to the levelling out of class distinctions; in sport, people were able to look beyond social categories, e.g. class, profession, and political affiliation.[22]

As the title of the speech suggested, Söderblom did not only see advantages in sport. The latter could also lead to considerable risks, which the speaker divided into three categories. First, there were sporting activities which were characterized by violence and brutality. Even if Söderblom did not mention any sport specifically, one must remember that the 1920s was the golden age of boxing in Sweden.[23] However, brutality could, according to Söderblom, befall any sport. Second, sport ran the risk of leading one into dissoluteness. To obstruct this, one had to keep in mind that the will must rule the body, not vice versa. Again, the ideal of self-restraint was put to the fore by the Archbishop. The last risk according to Söderblom was that of excessive commitment. Instead of becoming a 'sport freak', one should remember 'the large defining goal, which can be called by the Saviour's own name'.[24]

In the following years, members of the clergy would give speeches in connection to the opening ceremonies of sporting events and bless the participants.[25] A more thorough initiative to establish a connection between the Church of Sweden and the sports movement was taken in 1930. Manfred Björkquist, who was the leading figure of the Young Church Movement, arranged a conference at the Sigtuna Foundation outside Stockholm with delegates from the Church of Sweden on the one hand, and leaders from the sports movement on the other. The initial programme for the conference had four items: sport on Sundays, divine service for sportsmen, the sports press and character-building, and the question of a permanent body for collaboration. With regard to the view of sport as something politically as well as religiously neutral, a debate about the latter item was rapidly dismissed by representatives from the sports movement. In fact, the conference mainly treated sporting activities on the Sabbath and divine service for sportsmen.[26]

The conference, which was preceded by a service where Archbishop Söderblom gave a sport-related sermon, had Björkquist as its introductory speaker. He pointed to the fact that the aim of the meeting was not to put restraints on the sports movement or to make any final decisions, but rather to make it possible for the representatives from each side to – as he put it – get to know each other. Björkquist stressed the need for a uniform culture work, in which the youth would be taught sound human values based on physical culture on the one hand, and spiritual culture on the other. This coincided well with the aims and ideals that had been expressed within the Muscular Christianity movements mainly in Great Britain and the United States.[27]

Britain was also brought up as a paragon by the next speaker, Ernst Killander (1882–1958), and by others during the conference sessions. Killander, a front-runner in the sports movement and fervent advocate for closer church–sport relations, spoke about the worship services for the sporting youth in the outskirts of London. By adopting this sort of 'original, interesting, and short' service, the young men in the Swedish sports movement would establish a continuous relation to the church. In accordance with their British counterparts, he also claimed that students at the theological faculties in Sweden should devote more time to sport, in order to come into contact with other young men. If Söderblom attributed sport with important ideals in itself, Killander seemed to be more interested in the instrumental prerequisites of sport in relation to the church.[28]

A third and final speech from the conference should be mentioned here, given by a priest called Gabriel Grefberg (1892–1960). During the 1930s he published books and articles about the place of sport within the church, as well as a devotional for sportsmen. Grefberg agreed with the general consensus that the sports movement had to remain free from religious and political influences. Instead, he saw Juvenile's concept of a sound mind in a sound body (*mens sana in corpore sano*) as the sports movement's own creed. It was this creed that men of the church had to serve within the sports movement in order to preserve the true nature of sport. He claimed that sport must not only create 'heroes in muscle power and physical buoyancy', but also 'a type, in which a strong body, a noble way of thinking, and a warm heart shape complete human beings'. This combination of physical strength, nobility, and warm-heartedness is familiar from the ideals of masculinity, which prevailed within Muscular Christianity. Hence, it was not only Manfred Björkquist and Ernst Killander who were trying to adopt ideals and structures from the Anglo-Saxon context.[29]

During the discussion that followed, the participants often came to the same conclusion as Grefberg – that the sports movement had to be neutral in all aspects. This is not surprising, since the large-scale sporting federations in Sweden during the inter-war years decidedly claimed that sport and politics (in extension, also religion) should be separated. It was also presented as desirable that no sporting events should take place on Sundays between 11.00 am and 1.00 pm, nor at all on Good Friday, Easter Sunday, Christmas Day, or the Day of Penance (which until 1983 was a specific feast celebrated in February within the Church of Sweden). Regarding a divine service for sportsmen, most representatives from both sides were sceptical. The secretary general of the Swedish branch of the Young Men's Christian Association (YMCA), Hugo Cedergren (1891–1971), instead preferred a solution along the lines presented by Killander – namely that the priests to a wider extent would be part of the sporting organizations. In that way, a relationship to the church would be established among the male youth.[30]

The above developments in the Church of Sweden had an equivalent in one of the major revival movements in Sweden at the time. In her analysis of a journal for the youth within the Mission Covenant Church, historian Elin Malmer shows that the attitude towards the sports movement went from dire criticism to prudent appreciation during the first decades of the twentieth century. In the first years of the twentieth century, the readers of the journal were strictly advised to devote their time to work 'for God' rather than taking part in sporting activities. Not surprisingly, the problem of sport on the Sabbath was addressed as one of the major issues. This sort of critique was also directed towards other forms of leisure, not least dancing, which had become a popular pastime in the late nineteenth and early twentieth centuries. The problem, however, does not appear to have been sport in itself, but rather what involvement in the sports movement could lead to. Malmer reaches the conclusion that 'competitive sport and parlour games – like social customs within sports and rifle clubs – was associated with sin, and thus constituted a threat to the spiritual life of the born-again Christians'.[31]

Over the coming years, the editors of the journal became more obliging. In one article from 1908, the Swedish athletes who took part in the London Olympics were honoured. The author did, however, point out that the ultimate goal is higher than sport: the eternal life. This claim was supported with a reference to 1 Corinthians 9:25, where St Paul claims that the followers of Christ race to win an imperishable wreath. In a similar way to Nathan Söderblom, the author is anxious to point out that sport must not take too much of a person's time. In an article published in 1910, the preacher and editor of the journal in question, August W. Hellström (1857–1938), encouraged 'strengthening sporting activities during unoccupied hours' and urged the youth of the revival movements to strive after a sound mind in a sound body.³²

Ideological and Practical Motifs

In the beginning of the 1940s, the Church of Sweden National Board for Parish Life (*Svenska kyrkans diakonistyrelse*) set up a position as secretary for sports. The initiative in itself shows how strategically important the church considered the issue of leisure and sport to be. The first holder of this assignment was Samuel Norrby (1906–1955). Norrby, who was himself a successful athlete, for example a fivefold Swedish champion in shot-put, worked as a pastor in the outskirts of Stockholm.

As secretary for sports within the National Board for Parish Life, Norrby had the task to inspire his colleagues among the clergy to, as a part of their pastoral work, engage with young people and the sports movement. Furthermore, he was supposed to work as a mediator between the Church of Sweden and the rapidly growing sports movement.³³ Some of Norrby's speeches and sermons from these different occasions were later to be published. As a consequence of his own successful athletic career, one should not underestimate the impact that Norrby may have had on the boys and girls that he met during the course of his work.

Norrby was strongly influenced by the ideas of the above-mentioned Young Church Movement and men like J.A. Eklund (1863–1945), Nathan Söderblom, and Manfred Björkquist. In one of his speeches, he even paraphrased a popular nationalistic hymn significant for this movement. In the hymn it was emphasized that the well-being of the Swedish society was dependent upon the Christianization of the Swedish youth, but in Norrby's phrasing the well-being of the country was dependent on whether or not the sports movement was Christianized.³⁴ In that sense, Norrby equated the importance of counteracting a perceived feminization by proselytizing among boys and young men within the sports movement. For Norrby and his like-minded, the overall purpose was to reconcile any differences between the church and the surrounding society. In doing so, Norrby, from a practical perspective, gave voice to something similar to *Kulturprotestantismus*. When Norrby expressed this view he spoke in terms of 'everyday Christendom' (*vardagskristendom*), and emphasized that Christian faith should not be confined to the Sabbath, but rather should be an important part of everyday life, including sport activities.³⁵

In his essays and speeches, Norrby frequently pointed out that a Christian belief could be combined with a sound engagement in athletic activities, resulting in positive consequences. Norrby frequently returned to the idea of a sound mind in a sound body. He also emphasized that there were important societal gains to be made if the sports movement and the church cooperated, and if the church took on a positive attitude to different athletic activities. Norrby underlined that sport gave rise to important virtues, especially when it came to the education of boys and young men. For example, sport fostered democratic and patriotic citizens, and it introduced the idea of fair-play and thus helped in encouraging people to become 'better humans'. Additionally, the exaltation that came with athletic exercise or a victory gave a perception of God.³⁶

Frequently, Norrby pondered on the idea that the industrial society in which he worked was in need of organized leisure activities for the youth. It is important to note that Norrby used the term 'youth' (*ungdom*) as a synonym for boys or young men. Only occasionally, and in passing, did he mention girls or young women in connection to sports. When speaking about women, Norrby kept to a strict traditional gender division, underlining the role of women as mothers within the private domain.[37] Emphasizing the need for boys and young men to engage in athletic activities, Norrby used a rhetoric typical of the period, viz. the idea that men during their adolescence needed to have a fling. This idea, highlighted by historian David Tjeder, meant that boys or young men needed to give way to different passions or to have 'their fling' in order to be able to live settled lives as adults.[38] For Norrby, sport appeared as a useful means to channel this need for a fling, and at the same time helped in reducing violent behaviour among boys and young men. A collaboration between the sports movement and the church would also educate youth in more ethical and spiritual matters.[39] Sport was seen as a serious form of play. This kind of play was considered as a necessary component in contemporary society, since it constituted a means for people to better understand themselves and others. Additionally, Norrby pointed out that athletics, probably referring to track and field, was a type of play which suited men.[40] Altogether, sport was seen as vital part in shaping democratic and Christian citizens.

Parts of Norrby's text seem to be strongly influenced by the notion of a perceived feminization. As others influenced by the Young Church Movement, Norrby tried to persuade his readers and listeners that Christianity was a masculine matter; that the spirituality that he belonged to was genuinely manly and that there was nothing effeminate about it.[41] It thus seems that a faith with masculine traits was a prerequisite for Norrby in order to engage with representatives of the sports movement.

Norrby was not convinced about the idea that sport and the sports movement should be neutral with regard to religion. Since he perceived Sweden to be a Christian country, he did not accept that religion was relocated to the private sphere. Instead, he claimed that 'Christianity is the ideology and life form of all Swedes – including athletes!'[42]

Of course, Norrby recognized the different down-sides of sport, too. One of the negative aspects of sport was the increasing professionalization. Norrby regarded professionalism as a problem since its outcome was that the joy that came with sport was superseded by the pursuit of earning money.[43] Additionally, Norrby could be sceptical towards sport activities during Sundays. Thus, it seems as if the question of sabbatarianism was still important within Broad Church circles of the Church of Sweden during the 1940s. However, Norrby was not rigid in his opinion, and in a personal reflection he mentions how he as a competing athlete found it difficult to attend service on Sundays. He nevertheless found a strategy to be able to attend service at the place of the contest, thus successfully combining the requirements of the third commandment and his career as an athlete.[44]

Critical Voices within the Church of Sweden

The positive approach to the sports movement common to the Young Church Movement and Samuel Norrby was not shared by the entire clergy of the Church of Sweden. On the Swedish west coast especially, proponents of the conservative revival tradition were sceptical.

This particular revival was influenced by Lutheran orthodoxy and Pietism, and had its key figure in Henric Schartau (1757–1825) who served as a minister in the cathedral of Lund from 1785 until his death 40 years later. In that position he practiced considerable influence on the numerous theology students in the city. After him, the revival movement is known as Schartauanism. The advocates consider the preaching of the word the principal means of grace, which is why liturgical reforms and new work models within the church are looked upon with disapproval. The essential element is instead the intellectual aspects of faith, i.e. preaching, education, cure of souls, and individual reading of edification literature.[45]

Based on this short introduction it is not difficult to see why exponents of Schartauanism took a stand against sport and the sports movement. They saw two major problems with sport and how it was praised by an increasing amount of representatives from the church. First, sport was viewed as a rival activity to listening to the sermon during the Sunday service. The fact that the Sunday issue was of major importance to the conservative revival tradition was not coincidental. Its high esteem of the ministry and the significance it placed on preaching made the Sunday services protracted and of utmost importance to the faithful. There was simply not room for sporting activities on the Sabbath, which instead was to be devoted entirely to spiritual undertakings and serenity. Even after the introduction of work-free Saturdays in Sweden during the 1960s, the sports movement was criticized on Sabbatarian grounds.[46]

The second problem was of more substantive character, viz. that the proponents of the sports movement within the Church of Sweden valued sport because of its potential to improve (male) youth morally. To neglect the aspect of faith in favour of morals was considered theologically dubious by the leaders of the revival. Personal improvement could not be reached by any outward activity, but was the consequence of deepened belief.[47] These objections indicate that it was not sport in itself which was considered the problem, but rather that sport – as much as any other leisure activity – would lead to a misguided focus.

The 1920s saw the establishment of a High Church movement within the Church of Sweden, influenced by the ecumenical aspirations of the time. With Anglo-Catholicism and the Roman Catholic Liturgical Movement as prototypes, it strove for a liturgical revival within the Church of Sweden. The life of the church was to be based around the divine service with mass being celebrated every Sunday. The word and the sacraments were at the centre of parish life.

The leading character in the Swedish High Church movement was Gunnar Rosendal (1897–1988). He authored the book series *Kyrklig förnyelse* ('Church Renewal'), published in nine volumes between 1935 and 1972, which came to be programmatic to the movement. In the prologue to the first volume, Rosendal comments on the growing popularity of sport as an element in the youth work of the parishes:

> Many clergymen were imaginative enough to use sport as bait on the hook in order to catch the young, but the youth took the bait and skilfully avoided the hook. They sometimes came across their clergy on the football pitch, but they seldom cared to hear him in church.[48]

Rosendal considered the church's attempt to attract male youth through sport futile. Only by conducting and creating an interest for the divine service could the clergy attract new devotees.

In conclusion, a theological divide can be observed when clergy and other representatives from the Church of Sweden discussed the place of sport in parish life. Proponents of the conservative revival tradition on the west coast and the members of the High Church movement saw sport as a distraction from what they believed to be essential to the church. The results indicate that neither of the two considered sport as something negative or harmful in itself, as long as it did not interfere with what they considered to be ecclesiastical obligations.

The Pentecostal Turnabout

In addition to the Mission Covenant Church discussed above, the Swedish twentieth-century revival had a stronghold in the Pentecostal movement. The latter was established in Sweden only a few years after the Azusa Street Revival in Los Angeles, and between 1911 and 1974 the spiritual leader of the Pentecostal movement in Sweden was Lewi Pethrus (1884–1974). Pentecostalism is part of the wider charismatic movement and characteristic of its piety is the focus on spiritual gifts, particularly glossolalia, generally known as speaking in tongues. Similar to the Mission Covenant Church, Pentecostals practice adult baptism, which means that a person must actively profess his or her faith in order to be baptized and become a member of a congregation. Being baptized thus means that you are born-again and have chosen a life with God, which comes with obligations with regard to how you choose to live your life.[49]

Church historian Joel Halldorf argues that we have to understand the Pentecostal attitude towards sport in light of its theological roots. As stated above, the born-again Christian is to lead a life without sin in order to reach sanctification. This, in turn, means that this disposition should be characteristic for every single deed that he or she performs. Unlike traditional Lutheran theology, there are no actions deemed adiaphora in Pentecostalism; all acts are considered either spiritual or unspiritual and thus sinful. As a born-again Christian you are to give up all worldly pleasure-seeking and live a life entirely devoted to Christ. Any form of leisure might lead you in the wrong direction and must thus be avoided.[50] This was a notion that was also common among Baptists and members of the Mission Covenant Church as well as within certain factions of the Church of Sweden.[51]

Rather than the Sabbath issue, which was frequently discussed within the Church of Sweden, Pentecostals viewed sport as problematic because it was a rival for the souls and marked by destructive ethics.[52] Thus, in a 1950 article from a Pentecostal journal, the author asserted that 'many young people waste their time and energy on sport ... There is, however, something better to live for, which is seeking to win the heavenly and eternal prize that awaits the faithful at the end of the track'. Ten years later, in 1960, another journal article emphasized the rivalry aspect by arguing that 'if you go in for your mission, there will be no time left for sporting activities'. Instead of dedicating time to sport, one had to spend it in prayer and dealing with congregational duties.[53]

We have seen how representatives from the Church of Sweden endorsed the sports movement and claimed that sport brought both personal and societal virtues. Notwithstanding that there were pragmatics, the most common opinion expressed by Pentecostals in the 1950s and 1960s was that there was no connection between sport and virtue. Rather than discipline, self-restraint, and the other virtues listed by Nathan Söderblom and his peers, Pentecsostals often argued that sport was an idol or a demon characterized by competition mania, which resulted in selfishness and vanity.[54]

The scepticism towards sport and other expressions of popular culture was loosened within the Pentecostal movement from the 1960s. As a result, Lewi Pethrus published a book in 1967, called *Nöjesliv eller frälsningsfröjd* ('Entertainment or the Joy of Salvation'), where he defended traditional Pentecostal ethics and rejected the recent development. The book was subject to extensive criticism from younger pastors within the movement. Many seemed to have reached the conclusion that representatives from the Church of Sweden and the Mission Covenant Church had reached a few decades earlier: in order to keep the youth, the congregations have to employ a more pragmatic approach. Indicative of the shift in attitudes was the fact that a journal for Pentecostal youth leaders in 1975 published an article entitled 'Defuse the Element of Competition' accompanied with a picture of children playing football. Sport, the authors argued, would create solidarity and unity and arranging camps with sporting activities would sound more appealing to the youth than Bible camps. Now, sport was seen as a way to, rather than a distraction from, spiritual exercises. These changes came rapidly and without further reflection. In a sudden manner, the Puritan ideals were refused since the traditional prohibitions and restrictions seemed incomprehensible. According to Halldorf, a contributory cause to this process was that the mediation of Pentecostal tradition experienced a breach in the later part of the twentieth century. The pragmatic approach to sport was accomplished in 1995 with the establishment of Sport for Life, a Pentecostal organization with the explicit aim to help children and youth to grow and develop through sport.[55]

The development in the Swedish Pentecostal movement is similar to that which took place after the First World War in the American South. In the North, Muscular Christianity had left a remaining impact, while Evangelical Christians in the rural South remained sceptical to such intermingling until the 1920s. Much like the Pentecostals in Sweden, the Southerners were hesitant at best when it came to sport because it represented ideals in society of which they disapproved. Historian William J. Baker also provides an additional account for why Evangelicals in the South called the combination of religion and sport into question, viz. because it was associated with their opponents in the North.[56] There was no corresponding geographical divide in Sweden, but the confessional divide was all the more manifest. Hence, the hostility to sport expressed within the Swedish Pentecostal movement from the 1940s until the 1970s might also be interpreted as an objection to the friendly advances to the sports movement that was made by representatives of the Church of Sweden.

Conclusion

There are several parallel histories of the relation between the church and the sports movement in twentieth-century Sweden. Nonetheless, it is clear from the results presented above that a hesitant attitude to sport among representatives of the major Christian denominations in Sweden during the early years of the twentieth century was later renegotiated – first by the Church of Sweden and the Mission Covenant Church in the 1920s and 1930s and later, in the 1960s and 1970s, by the Pentecostal movement. While representatives of the Church of Sweden – particularly those representing the Young Church Movement – wanted the church to adapt to society at large, the Pentecostals wanted to demarcate themselves from a leisure trend which they perceived as sinful.

We have argued that the approaching attitude to the sports movement by the Church of Sweden must be understood from a gender perspective. In the early 1900s the sports movement was – and to a large extent still remains – dominated by men. Simultaneously, Nathan Söderblom, Manfred Björkquist, Samuel Norrby, and many of their peers were expressing their concern that the church was running the risk of becoming 'feminized'. It is therefore not surprising that their depictions of sport were drenched in stereotypically 'masculine' traits of the time, such as strength, prowess, chivalry, and self-control. In this sense, they could be said to represent a Swedish version of Muscular Christianity, largely influenced by its British predecessor. By connecting these ideals to sport – and by extension to the church – the latter was portrayed as hypermasculine rather than effeminate. In other words, sport can be said to have been used as a tool in an attempt to 'masculinize' the Church of Sweden.

It can thus be argued that the church was presented as in need of the sports movement. At the same time, however, the sports movement was similarly presented as if it was in need of intervention from the church. There were negative aspects of sport that Christian ideals could remedy. The main issue was, not surprisingly, sport on the Sabbath, but violence, professionalization, and a misguided focus in life were also problems which could be countered if there was a collaboration between the clergy and the sporting youth. This kind of double-sided influence was to foster the frequently addressed ideal of a sound mind in a sound body.

Notes

1. Manfred Björkquist, '1929 års Generalkonvent', *Kyrkobröderna* 5, no. 8 (1929), 87, authors' translation.
2. Anders Jarlert, 'Introduction', in Anders Jarlert (ed.), *Piety and Modernity: The Dynamics of Religious Reform in Northern Europe 1780–1920, III* (Leuven: Leuven University Press, 2012), 7–24; Lars Österlin, *Churches of Northern Europe in Profile: A Thousand Years of Anglo-Nordic Relations* (Norwich: Canterbury Press, 1995), 153–79; Oloph Bexell, *Sveriges kyrkohistoria: 7. Folkväckelsens och kyrkoförnyelsens tid* (Stockholm: Verbum, 2003), 198–245; Alexander Maurits, *Den vackra och erkända patriarchalismen: Prästmannaideal och manlighet i den tidiga lundensiska högkyrkligheten, ca 1850–1900* (Lund: Universus Academic Press, 2013), 42–50.
3. Jan Lindroth, 'Kors eller boll? Kyrkan och idrotten i Sverige 1900–1914', *Idrott, historia och samhälle* (1986), 103.
4. Ibid., 104, authors' translation.
5. Hugh McLeod, 'Sport and Religion in England, c. 1790–1914', in Nick J. Watson and Andrew Parker (eds), *Sports and Christianity: Historical and Contemporary Perspectives* (New York: Routledge, 2013), 120.
6. Bexell, *Sveriges kyrkohistoria*, 11. For an international example, see L. Dean Allen, *Rise Up, O Men of God: The Men and Religion Forward Movement and Promise Keepers* (Macon: Mercer University Press, 2002), 24–5.
7. Johnny Wijk, 'Idrott, ungdom och "dansbaneelände": Om den svenska idrottsrörelsens begynnande engagemang som ungdomsfostrare på 1940-talet', *Idrott, historia och samhälle* (2001), 99. Another male-dominated movement whose activities were accused of Sabbath violation was the voluntary defence movement established in 1860, known as the 'sharpshooter's movement' (*skarpskytterörelsen*). Cf. Alexander Maurits, 'Kyrkan och skarpskytterörelsen: En mikrohistorisk konfrontation', in Mikael Ottosson and Thomas Sörensen (eds), *Borgerlighet i vapen: En antologi om 1800-talets milisrörelse* (Malmö: Malmö University Press, 2008), 58–90.
8. Barbara Welter, 'The Cult of True Womanhood: 1820–1860', *American Quarterly* 18, no. 2 (1966), 151–74; Barbara Welter, 'The Feminization of American Religion: 1800–1860', in Mary S. Hartman and Lois W. Banner (eds), *Clio's Consciousness Raised: New Perspectives on the History of Women* (New York: Harper and Row, 1974), 137–57.
9. Tine Van Osselaer and Thomas Buerman, 'Feminization Thesis: A Survey of International Historiography and a Probing of Belgian Grounds', *Revue d'Histoire Ecclésiastique* 103, no. 2 (2008), 497–544; Bernhard Schneider, 'Feminisierung der Religion im 19. Jahrhundert: Perspektiven einer These im Kontext des deutschen Katholizismus', *Trier Theologische Zeitschrift* 111 (2002), 123–47; Patrick Pasture, Jan Art, and Thomas Buerman (eds), *Gender and Christianity in Modern Europe: Beyond the Feminization Thesis* (Leuven: Leuven University Press, 2012); Olaf Blaschke, 'The Unrecognised Piety of Men: Strategies and Success of the Re-Masculinisation Campaign around 1900', in Yvonne Maria Werner (ed.), *Christian*

Masculinity: Men and Religion in Northern Europe in the 19th and 20th Centuries (Leuven: Leuven University Press, 2011), 21–45.
10. Olaf Blaschke and others have called these initiatives strategies of remasculinization, but as Tine Van Osselaer argues, it is more adequate to use the term differentiation. Tine Van Osselaer, '"From That Moment On, I was a Man!": Images of the Catholic Male in the Sacred Heart Devotion', in Patrick Pasture, Jan Art, and Thomas Buerman (eds), *Gender and Christianity in Modern Europe: Beyond the Feminization Thesis* (Leuven: Leuven University Press, 2012), 135.
11. Jens Rydström and David Tjeder, *Kvinnor, män och alla Andra: En svensk genushistoria* (Lund: Studentlitteratur, 2009), 134–55; Yvonne Hirdman, Urban Lundberg, and Jenny Björkman, *Sveriges historia, 1920–1965* (Stockholm: Norstedts, 2012), 77–82.
12. Claes Annerstedt, *Idrottslärarna och idrottsämnet: Utveckling, mål, kompetens – ett didaktiskt perspektiv* (Gothenburg: Acta Universitatis Gothoburgensis, 1991), 107–8.
13. Jens Ljunggren, 'The Masculine Road through Modernity: Ling Gymnastics and Male Socialisation in Nineteenth-Century Sweden', in J.A. Mangan (ed.), *Making European Masculinities: Sport, Europe, Gender* (London: Frank Cass, 2000), 93. Cf. George L. Mosse, *The Image of Man: The Creation of Modern Masculinity* (Oxford: Oxford University Press, 1996), 40–55.
14. Annerstedt, *Idrottslärarna och idrottsämnet*, 107–14.
15. Ann-Katrin Hatje, 'The Struggle Over Christianity as a School Subject: The Democratic Role of the Press in a Church Campaign in 1963', in Anna-Sara Lind, Mia Lövheim, and Ulf Zackariasson (eds), *Reconsidering Religion, Law, and Democracy: New Challenges for Society and Research* (Lund: Nordic Academic Press, 2016), 235–54.
16. Jan Falk, Kjell Löfberg, and Sverker Tirén, *Hellas: Idrottshistoria under ett sekel, 1899–1999* (Stockholm: Sim- och idrottsklubben Hellas, 1999), 2–10, 278; Henrik Sandblad, *Olympia och Valhalla: Idéhistoriska aspekter av den moderna idrottsrörelsens framväxt* (Grillby: Lärdomshistoriska samfundet, 1985), 258, 364–7; Klefbeck established an athletic association as early as 1892, two years after his ordination, but with no obvious connection to the church. Anders Jarlert, *Göteborgs stifts herdaminne, 1620–1999: III. Fässbergs, Älvsyssels södra och norra kontrakt* (Gothenburg: Tre böcker förlag, 2016), 147–9.
17. McLeod, 'Sport and Religion in England', 118–19.
18. Cf. Nils Martinius Justvik, *Idrett og kristendom på Sørlandet 1945–2000* (Kristiansand: Portal Akademisk, 2012), 75.
19. About the Young Church Movement, see Tobias Harding, 'The Dawn of the Secular State? Heritage and Identity in Swedish Church and State Debates 1920–1939', *International Journal of Cultural Policy* 22, no. 4 (2016), 631–47; Stephen A. Mitchell and Alf Tergel, 'Chosenness, Nationalism, and the Young Church Movement: Sweden 1880–1920', in William R. Hutchinson and Hartmut Lehmann (eds), *Many Are Chosen: Divine Election and Western Nationalism* (Minneapolis, MN: Fortress Press, 1994), 231–49.
20. 1 Corinthians 9:24, English Standard Version (ESV). This passage is recurring in discussions about sport and Christianity. While some, like Söderblom, used it in order to prove that sport was an activity worthy of an apostle, others claimed that St Paul pointed to the negligible use of sport. Cf. Lindroth, 'Kors eller boll?', 113, 118, 125.
21. 1 Corinthians 9:25; 2 Timothy 2:5, ESV.
22. Martin Nykvist, 'För männens skull: Svenska kyrkan och idrottsrörelsen 1929–1930', in Martin Nykvist and Alexander Maurits (eds), *Kyrkan och idrotten under 2000 år: Antika, medeltida och moderna attityder till idrott* (Malmö: Universus Academic Press, 2015), 188–93. The speech can be found in Nathan Söderblom, *Tal och skrifter: Tal* (Stockholm: Åhlén och söners förlag, 1933), 286–95.
23. Cf. Justvik, *Idrett og kristendom*, 69.
24. Nykvist, 'För männens skull', 193–4.
25. E.g. Gabriel Grefberg, *I tävlingskampen – andaktsbok för idrottsmän och friluftsfolk: Betraktelser och tal* (Stockholm: Svenska kyrkans diakonistyrelses bokförlag, 1939); Samuel Norrby,

Vasalopp och kyrkmarsch (Stockholm: Svenska kyrkans diakonistyrelses bokförlag, 1943), 118–26.
26. Nykvist, 'För männens skull', 198–9.
27. Ibid., 204. The Muscular Christianity movement, which has its origins in 1850s Great Britain, stressed the importance of both physical and moral strength. As Hugh McLeod has summarized, Muscular Christianity 'was not merely advocating sport as a remedy for social ills or an alternative to more disreputable recreations: it was a part of the full life that God intended us to live, and thus should be enthusiastically enjoyed by Christians, including clergymen'. McLeod, 'Sport and Religion in England', 115–17. For an introduction to Muscular Christianity, see Clifford Putney, *Muscular Christianity: Manhood and Sports in Protestant America, 1880–1920* (Cambridge, MA: Harvard University Press, 2001); Norman Vance, *The Sinews of the Spirit: The Ideal of Christian Manliness in Victorian Literature and Religious Thought* (Cambridge: Cambridge University Press, 1985).
28. Nykvist, 'För männens skull', 204–5.
29. Ibid., 205–6.
30. Ibid., 206–8.
31. Elin Malmer, 'Muskelkristendom på svenska: Idrotten och det maskulina ungdomsidealet i *Ungdomsvännen* 1900–1914', in Martin Nykvist and Alexander Maurits (eds), *Kyrkan och idrotten under 2000 år: Antika, medeltida och moderna attityder till idrotten* (Malmö: Universus Academic Press, 2015), 175–6, authors' translation.
32. Ibid., 172–4.
33. Norrby, *Vasalopp och kyrkmarsch*, 5.
34. Ibid., 47. The paraphrase of the hymn reads: 'Idrotten kristnad är Sveriges vår, Sveriges framtid och hälsa!'
35. How theologians, for example Bishop J.A. Eklund, by different means strove for a culture synthesis is developed in Johan Sundeen, *Andelivets agitator: J A Eklund, kristendomen och kulturen* (Lund: Avdelningen för idé- och lärdomshistoria vid Lunds universitet, 2008), 24–8. See also Samuel Norrby, *Fritt fram* (Stockholm: Svenska kyrkans diakonistyrelses bokförlag, 1954), 74–5, 89.
36. Norrby, *Vasalopp och kyrkmarsch*, 5–6, 11, 17–18, 30.
37. Cf. Norrby, *Fritt fram*, 51–3.
38. David Tjeder, *The Power of Character: Middle-Class Masculinities, 1800–1900* (Stockholm: Stockholm University, 2003), 97–128.
39. Norrby, *Vasalopp och kyrkmarsch*, 21–4.
40. Norrby, *Fritt fram*, 42.
41. Norrby, *Vasalopp och kyrkmarsch*, 33–4.
42. Ibid., 42.
43. Ibid., 12–19.
44. Norrby, *Fritt fram*, 85.
45. Cf. Lars F. Qualben, *A History of the Christian Church* (Eugene, OR: Wipf and Stock, 2008), 397.
46. Anders Jarlert, 'Idrotten och den kyrkliga skepsisen', in Martin Nykvist and Alexander Maurits (eds), *Kyrkan och idrotten under 2000 år: Antika, medeltida och moderna attityder till idrotten* (Malmö: Universus Academic Press, 2015), 216–8.
47. Ibid., 219.
48. Gunnar Rosendal, *Kyrklig förnyelse* (Osby: Pro Ecclesia, 1935), 9, authors' translation.
49. For an introduction to Pentecostalism, see William K. Kay, *Pentecostalism* (London: SCM Press, 2009).
50. Joel Halldorf, 'Avvisad och omfamnad: Idrott i den svenska Pingströrelsen 1940–1980', in Martin Nykvist and Alexander Maurits (eds), *Kyrkan och idrotten under 2000 år: Antika, medeltida och moderna attityder till idrott* (Malmö: Universus Academic Press, 2015), 230–2.
51. For a discussion on this topic within the Free Church movement, see Owe Kennerberg, *Innanför eller utanför: En studie av församlingstukten i nio svenska frikyrkoförsamlingar* (Örebro: Libris, 1996). On Schartauanism within the Church of Sweden, see Katarina Lewis,

Schartauansk kvinnofromhet i tjugonde seklet: En religionsetnologisk studie (Uddevalla: Bohusläns museums förlag, 1997), 125–31, 190–1.
52. Cf. Justvik, *Idrett og kristendom*, 73–4.
53. Halldorf, 'Avvisad och omfamnad', 234–8.
54. Ibid., 238–42.
55. Ibid., 244–8.
56. William J. Baker, *Playing with God: Religion and Modern Sport* (Cambridge, MA: Harvard University Press, 2007), 85–107.

Disclosure Statement

No potential conflict of interest was reported by the authors.

Cultural Imperialism, Nationalism, and the Modernization of Physical Education and Sport in China, 1840–1949

Huijie Zhang, Fan Hong and Fuhua Huang

ABSTRACT
This paper examines how missionary educational institutions and Young Men's Christian Association physical education and sport programmes, in conjunction with the nation-building project of the Nationalist government, transformed and modernized physical education and sport in China from 1840 to 1937. The concepts of cultural imperialism and nationalism are central to this study, to understand how the two interacted in the process of the development of modern physical education and sports in China. This paper argues that the cultural imperialism model is ineffective for an understanding of the impact of missionaries on Chinese society and the subsequent transformation and indigenization of physical education and sport in modern China. More precisely, the way in which Chinese nationalism played an active role in resisting, selecting, and reshaping the cultural products (modern physical education and sport) evidences a process that was an active negotiation, rather than a passive consumption, of Western culture. This said, Christian physical education and sport programmes had long-lasting effects on how physical education and sports became the way to define 'modern' bodies as they were incorporated into the wider education programme of modernizing China under the Nationalist government.

Modern physical education and sport in China, as they exist in their current form, are not products of indigenous Chinese culture. They are, as Fan Hong and Tan Hua argue, 'foreign import[s] and developed in a hot-house of modernization' in the early twentieth century.[1] Before the start of the First Opium War,[2] under the influence of traditional Chinese Confucian-informed culture, strenuous physical exercise, and sports were linked to low class and status. They were looked down upon by mainstream Chinese society and the upper classes in particular. Consequently, modern Western physical education and sport were virtually non-existent until the 1840s, when Western powers began making military and trading incursions into

China. Christian missionaries arrived in China in the wake of these inroads;[3] until then, religious proselytization by foreigners had been prohibited in China. Modern Western physical education and sport were introduced to China primarily by Western missionaries and physical (education) directors of the Young Men's Christian Association (YMCA). Under the influence of the missionary schools and the YMCA, physical education and sport in China modernized rapidly in the early twentieth century. From small beginnings, and in less than 50 years, modern Western physical education and sport were gradually embraced by the Chinese and became important tools for Chinese nation building.

The Development of Chinese-Led Western Military Physical Education and Sport

After its defeats in both Opium Wars, China's political and geographic integrity was threatened by both domestic instability and Western military incursions. Internally, China was ravaged by social upheaval and economic recession, rapid population growth, food shortages, political corruption, and bloody insurgencies by ethnic minorities, workers, and peasants. This placed increasing pressure on the Qing government and initiated a period of dynastic decline. Alongside this internal strife, China was defeated by external forces in a series of wars, including the two Opium Wars and the First Sino-Japanese War.[4] Consequently, the Chinese regime lost much of its international political standing, in particular after a series of unfavourable treaties were signed with Western countries and Imperial Japan. This situation turned China into a semi-colonial, semi-feudal society.[5]

In view of both domestic strife and foreign aggression, the Qing government was forced to take stock and re-evaluate itself and its opponents. Eventually, a series of reforms were introduced. Qing officials, scholars, and even the emperor himself launched a number of self-actualization initiatives, including the Self-Strengthening Movement (1864–1895) and the Hundred Days' Reform (11 June–21 September 1889). One of the important purposes of these reform movements was to 'learn with a sense of caution' so as not to be overawed by various aspects of the West's military training, technology, education and political systems.[6] These reform movements also sought to learn from Western countries in order to enable China to become a strong and rich country and eventually subdue foreign threats to its sovereignty.

A similar attitude was adopted with the Chinese state's embrace of Western military sport.[7] While these state-led reform movements met with the same fate as the rebellions, they did leave an impression among the Chinese people. The real legacy of these reforms was that they led to an overhaul of political culture and the economy, and to an increased emphasis on military training and improving the physical strength of the Chinese people. These reforms also facilitated China's path to Western-style modernity in Chinese physical education and sport.

These movements, even in their demise, ushered in a new era and facilitated the introduction of subsequent reforms from 1901 to 1911. These were so successful that the Empress Dowager Cixi and her court became convinced of the indispensability of the reform movement, not only to 'save China from Western imperialism' but also to 'restore the prestige and power of the Qing dynasty in China itself'.[8] As a result, a series of reform decrees were issued by the Qing government. In terms of education, the reforms included abolishing the eight-part essay in the Imperial Civil Examination,[9] adopting Western-style teaching systems in schools, establishing a Ministry of Education, translating Western books and sending students abroad to study.[10]

The first modern school system, the Qinding Regulation for Schooling (QRS), was introduced by the Qing government in 1902. This educational system was an experiment designed to assess the efficacy of a programme that emulated the Japanese educational system.[11] The Japanese educational system was modelled on military training principles and drew on German-style gymnastics. This system was thoroughly revised the following year and put into effect as the Zouding Regulation for Schooling (ZRS). The ZRS specified the goals and expectations of the four tiers of local educational institutions across China—primary, middle and secondary schools, and higher institutions.[12] This reorganization of the educational system was followed by the introduction of many 'Western' subjects into the curriculum, which now also included a compulsory gymnastics class.[13] The ZRS became the earliest nationwide official national regulation for schooling instituted by the Chinese government for local government and private schools. This programme, for the first time, signified the role of physical education in the local educational system of modern China. Gymnastics, especially military gymnastics, was emphasized by schools and the government, and used to improve the military force of the Chinese army and the physical strength of Chinese youth.

These reforms in indigenous education did result in the advancement of physical education, especially military sports, to promote the physical strength of Chinese youth and to improve the force of the Chinese military. However, more comprehensive and differently styled physical education and sport initiatives were being undertaken by the Christian missionary educational institutions and the YMCA with a different goal in mind, running in parallel to military physical education in local schools and sports societies.

Christianity and the Development of Physical Education and Sport in Modern China

Christianity and the Emergence of Western Physical Education and Sport in China, 1840–1908

From 1840 to 1908, evangelists and missionaries became significant agents of change who were able to take advantage of the precarious political situation in China to promote religion and Western-style education and sport to the Chinese people. By virtue of a series of unequal treaties signed between China and Western countries, such as the Treaty of Nanking and the Treaty of Peking, the missionaries gained the right to travel and live anywhere in China and to carry out their missionary work. These early missionaries of this period had little intention to revolutionize Chinese society, as their main concern was to convert the Chinese, but when faced by obstacles put in their way by both the Chinese people and their traditional customs, they focused on developing Christian education. For example, missionaries from the Congregational Church came to China in 1847 but baptized their first convert only in 1865.[14] John Leighton Stuart, a Presbyterian Church missionary and later president of Yenching University in Peking, said: 'It was very well to talk of the importance of direct evangelism, but it was difficult to maintain enthusiasm [among missionaries] for preaching tours which brought few tangible results'.[15] Frequent illnesses and high death rates among missionaries and their wives and children, harsh living conditions, and the indifference of Chinese people to their preaching made for a difficult experience, forcing the missionaries to devise new strategies for proselytizing. The educational route offered the best prospects, and as a result more attention was paid to providing Christian education and to establishing various missionary schools and colleges. This is how these missionaries then 'moved beyond simple evangelism to a broader effort to reshape Chinese society'.[16]

Thus, it was to fulfil the aims of Christianizing and 'civilizing' China that the missionaries gradually began to emphasize Christian educational enterprise. By the end of the nineteenth and the beginning of the twentieth century, a comprehensive educational system from elementary to tertiary education had been set up, and a chain of missionary educational institutions spread throughout China.[17] In this context, modern Western physical education and sport were initially intended to improve students' health and to build up 'good Christian character'. The missionaries saw themselves as instrumental in changing the image of China as the 'Sick Man of East Asia' by addressing aspects of Chinese traditional customs and culture which were seen to perpetuate poor physical health among Chinese youth.[18] Physical education in these schools and colleges was carried out through either formalizing extracurricular activities or conducting compulsory physical education classes.[19] In addition, interscholastic athletic games started to be held in cities such as Shanghai, Tientsin and Peking, heralding a popularization of Western sport among students and the general public.

The further development of the missionary schools and Christianity also paved the way for the YMCA's arrival in China. Since the International Committee of the YMCA had established a presence in Tientsin in 1895, its work had proved instrumental in the development of physical education and sport in big cities. By 1908, the YMCA had started organizing very successful sport exhibitions and matches in Tientsin and Shanghai,[20] despite having been in China for less than 20 years with a limited presence of only a small number of branches. However, this proved to be a real milestone—more and more Chinese students in these two cities started taking part in sporting activities.

At the initial stage, the missionaries and YMCA directors met with some indifference and even resistance from Chinese students. First, at that time there was an emphasis on literary endeavours, with physical activities held in contempt by mainstream Chinese society. Some students thought that participating in sports activities would decrease their dignity.[21] Second, these Western sports activities greatly emphasized athleticism, and many students were reluctant to participate in sports competitions for fear of losing face if they were defeated.[22] Third, some traditional Chinese customs constrained students from taking part. Edward Alsworth Ross notes: 'Lissom young men with queues were skipping about the tennis courts, but they wore their hampering gowns and their strokes had the snap of a kitten playing with a ball of yarn'.[23]

Women were also discouraged from taking part in physical activities. In the Confucian-dominated Qing dynasty, women were expected to practise the 'Three Obediences' (*Sancong*); namely, to obey her father before marriage, her husband after marriage, and her sons after the death of her husband. She was also required to practise the 'Four Virtues' (*Side*)—morality, proper speech, modest manners, and diligent work. Taking part in sports was seen as countering such desired behaviour. Another tradition that prohibited women from participating in sports was the practice of footbinding. Upper class women had their feet bound with several metres of bandages from the age of four or five to prevent further growth. This binding process normally lasted from 10 to 15 years. As a result, women with bound feet had difficulty walking steadily or quickly, which made participation in sporting activities virtually impossible.

Nevertheless, by the end of the nineteenth and beginning of the twentieth century, with the changing physical ideology as a result of this series of social and political reforms, and the strenuous efforts of missionaries and YMCA directors, Western sports attracted increasing attention from both Chinese students and the public, despite being limited to the big treaty port cities. Students from missionary schools and even some government schools started participating.

Christianity and the Expansion of Western Physical Education and Sport in China, 1908–1919

From 1908 to 1919, the expansion of modern Western physical education and sport reached its peak in China. The downfall of the Qing government, the creation in 1912 of the Republic of China and the later restoration by Yuan Shikai which led to in-fighting among warlords rendered the country extremely unstable, with no central sovereign authority. Under these socio-political conditions, missionary educational institutions and the YMCA continued to thrive.

However, the dissemination of modern Western physical education and sport was certainly not an overwhelming infusion process. In this period, Chinese intellectuals, patriots and nationalists continued to learn from the West in order to build a 'strong and prosperous nation'.[24] In the 1910s, new educational systems were set up by the Republic of China, such as the Renzi-Guichou Regulation for Schooling (RGRS, 1913). The RGRS clearly positioned the provision of physical education in schools as one of its main objectives. In this context, the content of the physical education class, or gymnastics class as it was called in this new school system, included basic military and general gymnastics exercises.[25]

Nevertheless, the development of Western sports in local schools gained its momentum. Above all, although Western ball games and athletics were only in a nascent state in China, Chinese sports ideology was gradually changing. Missionary schools and the YMCA became the main initiators of this significant change in society, though local educators and nationalists later followed suit. This period witnessed the further expansion of missionary schools and YMCAs throughout China. The physical education work of the missionary schools brought a functional sophistication which popularized Western sports and Western sports ideology, not only among students in Christian schools but also among those in local schools and among the general public.[26] Their physical education and sport work was increasingly acknowledged by the Chinese elites, who perceived the missionaries' educational endeavours as helpful in inculcating self-belief among Chinese youth.[27] More importantly for the development of sports education in China, the missionary educational institutions were effective in instilling an enthusiasm for sports, and changed the mindset of young people by denting the derogatory notions of physicality formerly prevalent in China.[28] Their reach was broad and comprehensive, encompassing the inculcation of modern Western attitudes toward the body, the design of physical education curricula and teaching methodology, and a focus on developing infrastructure for sports education. Their activities covered elementary, high school, and tertiary education, and they moved towards mass reform by not only introducing basic reforms in classroom curricula, but also conducting regular sports, athletic, and extracurricular activities. Infrastructure was developed, sports facilities were constructed and professional physical education training was provided to teachers. Seasonal intramural and interscholastic athletic contests also became a regular feature of the physical education programme of the missionary educational institutions. The influence of these activities is evident in how they brought great functional sophistication of national sports activities, leading to the wide-scale popularity and adoption of Western sports and Western sports ideology not only among students in Christian colleges and schools, but also in government-run non-religious local schools across China. Most importantly, Western-style sport was made popular beyond educational institutions, through intramural competitions.[29]

However, it was the YMCA's educational programmes in particular that galvanized the development of Western-style physical education with a Christian ethos during this period. Most significantly, the establishment of the physical department of the YMCA in 1908 further enhanced the physical education and sport programme.[30] This comprised physical education in missionary and indigenous educational institutions, lectures on physical education and sport, leadership training, physical education activities and exhibitions inside and outside YMCA buildings, and the organization of regional, national, and international athletic games. The YMCA and other missionary institutions laid the foundations of modern physical education and sport in Chinese society. First, a large number of talented Chinese sports people and educators cultivated by the YMCA later became responsible for the development of modern physical education and sport.[31] Second, more basic sports facilities were constructed and developed.[32] Third, due to special lectures, training classes, and teaching in missionary schools and some local schools, more and more Chinese youth, educators and even government officials changed their mindset on Western physical education and sport.[33]

Under the influence of the YMCA, Western sports such as athletics and basketball gained greater currency in local schools. In this way, a Dual-Track Physical Education System (*Shuanggui tiyu*, DPES) developed in modern China. Thereafter, in a large number of local government and private schools, the official physical education class consisted largely of military gymnastics based on RGRS, while Western sports such as ball games and calisthenics were popular only as extracurricular activities.[34] Some schools even added ball games and track and field to their official physical education classes, and cut down on military gymnastics.[35] These Western games were used to educate young people in new and desired modern Chinese characteristics of cooperation, equality, and national unity.[36]

It is noteworthy that the missionary schools and the YMCA played a pivotal role in leading physical education and sport in China, until their activities were effectively subsumed by the Nationalist government nation-building agenda from the late 1920s on. For instance, they took charge of the sports organizations in most of China, and organized the National Games. They were also responsible for preparing for China's participation in international sports events such as the Far Eastern Championship Games (FECG), including the selection and training of athletes.

The Indigenization of Modern Western Physical Education and Sport in China

The Nationalist Movements and the Decline of Physical Education Programmes in Missionary Schools and the YMCA, 1919–1928

The New Culture Movement[37] and the May Fourth Movement[38] of the late 1910s and 1920s can be seen as harbingers of the later anti-imperialist and nationalist movements in China. After these movements, nationalism continued to spread among the Chinese people, especially among intellectuals. These two movements paved the way for the Anti-Christian Movement of the 1920s by creating a unifying narrative of paranoiac projection outward of a foreign threat that could only be overcome through a process of Sinification. During this period, in the context of widespread nationalist sentiment, Christianity came to be regarded as a tool of Western cultural and political imperialism and was denigrated accordingly. Within the short span of five years from 1922 to 1927, three waves of the Anti-Christian Movement erupted, occasioning a tragic denouement of the years-long efforts of Christian missionaries and the YMCA's foreign directors in China.[39] As a result, by the end of 1927 many churches had been forced to close or had been seized by the Northern Expedition Army. Many foreign missionaries and their converts were killed, and numerous foreign missionaries and YMCA secretaries were sent back to their own countries.[40] At the same time, the trend towards the indigenization of Christian organizations was growing across the general population, as can be seen from the increasing number of Chinese Christians who took up leadership roles in organizations like the missionary educational institutions and the YMCA. They wished to demonstrate the compatibility of Christianity and Chinese nationalism by redefining Christianity in terms of China's own religious culture.[41]

Sport provided 'important insights into varieties of imperialism, the cultural politics of the anti-imperialist struggle and postcolonial legacies'.[42] The role of the missionary educational institutions and the YMCA in physical education and sport declined between 1919 and 1928, and Western sport in China underwent a process of indigenization in terms of leadership. First, as a result of the Anti-Christian Movement, many missionary educational institutions and YMCAs closed and many others could not carry on their activities and educational work as effectively as before. Some talented young Chinese sports people left the missionary educational institutions and the YMCA to study or work in Chinese schools or indigenous sports communities.[43] In addition, as a result of a nationwide boycott, teams from missionary educational institutions and universities were banned from taking part in some interscholastic athletic contests, and new interscholastic athletic contests were organized to rival the Christian ones.[44]

Second, alongside the declining role of the missionary educational institutions and the YMCA, indigenous sports and in particular martial arts began to receive greater attention from the Chinese people—to the extent that for some nationalists martial arts were seen as a counterweight to Western sports, even if this did not happen in practice.[45]

Third, the failure of the Chinese team at the sixth FECG resulted in a series of discussions and reflections on sporting sovereignty. The absence of an indigenous community or organization to manage Chinese sport, and a lack of support from the government, were concluded to be the main reasons for this. Therefore, it was decided to replace the China National Athletic Union (CNAU),[46] set up by the YMCA, with the China National Amateur Athletic Federation (CNAAF). This was made responsible for the organization of athletic activities, especially international competitions such as the FECG. One noteworthy aspect of this development was that all the members of the new CNAAF were Chinese. Even though a large number of the leaders in sports communities had once been trained by or had worked for the YMCA, the leadership of Chinese competitive sport and physical education was put in Chinese hands.[47] The Chinese nationalists used Western physical education and sport to wake up a national sentiment of 'China under threat'. They also used competitive sport to foster a nationalistic spirit and patriotism.

In sum, the New Culture Movement, May Fourth Movement and Anti-Christian Movement between 1919 and 1927 resulted in widespread hostility towards Christianity in modern China, so much so that opposition to the religion was even officially sanctioned during this era.[48] Under the influence of these nationalist movements, the Chinese began to take control of education, physical education, and sport, hitherto mostly run by foreign missionaries.

Nationalism and the Indigenization of Physical Education and Sport in China, 1928–1937

The Nationalist Party overcame the warlords, occupied Peking and officially established a new capital in Nanking in 1928. The Nationalist government then began to take away sovereign rights in different areas from foreigners around China.[49] Missionary educational institutions and the YMCA were required to register and be supervised by the Nationalist government, and their activities had to be in accordance with government regulations and policies. At the same time, Chinese personnel were officially favoured and gradually acquired most of the administrative positions in these Christian institutions.[50] For example, by 1933 almost all Christian higher education institutions had registered with the Nationalist government and integrated their education more closely with the state school system.[51]

Despite the strict supervision, the Nationalist government generally adopted a lenient policy towards Christianity. Moreover, the 'localizing' missionary educational institutions and the YMCA became active promoters of 'a nation state identity among contemporary Chinese'.[52] Consequently, the Christian institutions and their physical education and sport programmes recovered to some extent shortly afterwards, despite no longer holding a leadership position in physical education and sport in China. Under the leadership of the Nationalist government and along with the development of nationalism among Chinese people, there was further indigenization of Christian institutions and their physical education and sport programmes, as well as modernization of sport in China.

In the educational system, the Nationalist government had official control over physical education and sport in China by the 1930s. In April 1929, it established the National Sports Law, which positioned physical education and sport as a viable means of developing a national spirit of unity to help China emerge as an independent modern state.[53] The first official Nationalist government administrative body for physical education and sport—the National Sport Committee of the Ministry of Education (NSC)—was constituted in October 1932, and provincial and local physical education committees followed soon afterward.[54] The NSC's achievements include planning the national curriculum for physical education. This mandated 150 minutes of physical education per week for primary schools, further suggesting activities like games, outings, traditional sports, hill climbing, calisthenics, ball games, and other modern sports. All students were also required to participate in after-school sports and exercise programmes.[55]

Outside the campus, the Nationalist government used physical education and sport as a tool to popularize its ideology of developing a new way of life among the Chinese people through civic education and a return to traditional morals, and to inculcate in them the notions of Chinese nationalism and a national consciousness. To do so, the Nationalist government initiated the New Life Movement in 1934. On 2 March 1935, the Nationalist government issued an open letter—'the Promotion of Physical Education and Sport'—to the nation, seeking general approval for its plan to implement a mass physical exercise programme. Following this directive from Chiang Kai-shek, not only was the Physical Education and Sport Department founded by the New Life Promotion Committee in 1935, but several provincial Physical Education and Sport Councils were also subsequently founded to promote the regional mass sports campaign by training physical education instructors and organizing a variety of physical activities for the Chinese people, such as basketball.[56]

Furthermore, the Nationalist government began to use the modern operational modes of physical education and sport, namely sporting competitions, to unite the nation, and to strengthen the people's political will, by instilling national consciousness through projecting the country's national image on the international stage through competitive sport. This propaganda goal was mainly achieved through China's organization of the National Games and participation in the Olympic Games.

For instance, at the opening ceremony of the fifth National Games (1933), when all the delegations had marched into the centre of the stadium, an athlete from the northeast read out a public letter lamenting the loss of Chinese territory in the northeast of China so as to incite anti-Japanese sentiment and patriotic fervour in spectators.[57]

China's first participation in the Olympic Games was also linked to its political appeal. After the 'September 18 Incident',[58] the Japanese government tried to send Chinese athletes Liu Changchun and Yu Xiwei to the 1932 Olympic Games in order to legitimize the Manchukuo puppet regime in the international community. This failed due to Liu and Yu's strong rejection and the IOC's disapproval. In response, the Nationalist government sent Liu to the Games, sponsored by some patriots, to proclaim the autonomy of China.[59]

Between Cultural Imperialism and Nationalism: The Modernization of Physical Education and Sport in China

Despite the notion that sports and physical education were eventually indigenized and led by the Chinese themselves, the question now remains as to whether this all represents a form of cultural imperialism that was simply introduced by Western missionaries and consequently merged into the very core of notions of modern Chinese national identity. In this concluding part, it is asserted that the answer lies somewhere between these two positions, as cultural imperialism as a tool for foreign encroachment was by and large made ineffective due to the way in which the Chinese Nationalist government appropriated Western sports in its own nation-building projects.

The missionaries were in general driven to work in China by their belief in the Christian doctrine of salvation of the soul through a personal relationship with God and through Christ's sacrifice, and the obligation of each believer to respond to this sacrifice by proclaiming the Gospel of Christ to all of humanity. However, while the religious aspect was driven by personal belief in God and evangelism was perceived as an individual response to it, the missionary and YMCA educators also strove to promote modern Western knowledge and culture, in the belief that it was only through moulding China into a Christian country that it could survive in the modern world. While the spiritual mission was their primary focus, the missionaries saw China as in need of Western religion and civilization in order to adopt modern values and make progress.[60] For this reason, other aspects of Western culture and knowledge were also introduced by the missionaries, such as customs, language, and Western knowledge of mathematics and geography. Missionary educational institutions and the YMCA used modern physical education and sport to bring social change and Western civilization to China.

One of the most significant changes for the Chinese was that the adoption of Western physical education and sports brought about a significant change in cultural attitudes toward muscular bodies. Western sports set and demanded high standards of physicality (as opposed to the traditional Chinese view), providing a strong justification for extending Western rule 'as necessary for bringing [the] local population up to Western [physical] standards'.[61] The physical education work of missionary educational institutions and the YMCA in China, though integrally connected to evangelical work, was an enterprise for the missionaries to 'transform the world's most populous nation' into the mould of a global civilization.[62]

This change was envisaged based on the idea of 'muscular Christianity', a concept then popular in Europe and America. The basic premise of muscular Christianity was that taking part in sport contributed to 'the development of Christian morality, physical fitness and "manly" character' in individuals.[63] The widely held Christian belief at that time was that one's physical condition had religious significance and that the body was an instrument in the service of God, meaning 'the effort to have a sound body was an effort to be a good Christian'.[64] Adherence to the idea of muscular Christianity in the second half of the nineteenth century had a sustained impact on the seriousness with which Anglo-American and other European Christians viewed the relationship between sport, physical fitness, and religion.[65] It was no wonder that sporting activities became ever more popular not only in Christian institutions and the modern educational system, but also throughout the West. These Western countries, especially the United States and Britain with their well-equipped Christian institutions, later became the vanguards of Western imperialism. Through them, modern sports were introduced, promoted and regulated in other countries around the world, including China, at this time labelled the 'Sick Man of East Asia' due to political instability and vulnerability.[66] The missionaries found the Chinese to be physically weak and living a hand-to-mouth existence. Physical education and sport were thus greatly emphasized by missionary educational institutions and the YMCA, as part of nurturing a Western and essentially Christian image of manhood.

Confucianism emphasized civility and held martial attitudes and practices in contempt, and accordingly exercise and manual labour were also disparaged by educated and wealthy Chinese in the late Qing period. The men of the upper classes wore flowing gowns, grew their fingernails and prioritized intellectual pursuits, while the women practiced the 'Three Obediences', 'Four Virtues', and footbinding. However, with the popularity of modern Western physical education and sport in China, the Chinese, especially Chinese youth (including young women), began to actively participate in various Western sporting activities and games, and in general sportsmanship, fair play, friendship, and goodwill were witnessed. This method of introducing and popularizing physical education and sport among Chinese people signalled a transformation of traditional Chinese cultural norms toward the body.[67] Modern Western physical education and sport were instruments offered to Chinese people converting to Christianity. Physical education and sport were presented as elemental modalities of Western culture; also, once the conquered accept antecedents such as the physical education and sport of a foreign culture, this is a crucial further step toward accepting its religion and customs. Therefore, the attempts of missionary educational institutions and the YMCA to Christianize China were among the most important reasons for the introduction and promotion of modern Western physical education and sport. In fact, physical education and sport were used as agents of change for the propagation of religion and culture by the missionary educational institutions and the YMCA in their project to Christianize China.

Particularly during the period from 1840 to 1920s, the morale of Westerners in China was high, due to the success of the physical education and sport programmes. They saw themselves as having the 'right and indeed the responsibility' to 'help' the Chinese—a people 'of different and, by implication, lesser religion or civilization than their own'.[68] Prior to the dramatic rise of Chinese nationalism in 1920s, foreigners held the major leadership roles in the management of physical education and sport in China. In missionary educational institutions and the YMCA, most leaders and directors were foreigners, and they alone developed policies for Christian organizations and institutions. This fact was never more evident than at the time of the first three FECGs from 1913 to 1917. Most of the leaders of Chinese delegations at these events were foreigners who both selected and trained the athletes. Even the rules of competitive events in the first two National Games were written in English, and the commentary was also in English. In this sense, Christian missionaries and YMCA directors thus played a significant part in instigating a process of social and cultural change in modern China and—both intentionally and unintentionally—inculcating a particular set of beliefs, values, knowledge and behavioural norms in China.[69]

However, it is argued that the transformation in beliefs about physicality and the approach to Western physical education and sport evidences a negotiated process that complicates simplistic claims that the activities of Christian institutions in China during this period were simply straightforward imperialism that the local population was unable or defenceless to resist. This is because reading this historical process as a simplistic act of cultural imperialism renders the native response to it passive and meaningless, and affords the missionaries' intentional or unintentional drive to introduce aspects of Western values and culture too significant a role in moulding modern Chinese society. Reflecting objectively on, and analyzing, the historical trajectory in the light of the evidence in this research, it becomes clear that for missionaries and physical directors, their continued presence and success in China depended on 'their value and usefulness, the willingness of local leaders and their people to cooperate with them, the possibility of Christianity being constructed in a manner answering to local circumstances'.[70] The missionaries brought their cultural and religious beliefs to China, but the Chinese people eventually consumed them for their own benefit, and capitalized on them especially to nurture Chinese nationalism, an example of the historically demonstrated Middle Kingdom way of handling foreign influences: they are either absorbed or indigenized.[71] As a result, when Western culture came into China, the Chinese responded by resisting, selecting, and reshaping the cultural products they chose to absorb.[72]

The history of sport thus has a close relationship with the development of nationalism in modern China. Nationalism also holds that as a contributor to the development of nationalism and national identity, sport is frequently taken as 'a vehicle for the expression of nationalist sentiment' and is used by existing nation states or politicians for specific purposes.[73] These purposes include nation-building, promoting the nation state, consolidating and promoting national identity and sovereignty, giving cultural power to separatist movements, inculcating the notion of national consciousness, securing legitimacy, and enhancing international standing and image.[74]

For China, the people's resilience was boosted by the very strong and uncompromising nationalist stand of the Chinese Qing government. The Self-Strengthening Movement and Hundred Days' Reform were initiated by government officials and scholars. These reform movements awakened the Chinese people to the fact that they could not submit unquestioningly to foreigners, but could still learn some positive things from the West, whether in terms of military training, education, politics, economics, or culture. The need for physical education, especially military gymnastics, was thus stressed by both nationalists and revolutionaries as crucial to cultivating the fighting force of the Chinese people. The situation already favoured transformation, as the equal opportunities for all provided by the missionary education institutions and the YMCA in China were encouraging more and more Chinese youth from the middle and upper classes to learn Western ways, with some of them joining these institutions.

Local institutions also began to emulate the Western model of modern physical education and sport. With the expansion of the work of the missionary educational institutions and the YMCA, the corporeal and somatic signs of Western modernity took hold as signs of progress and modernity through their activities. Modern Western sport, especially international competitions, provided the Chinese with a good chance to understand the boons of modernizing the Chinese body, nurturing nationalist feelings and experiencing an emerging sense of nationalist pride. Once their passion and intellect had been ignited, the Chinese, especially the youth, made their mark in every athletic activity. The success of the Christian institutions' physical programme thus did not depend only on the efforts of missionaries and physical directors, but also greatly on the changing attitude of the Chinese towards modern physical education and sport, and on their readiness to seek help in this regard. The willingness of local governors, educators, and students to cooperate with the YMCA personnel and missionaries to positively transform Chinese society was crucially significant in its own right as well. In fact, the embrace of modern Western physical education and sport by elite Chinese, government officials and the public was arguably the first collective experience of self-actualization, through the development of a common cause of competitive sport for all to cherish and as a tangible expression of Chinese nationalism.

Summary

This paper focuses on the development of missionary educational institutions and the YMCA's physical education and sport programmes and how they, along with burgeoning Chinese nationalism, transformed physical education, and sport in modern China between 1840 and 1937. While missionary educational institutions and the YMCA used physical education and sport as agents of religious conversion and cultural propagation in an attempt to Christianize China, they also significantly influenced the development of modern physical education and sport in China by introducing and promoting Western sports, advocating physical education in schools, training and cultivating sport talent and leadership, and organizing various athletic activities. Christian missionaries and YMCA directors thus played a significant part in instigating a process of social and cultural change in modern China and—both intentionally and unintentionally—inculcating a particular set of beliefs, values, knowledge, and behavioural norms in China.

This process of inculturation and indigenization has been described in some literature as a process of cultural imperialism and an imperialist tool for foreign encroachment. However, this paper illustrates how any such intended direct form of imperialism was made by and large ineffective due to the way the Chinese Nationalist government appropriated Western sports in its own nation-building projects. This said, these programmes had long-lasting effects on how physical education and sports became the way of defining 'modern' bodies, as the missionary education institutions and YMCA programmes in particular were incorporated into the wider educational project of modernizing China under the Nationalist government. While doing away with the religious aspects of Christian faith, this rational-instrumental form of modernity based on the Christian ethics of the body informed the way in which the Chinese elite adopted Western physical education and sport as a means to achieve their political and cultural ambitions. These values were put in the service of the nation through a process of imbuing the spirit of unity and patriotism in the Chinese people, supporting the enterprise of nation-building, educating the Chinese people and signifying independent nationhood, as well as projecting outward an image of a modern state in international relations.

Notes

1. Fan Hong and Tan Hua, 'Sport in China: Conflict Between Tradition and Modernity, 1840s to 1930s', in J.A. Mangan and Fan Hong (eds), *Sport in Asian Society: Past and Present* (London: Frank Cass, 2005), 155.
2. The Opium Wars occurred as a result of China's attempts to suppress the illegal trade of opium in China by the British. The First Opium War took place from 1839 to 1842 as a result of the Chinese government's confiscation of opium stores in Canton and continued attempts by the British to force China to open up to trade. The Second Opium War, from 1856 to 1860, saw China invaded by British and French forces who wished to extend their trading rights and gain control of additional territories in China. Despite their initial refusal to ratify the treaties of Tientsin in 1858, the Qing government eventually succumbed and signed the so-called 'unequal treaties' which legalized the opium trade, opened several additional Chinese ports for trade and gave freedom of travel and movement in the interior of China to foreigners and missionaries.
3. These Westerners were from imperial countries (the United Kingdom, the United States, France, Germany, Italy, Austria–Hungary) which had all taken part in a series of conflicts in China.
4. The First Sino–Japanese War was fought between the Qing dynasty China and Meiji Japan from 1 August 1894 to 17 April 1895, primarily over control of Korea. After more than six months of continuous successes by the Japanese army and naval forces, the Qing leadership sued for peace in February 1895 and was forced to sign the humiliating Treaty of Shimonoseki.
5. Michael Dillon, *Dictionary of Chinese History* (London: Routledge, 2013), 61.
6. Shiming Luo, *Zhongguo tiyu tongshi di san ji* ['General history of Chinese physical education and sport: Volume 3'] (Beijing, Renmin tiyu chubanshe ['People's Sports Publishing House of China'], 2008), 22, 35.
7. Ibid.

8. Jessie G. Lutz, *China and the Christian Colleges, 1850–1950* (Ithaca, NY: Cornell University Press, 1971), 96.
9. The eight-part essay was a style of essay writing in the Imperial Civil Examination system during the Ming and Qing dynasties.
10. Lutz, *China and the Christian Colleges*, 96.
11. Xingzhi Tao, 'Zhongguo jianshe xinxuezhi de lishi ['The history of China's new schooling system'], *Xin jiao yu* ['New Education'] 4, no. 2 (1922), 240.
12. Tze-Ki Hon and Robert J. Culp, *The Politics of Historical Production in Late Qing and Republican China* (Leiden: Brill Publishers, 2007), 82.
13. Lutz, *China and the Christian Colleges*, 97.
14. Ellsworth C. Carlson, *The Foochow Missionaries, 1847–1880* (Cambridge, MA: Harvard University Asia Center, 1974), 64.
15. John Leighton Stuart, *Fifty Years in China – The Memoirs of John Leighton Stuart, Missionary and Ambassador* (New York: Random House, 1954), 28.
16. Graham Gael, 'Exercising Control: Sports and Physical Education in American Protestant Mission Schools in China, 1880–1930', *Signs* 20, no. 1 (1994), 24.
17. Chinese Educational Commission, Foreign Missions Conference of North America. Committee of Reference Counsel, and Conference of Missionary Societies in Great Britain & Ireland, *Christian Education in China: The Report of the China Educational Commission of 1921–1922* (Shanghai: Shangwu yinshuguan ['Commercial Press'], 1922), 67.
18. Ibid., 68–9.
19. Editorial Committee of Fuzhou Chronicals, 'Jiaohui banxue ['Christian-Run Schooling'], in Editorial Committee of Fuzhou Chronicals (ed.), *Fuzhou shizhi* ['Fuzhou Chronicles'] (Fuzhou: Publishing House of Local Records, 1998), 124; Luo, *Zhongguo tiyu tongshi di san ji*, 83; Xiaoxia He and Jinghuan Shi, *Jiaohui xuexiao yu zhongguo jiaoyu xiandaihua* ['Missionary schools and the modernization of education in modern China'] (Guangzhou: Guangdong jiaoyu chubanshe ['Guangdong Education Publishing House'], 1996), 152.
20. *Tientsin Young Men* 7, no. 2 (29 February 1908); *Tientsin Young Men* 7, no. 18 (4 July 1908). Charles Howard Hopkins, *History of the Y.M.C.A. in North America* (New York: Association Press, 1951), 699; Judy Polumbaum, 'From Evangelism to Entertainment: The YMCA, the NBA, and the Evolution of Chinese Basketball', *Modern Chinese Literature and Culture* 14, no. 1 (2002), 278–30; and Zhongyuan Wu and Yongwu Que, 'Organizational Structure of China's Physical Culture', in Howard G. Knuttgen, Qiwei Ma and Zhongyuan Wu (eds), *Sport in China* (Champaign, IL: Human Kinetics, 1990), 41–57.
21. Gerald R. Gems, *The Athletic Crusade: Sport and American Cultural Imperialism* (Lincoln, NE: University of Nebraska Press, 2006), 20.
22. Ibid., 21; Gael Norma Graham, *Gender, Culture, and Christianity: American Protestant Mission Schools in China, 1880–1930* (Michigan: University of Michigan, 1990), 101–4.
23. Gems, *The Athletic Crusade*, 21; Susan Brownell, *Training the Body for China: Sports in the Moral Order of the People's Republic* (Chicago: University of Chicago Press, 1995), 40.
24. Yongnian Zheng, *Globalisation and State Transformation in China* (Cambridge: Cambridge University Press, 2004), 43.
25. Xiushu Zhang, 'Qingmo Minchude Xuexiao Tiyu' ['Physical Education in Schools of the End of the Qing Dynasty and the Beginning of the Republic of China'], in Editorial Committee of Historical Documents of Sport in Sichuan (ed.), *Sichuan tiyu shiliao* ['Historical document of sport in Sichuan'] (Chengdu: Editorial Committee of Historical Documents of Sport in Sichuan, 1984).
26. Gengsheng Hoh, *Hao Gengsheng huiyilu* ['The memoirs of Hao Gengsheng'] (Xinbei, Taiwan: Zhuanji wenxue chubanshe ['Zhuanji Wenxue Press'], 1969), 92.
27. Shiliang Gao, *Zhongguo jiaohui xuexiaoshi* ['The history of the missionary schools in modern China'] (Hunan: Hunan jiaoyu chubanshe ['Hunan Education Press'], 1994), 192.

28. Ibid.
29. Hoh, *Hao Gengsheng huiyilu*, 96.
30. Xiaoyang Zhao, *Jidujiao qingnianhui zai zhongguo: Bentu he xiandai de tansuo* ['The YMCA in China: A quest to indigenize and modernize'] (Beijing: Shehui kexue wenxian chubanshe ['Social Sciences Academic Press'], 2008), 192.
31. Jonathan Kolatch, *Sports, Politics, and Ideology in China* (New York: Jonathan David Publishers, 1972), 22–5.
32. Alfred H. Swan, 'Annual Report for the Year Ending September 30, 1915', *Annual Reports of the Foreign Secretaries of the International Committee October 1, 1914 to September 30, 1915* (1915), 422–40.
33. J.H. Crocker, 'Report for the Year Ending September 30, 1916', *Annual Reports of the Foreign Secretaries of the International Committee October 1, 1915 to September 30, 1916* (1916), 42–6.
34. Zhouxiang Lu, 'Sport, Nationalism and the Building of the Modern Chinese Nation State (1912-49)', *The International Journal of the History of Sport* 28, no. 7 (2011), 1031.
35. Editorial Committee of Historical Documents in Sports, *Historical Document of Sport* (Beijing: Renmin tiyu chubanshe ['People's Sports Publishing House of China'], 1982), 27.
36. National Sports Commission, The Committee of Sport History and Culture, and Chinese Sport History Association, *Zhongguo jindai tiyushi* ['Sport History in Modern China'] (Beijing: Beijing tiyu daxue chubanshe ['Beijing Sport University Press'], 1989), 13.
37. The New Culture Movement was launched by modern Chinese intellectuals including Chen Duxiu, Cai Yuanpei and Li Dazhao, to rebel against traditional Chinese feudal culture and to create a new collective consciousness, particularly among the upper class. This movement gave rise to Chinese nationalism and paved the way for the May Fourth Movement.
38. The May Fourth Movement marked the starting point of the nationalist movement in China as a form of protest against the imperialists. This movement is a symbolically important milestone on the Chinese nation's path to self-assertion and self-actualization.
39. Ka-che Yip, *Religion, Nationalism, and Chinese Students: The Anti-Christian Movement of 1922–1927* (Bellingham, Center for East Asian Studies: Western Washington University, 1980), 84.
40. Ibid.
41. Ibid.
42. Alan Bairner, 'Sport, Nationalism and Globalisation: Relevance, Impact, Consequences', *Hitotsubashi Journal of Arts and Sciences* 49, no. 1 (2008), 44.
43. Ibid.
44. Alumni Association of Jinling University, *Jinling daxue shi* ['The History of Jinling University'] (Nanjing: Nanjing University Press, 2002), 461.
45. Tingguang Luo, 'Guojia zhuyi yu zhongguo xiaoxue kecheng wenti' ['Nationalism and the primary curriculum in modern China'], *Zhonghua Jiaoyujie* ['The Chinese Education'] 15, no. 2 (1924), 31–2; Geng Wang, 'Guojia zhuyi yu xuexiao tiyu de gaizao' ['Nationalism and the Reformation of Physical Education in Schools'], *Zhonghua jiaoyu jie* ['The Chinese Education'] 15, no. 1 (1924), 9–10.
46. It served as both an advisory and a supervisory body in organizing various athletic contests at the national level.
47. Fan Hong (ed.), *Sport in the Global Society* (London: Routledge, 2006), xxiv, 129; Yujun Lu and Liang Bo, 'Minguo shiqi de zhonghua quanguo tiyu xiejinhui' ['The China National Athletic Union in the Republic of China'], *Lishi Dangan* [Historical Archives], no. 4 (2001), 106.
48. Ka-che Yip, *Religion, Nationalism, and Chinese Students*, 1.
49. Yongnian Zheng, *Discovering Chinese Nationalism in China: Modernisation, Identity and International Relations* (Cambridge: Cambridge University Press, 1999), 23.

50. 'Quanguo gongsili daxue, duli xueyuan, zhuanke xuexiao yilanbiao ['Table of the list of universities and colleges in modern China'], in The Second Historical Archives of Chinese Museum (ed.), *Zhonghua minguoshi dangan ziliao huibian* ['Compilation of archive documents of the Republic of China'] (Nanjing: Jiangsu renmin chubanshe ['Jiangsu People's Press'], 1936), 306–16.
51. Ibid.
52. Chuxiong George Wei and Xiaoyuan Liu, *Chinese Nationalism in Perspective: Historical and Recent Cases* (Westport, CT: Greenwood Press, 2001), 47.
53. 'National Sports Act (No. 262 of the Governmental Instructions)', *Guomin zhengfu gongbao* ('The official gazette of the Nationalist Government), no. 143 (16 April 1929), 77–9.
54. Luo, *Zhongguo tiyu tongshi di san ji*, 42.
55. Zhongshu Gui, *China Yearbook (1935–1936)*, (Tianjin and Shanghai: Tianjin Press, 1936), 541–3.
56. National Sports Commission, The Committee of Sport History and Culture, and Chinese Sport History Association, *Zhongguo gudai tiyushi* ['Sport history in ancient China'] (Beijing: Beijing tiyu daxue chubanshe [Beijing Sport University Press], 1990), 247.
57. 'Quanguo yundong dahui gaikuang' ['Overview of the National Games'], *Qiaowu yuebao* ['Qiaowu Monthly'], no. 1 (1933), 88.
58. The 'September 18 Incident' is also known as the 'Manchurian Incident' or the 'Mukden Incident'. On 18 September 1931, the Japanese Army blew up a section of the Liutiaohua Railway near Mukden (Shenyang, Dongbei), which the Japanese owned and operated. They then claimed that the Chinese Army had set off the explosion, using this ruse to justify the invasion of China. They took over a number of important cities such as Changchun and then took Manchuria, setting up a puppet regime named Manchukuo. The Mukden Incident was a pretext for the Japanese army to begin its invasion of China.
59. 'Wo xuanshou chuxi shijiehui' ['Chinese on the stage of the Olympic Games'], *Tiyu zhoubao* ['Sports News Weekly'] 20, no. 1 (1932), 19.
60. Oi Ki Ling, *The Changing Role of the British Protestant Missionaries in China, 1945–1952* (New Jersey: Fairleigh Dickinson University Press, 1999), 193; John King Fairbank and Denis Twitchett, *The Cambridge History of China: Republican China, 1912–1949* (Cambridge: Cambridge University Press, 1978), 172.
61. Stefan Hübner, 'Muscular Christianity and the "Western Civilizing Mission": Elwood S. Brown, the YMCA, and the Idea of the Far Eastern Championship Games', *Diplomatic History* 39, no. 3 (2015), 185–203.
62. Mark Dyreson, 'Imperial "Deep Play": Reading Sport and Visions of the Five Empires of the "New World", 1919–1941', *The International Journal of the History of Sport* 28, no. 17 (2011), 24–9.
63. Nick J. Watson, Stuart Weir and Stephen Friend, 'The Development of Muscular Christianity in Victorian Britain and Beyond', *Journal of Religion and Society* 7, no. 1 (2005), 2.
64. Koen De Ceuster, 'Wholesome Education and Sound Leisure: The YMCA Sports Program in Colonial Korea', *European Journal of East Asian Studies* 2, no. 1, (2003), 57.
65. Jim Parry et al., *Sport and Spirituality: An Introduction* (London: Routledge, 2007), 80.
66. Fan Hong, 'Preface', in Fan Hong (ed.), *Sport, Nationalism and Orientalism: The Asian Games* (London: Routledge, 2007), 85.
67. Elwood S. Brown, 'Far East Olympic Games', *Physical Training* 10 (1913), 173–4.
68. Robert Jackson, *Sovereignty: The Evolution of an Idea* (Cambridge: Polity Press, 2007), 74.
69. See also a very nuanced discussion on cultural imperialism and sport in the context of colonized Singapore and Australia: Peter A. Horton, 'Singapore: Imperialism and Post-Imperialism, Athleticism, Sport, Nationhood and Nation-Building', *The International Journal of the History of Sport* 30, no. 11 (2013), 1221–34; Peter A. Horton, '"Padang or Paddock": A Comparative View of Colonial Sport in Two Imperial Territories', *The International Journal of the History of Sport* 14, no. 1 (1997), 1–20.

70. Andrew Porter, '"Cultural Imperialism" and Protestant Missionary Enterprise, 1780–1914', *Journal of Imperial and Commonwealth History* 25, no. 3 (1997), 386.
71. Ibid., 375.
72. Ryan Dunch, 'Beyond Cultural Imperialism: Cultural Theory, Christian Missions, and Global Modernity', *History and Theory* 41, no. 3 (2002), 311.
73. Alan Bairner, *Sport, Nationalism, and Globalization: European and North American Perspectives* (Albany, NY: State University of New York Press, 2001), 1.
74. Jennifer Hargreaves, 'Sex, Gender and the Body in Sport and Leisure: Has There Been a Civilising Process?', in Eric Dunning and Chris Rojek (eds), *Sport and Leisure in the Civilising Process* (London: Macmillan, 1992), 161–82; Bairner, *Sport, Nationalism, and Globalization*, xi, 18; Zhouxiang Lu and Fan Hong, *Sport and Nationalism in China* (London: Routledge, 2014), 1; Colin Brown, 'Sport, Modernity and Nation Building: The Indonesian National Games of 1951 and 1953', *Bijdragen tot de Taal: Land-en Volkenkunde*, 164 no. 4 (2008), 431–49.

Disclosure Statement

No potential conflict of interest was reported by the authors.

Mormon Missionaries and the Emergence of Modern Argentine Sport, 1938–1943

Ryan A. Davis

ABSTRACT
In 1938, Mormon missionaries from North America, under the leadership of Frederick Salem Williams, formed an athletic club, *Club Atlético Los Mormones* ('The Mormons Athletic Club', CALM), in Buenos Aires, Argentina. CALM would sponsor professional teams in baseball, softball, and basketball, all bearing the name *Los Mormones* ('The Mormons'). *Los Mormones* won three league championships in the four years they played baseball and four championships in the five years they played softball. Two of their basketball players would become national all-stars, one of whom would represent Argentina at the South American Championship in 1940. Williams served as president of the softball league and vice president of the baseball league. *Los Mormones'* story is outlined and situated in relation to the various discourses that, woven together, constitute the cultural context of modern Argentine sport: physical culture and modernity, United States-Argentine relations, amateurism versus professionalism, and the spread of North American sports to Latin America.

This afternoon we played Boca Juniors. We lost 9 to 3. The first time at bat I knocked a home run. Managed three hits out of four times at bat. Laid two guys out as they came sliding into home. I sometimes wonder if I'm playing catcher on a baseball team or lineman on a football team. I saw them coming down third base line with blood in their eyes. I braced myself and they crumpled. Boca has one of the better teams … They had all played semi-pro ball, so it was always a blood bath every time Los Mormones and Boca Juniors played … They dished out all the dirt they could, but when we didn't knuckle under like the other teams and fought back, they respected us. After they carried those two runners off the field, we never had another problem. Just prior to that, one of their players, as he was sliding into second, raked his spikes down Elder James Barton's face, cutting it and his shirt and trousers clear on down to his socks. Pres. Williams ran out and grabbed the guy. The next thing I knew both sides were mixing it up. Just as the bats were about to swing, we managed to get everybody separated. It must have been our Missionary spirit prevailing. That is when I decided they would need to know how it is to play rough. So, the next two runners into home were out. Out of the game, out of it, and out loony like. From that point on, we were friends. We respected each other, but we played hard, and I must say, clean ball.[1]

The foregoing anecdote comes from the journal of one Phil Davis, catcher for the *Los Mormones* ('The Mormons') baseball team, which played in Argentina's professional league from 1939 to 1942. The year of Davis's journal entry, 1941, one of Argentina's big five clubs, *Club Atlético Boca Juniors*, would narrowly pip *Los Mormones* for the league championship, restoring some of the local club's glory. For although Boca had won the League title in both 1937 and 1938, by 1941 *Los Mormones* were two-time defending champions, having won the title in 1939, their first year in the league, and 1940. In fact, *Los Mormones* would again reclaim the title in 1942, perhaps earning for themselves the right to challenge the characterization of *Boca* as 'the most powerful [baseball] team of the period'.[2]

For a time *Los Mormones*, which also fielded professional basketball and softball teams, became 'on a modest scale the darlings of the nation'.[3] However, their fame would prove to be as ephemeral as it was surprising, for just as they were reaching the pinnacle of their sporting success, their chapter in Argentine sports history would come to an abrupt close. With the shadow of World War II looming ever larger over the Argentine Republic, their players, virtually all of whom were foreign missionaries for the Church of Jesus Christ of Latter-Day Saints (LDS or Mormons), were forced to return home by the end of 1944. Although new crops of missionary sportsmen would return after the War, never again would *Los Mormones* experience such a golden age. The main objective here is to recover this largely untold story, focusing on the key people, places, and ideals that explain who these sporting Mormons were and why athletics figured so prominently in their ostensibly religious mission. The story weaves its own idiosyncratic and circuitous path through a forest of scholarship that includes such trees as Argentine physical culture and modernity; Mormon recreational ideology and proselytizing efforts; the tension between amateurism and professionalism in Argentine sports; United States-Argentine political relations; and, to borrow Joseph L. Arbena's phraseology, the spread of 'American sports across the Americas'.[4]

A word about primary sources. Nearly two and three decades ago, respectively, J.A. Mangan and Robert M. Levine suggested there was still much to discover about the origins of, and prominent figures involved in, the spread of European and United States (US) sports to Latin America, and they intimated that those who 'dig deeper into untouched archives and other sources' may yet find missing pieces of a broader puzzle.[5] Mangan offered a potentially fruitful avenue to pursue when, in response to Arbena's observation that 'sports entered Latin American countries through a capital or major port city and via middle to upper class foreigners or locals who travelled in Europe or the United States', he suggested, 'it would be both fascinating and valuable to locate these foreigners and locals'.[6] *Los Mormones* offer an example of one group of middle class foreigners whose role in the diffusion of sport in Argentina has faded with time.[7] In some cases—for example, the 12th National Basketball Championship—Mormon sources serve to fill in missing pieces to stories others have already commenced. In other cases, though—for instance, the creation of the Argentine Softball League—they may well constitute the beginning of an entirely new story, or, perhaps more appropriately, a newly rediscovered story.

Frederick Salem Williams

It is impossible to understand the place of Mormons in Argentine sports history without knowing something about Frederick Salem Williams. Joel Horowitz has highlighted the role of 'notable individuals' in the establishment of football clubs in pre-1943 Buenos Aires.[8] Williams played this role for the Mormons, though he was neither a politician nor wealthy like the 'notable individuals' Horowitz discusses. His contributions include coaching and managing professional teams in softball, baseball, and basketball (he also played on the baseball and softball teams); overseeing the construction of a sports club; serving as president of the Argentine Softball League and vice president of the Argentine Baseball League; and serving on the committee of the ill-fated Pan-American games of 1942.[9]

Born 15 June 1908 in the Mormon Colonies of Chihuahua, Mexico, Williams and his family moved to the US (Phoenix, Arizona) where he was heavily involved in sports as a youth. In high school, he played basketball, baseball, and football at Phoenix Union High School, which at the time boasted an enrollment larger than that of the University of Arizona.[10] At 18, Williams left home for the first of three religious missions for the LDS Church; the first two in Argentina (1927–1929, 1938–1942), with headquarters in Buenos Aires, and the third in Uruguay (1947–1951). On his first mission to Argentina, Enrique P. Rumbo, coach of the *Olimpia Basketball Club*, a first division team, invited Williams and two other missionaries to try out for the Club's team. Rumbo selected all three, who 'played first string for the Club, which nearly took the league championship that year, due in large measure to our efforts'.[11] During the nine-year period between his missions in Argentina, Williams played basketball on a Mormon M-Men team and served as president of the basketball and baseball leagues of the Phoenix branch of the Young Men's Christian Association (YMCA).[12] His extensive experience in Latin America later helped him land a position with the US State Department as business manager of the Institute of Inter-American Affairs, Division of Health and Sanitation. The position took him first to Venezuela and subsequently to Uruguay, and involved 'set[ting] up malaria control programs and vaccination drives, and construct[ing] hospitals'.[13]

Upon his arrival in Argentina as a freshly minted LDS mission president, Williams was quick to seize upon sports as a formal proselytizing tool. His decision was a mixture of personal preference, serendipity, and historical coincidence. He cites his 'own inclination towards sports' and the fact that there were 'a number of exceptionally gifted athletes among the missionaries' as contributing factors.[14] The most significant factor, however, was an exhibition event that took place on 29 October 1938. The Mormons travelled to San Nicolás, where they participated in a basketball game and put on a musical concert. When they arrived, they were greeted by a large crowd that included Dr José Leo Morteo, the city mayor, and Cayetano Cavalli, president of *Club Atlético Belgrano*. After a tour of the town and an *asado* at the Belgrano club, the visitors were led to the central square where they were greeted by a huge banner over the street that read 'WELCOME MORMONS'.[15] The mission orchestra, The Hill Billy Boys, entertained a local crowd with a musical concert, and afterwards the Mormons basketball team, *Los Mormones*, defeated a team from *Club Atlético Belgrano*.[16]

The different assessments of the San Nicolás event offered by Williams and Cavalli highlight the competing discourses at play in analyzing the role of Mormon missionaries in Argentine sports. For his part, Cavalli called attention to the value of US-Argentine cultural ties:

> Mr. Williams ... we feel that you are the best ambassadors your country has ever had. We know the United States has an ambassador in Buenos Aires and that there are many members of the diplomatic corps in Argentina ... but we never see them personally. You and your missionaries have met with the people to show us how North Americans really are. You little realize how much your government owes your church.[17]

For Williams, the event proved a watershed for a different reason: 'The favorable results and the possibilities of using this same approach elsewhere were not lost on us; from then on, we used the Argentine news media to introduce our sports teams and musical groups, which in turn introduced the gospel to Argentina'.[18] In short, Cavalli saw the event as a fulfilment of FDR's good neighbor policy, while the Mormons felt they were fulfilling the Biblical mandate to love their neighbors by spreading the good word.

Although Williams plays up the fortuitous events of San Nicolás, there were also powerful cultural pressures weighing on him that not only contextualize his decision to use sports to proselytize, but also show just how logical it was. In the late nineteenth and early twentieth centuries, the LDS Church developed an elaborate and wide-ranging recreational ideology that grounded sports and athletics on certain psychological ideas about human nature and doctrinal beliefs about body, mind, and spirit.[19] Richard Ian Kimball, borrowing a well-known term from Protestant and Catholic parlance, refers to this ideology as muscular Mormonism.[20] When Mormon youth engaged in athletic activities and sports, provided they did so according to the principles of muscular Mormonism, they were, in a sense, showing their faith by their works.[21]

Muscular Mormonism suffused the religious context in which Williams and other Mormon youth were raised. Thus, despite his belief that his decision to adopt sports in Argentina constituted a 'radical departure' from Mormon missionary praxis, in truth the approach was rather common at the time.[22] Scholars have identified numerous LDS missions where sports, mainly basketball and baseball, played a prominent role in Mormons' evangelizing efforts between 1911 and 1963, including missions in Germany, South Africa, Great Britain, Holland, Australia, New Zealand, Finland, Chile, Ireland, Japan, and of course Argentina.[23] The most interesting case may be that of Germany, where Hitler himself allegedly 'sought the services of the Elders' as a means of defending Germany's 1933 European basketball championship at the 1936 Olympics in Berlin.[24] That the Mormons agreed to help has less to do with their colluding with Nazis than with trying to arrest the 'pagan trend' spreading through 'Hitlerized Germany'.[25] The Australian national basketball team would similarly enlist the help of Mormon missionaries in preparation for the 1956 Olympics. Acquiescing, the Mormons formed a team of missionaries, The Mormon Yankees, who became national celebrities.[26] Although the part played by Christian missionaries in the diffusion of Anglo-American sports in the late nineteenth and early twentieth centuries is generally acknowledged, the specific role of Mormon missionaries in this historical process remains comparatively less well known.[27]

When considering the reception of Williams and his missionaries in Argentina, it is important to bear in mind two differences between muscular Mormonism and the 'evangelical athletes of the empire' model.[28] On the one hand, historical or creedal Christianity has typically rejected Mormons' claims to being Christian.[29] On the other hand, articulations of American national cultural identity have often taken issue with Mormonism, at times marking the religion as profoundly un-American.[30] The second issue was likely lost on Argentines, although it is important to note that the Mormon missionaries were often confused for Germans, not North Americans, a situation exacerbated by the fact that early Mormon converts in Argentina came from Germany and that a German-language congregation existed until Williams disbanded it in June 1940.[31] As to the first issue, the Mormons' unorthodox version of Christianity certainly did influence their reception in largely Catholic Argentina. To cite Williams, 'In those days, whenever people first heard the word "Mormon," they sought their priests for information, or looked us up in their old encyclopedias (published in Spain under the auspices of the Catholic Church): "A small sect living out in the western part of the United States where they practice polygamy"'.[32] Because of the religious idiosyncrasies of Mormonism, Williams and his missionaries do not fit neatly into scholarly categories; they represented neither a Christian (by historical standards) nor an unambiguously American empire.

In sum, Williams turned to sports as a way to present Mormons as 'healthy, clean-living sportsmen rather than as polygamists', and if the fame and reputation of the various *Los Mormones* teams are any indication, he was largely successful.[33] Indeed, *Los Mormones*' extraordinary success allowed the ideals of muscular Mormonism to flourish in an Argentine society in which '[p]hysical culture and sports promoted a distinctly modern idea of the individual and society'.[34]

Club Atlético Los Mormones

With the San Nicolás success fresh in their minds, the Mormons set out to formalize their approach to sports. At the centre of these efforts was the *Club Atlético Los Mormones* ('Athletic Club The Mormons', CALM), formed officially on 1 December 1938. Initial efforts by a group of missionaries and local Mormon youth had led to the creation of *Club Mejoramiento Mutuo* ('Mutual Improvement Club', CMM) in September of 1938, though the club was 'forced into dormancy' by the abrupt return to the United States of Williams's predecessor, W. Ernest Young, and the arrival of Williams as the new mission president.[35] The name change of the club from CCM to CALM signals a subtle shift away from the American cultural roots of Mormonism and towards the adoption of a type of institution more resonant with Argentine culture. The phrase 'Mutual Improvement' recalls the Church's name for its youth program, the Mutual Improvement Association. By contrast, *Club Atlético Los Mormones* resembles the names of myriad clubs that sprang up in Argentina in the decades before CALM's creation. The reinvigorated and renamed club would remain active in Argentina long after the end of Williams's mission, though it was during his tenure that it gained national recognition.

One of the Mormons' mission quarterlies, the *Gaucho Gazette*, informed its readers, most of whom were family and friends of the missionaries, that although the idea of a church sponsored club may have seemed superfluous given the Church's myriad programs, the absence of athletics in Argentine schools left those without a club essentially disconnected from organized sports.[36] As the publication stressed, the club was 'the axle around which ... Argentine Social life' revolved 'and the youth, boy or girl, who doesn't belong to at least one Club or more is the exception to the rule'.[37] It was, then, both a recognition of the place of clubs in Argentine society and the desire to provide Argentine Mormon youth a 'wholesome' recreational space that prompted the creation of CALM.[38] In this sense, the club's primary impetus and focus were not sports, but the moral development of (primarily, though not exclusively) Mormon youth through sports and other activities. On this issue, the Mormons shared common ground with various other clubs that considered themselves, and were widely considered by the sports media to be, the '"true" custodians of the amateur spirit' and the fair play ethic.[39] However, they also added a uniquely Mormon spin.

In the official mission quarterly, *El Mensajero*, Williams penned a lengthy editorial titled 'Youth and their Recreation' in which he defended 'healthy recreation' (*sana diversión*).[40] He warned that young people would seek out entertainment one way or another, and it was the moral obligation of parents and the Church to provide them an appropriate option. Not only would healthy recreation teach youth spiritual and moral values, but it was also, for Williams, a sign of Christ's true gospel. CALM thus embodied the Mormons' commitment to the joint tasks of morally uplifting Argentine youth and spreading their missionary message. As one missionary put it, 'as it [i.e., the Club] is an essential part of the missionary program of the Mission, it embraces and teaches the same Mormon ideals that we, as Missionaries, are sent to preach to all people, kindred and tongue'.[41] At times, prominent sports publications would introduce *Los Mormones* by making explicit reference to the beliefs that motivated the Mormons' participation in athletics. For instance, *El Gráfico*, Argentina's premier sports magazine of the early twentieth century, led off a full-page story about *Los Mormones* basketball squad by quoting the Church's thirteenth article of faith.[42] Other sources cited the Mormons' Word of Wisdom—a health code, which, among other things, proscribes the use of alcohol and tobacco—as an interesting 'training system' aimed at improving physical condition.[43]

Julio Frydenberg, Rodrigo Daskal and Cesar R. Torres have argued that Argentine clubs 'became nodes for the crystallization of symbolic identities'.[44] This was certainly the case for CALM, which mixed elements of Mormon culture with those of Argentine culture. Central to CALM's identity was its motto—good sportsmanship (see Figure 1). Rolf Larson, *Los Mormones*' star basketball player and one-time president of CALM, discussed the capacious meaning of the motto in the pages of *El Mensajero*:

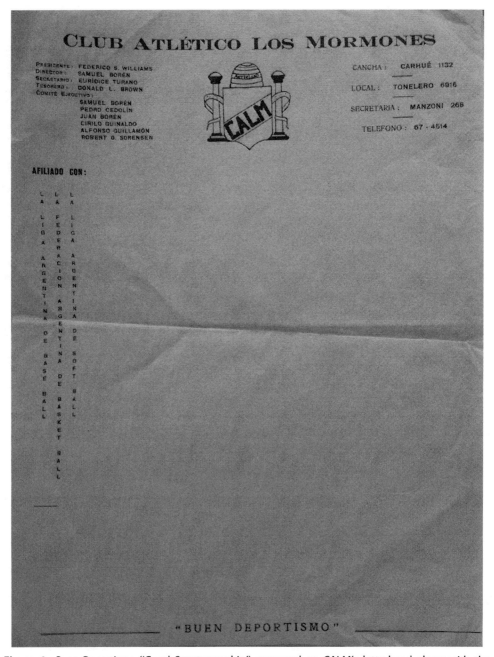

Figure 1. *Buen Deportismo* ('Good Sportsmanship') appeared on CALM's letterhead along with the club's league affiliations and insignia, a beehive with the word 'activity'. Utah, home of the Mormon Church's headquarters, is known as the beehive state. Image courtesy of the Frederick G. Williams collection.

There is no quality or attribute that a young man or woman could possess that is more attractive, more flattering for his or her personality than that of GOOD SPORTSMANSHIP. Often we think that sportsmanship refers only to active games where there is physical competition, but this is a grave error. GOOD SPORTSMANSHIP or its antonym are shown in every place where there is contact between human beings. This generosity of soul, this willingness to cede our rights for the benefit of others, either it is an integral part of our personality or it is a grave defect. No game, no special concession at a dance are worth it if we win by protesting, arguing, or through ill will. Let us all resolve that the good spirit of clean play, tolerance, and good behavior will govern our Club.[45]

Although Davis's anecdote above clearly indicates that the practice of good sportsmanship did not always come easy, the motto nevertheless served a 'citizenship building' function for the club.[46] In terms of the social debates about the role of sports, specifically the tension between amateurism and professionalism, the Mormons clearly came down on the side of amateurism, though they added to it an explicitly spiritual component.[47]

In keeping with both the LDS Church's recreational ideology and the practice of numerous Argentine clubs, CALM sponsored a variety of social events other than sports, including drama, speech, and music.[48] It also held regular dances for members and invitees, offered classes in calisthenics, initiated a library, and built a food storehouse as part of the Mission's Welfare Plan.[49] Once the construction of its facilities was completed, the Club could boast its own dressing room with bathroom and shower facilities, an outdoor court used for basketball and volleyball (which included cement standards, rare at the time), and badminton courts (see Figure 2).[50] Although one of the missionaries would proudly declare theirs 'one of the best outdoor basketball courts in the country', CALM's facilities were comparatively modest, at least by the standards of more established clubs.[51] The LDS Church's First Presidency, the Church's highest-ranking body, appropriated US$400 to purchase two vacant lots in the Liniers neighborhood of Buenos Aires, and both local members and missionaries

Figure 2. The basketball/volleyball court of *Club Atlético Los Mormones*. The surface of the court was made of finely ground brick powder. Image courtesy of the Frederick G. Williams collection.

donated much of the labor and material. The Club collected membership dues, with which it intended to cover expenses; though a month after its formal inauguration on 25 May 1940, it found itself in the red, a situation that would remain the norm.[52]

Club members were encouraged to invite their friends to join, thus opening up CALM to non-Mormons, at least in theory, provided they abided by the Club's standards, which included not smoking or drinking at or near club facilities, and also 'behaving correctly' and 'demonstrating at all times good manners and morality'.[53] Shortly after CALM's inauguration, Bryon C. Wheeler, then the Club's treasurer, was particularly bullish on the Club's prospects: 'With the fame of the sportsmanship and good playing of the Mormons spreading to all parts of the Nation, the potential membership of the club becomes unlimited'.[54] In reality, the majority of Club members were missionaries and, likely, early members of the Church. Friends of local Mormons may have frequented the Club's various social events, but it seems few were willing to pony up the requisite pesos to become full-fledged members.[55] Compared with other clubs, *Los Mormones* simply could not compete when it came to membership size. For example, the Mormons' biggest rival club in baseball and softball, *Boca Juniors*, boasted 17,500 members in 1939, while CALM claimed a comparatively miniscule 138.[56] Even smaller clubs like *Temperley*, with a membership of 1,860 in 1939, dwarfed the Mormons.[57]

Through their club, the Mormons established close ties with some of the biggest names in Argentine sports. The biggest was probably Federico W. Dickens, whom Enrique Romero Brest called the 'founder of Argentine sport'.[58] Dickens had served as Director of the Department of Physical Education for the YMCA in Buenos Aires and Technical Director of the Argentine Olympic delegation for the 1924 and 1928 games. When he met the Mormons, he was Director of the Department of Physical Education for *Ateneo de la Juventud*, a private Catholic club.[59] Dickens was one of the 'distinguished persons associated with the world of sports' among the 400 in attendance at CALM's inauguration celebration.[60] In his life history, Williams says the two became 'close friends' and that thanks to Dickens, *Los Mormones* were often permitted to use the Catholic Club's facilities.[61]

Federico Forrest was another meaningful contact for the Mormons, though less famous than Dickens. An instructor of physical education at *Club Gimnasio Chacabuco*, Forrest met Williams in late 1938 when the two joined others to formally organize the Argentine Softball League. The Mormons found in Forrest a kindred soul, commending him in the Mission's official publication for contributing to the 'upbuilding of the youth of that district by teaching them high ideals of sportsmanship, fair play and clean living and thinking'. The feeling was apparently mutual, for 'According to Mr. Forrest "Los Mormones" are idolized by the lads of the Club because of their evident physical fitness, standards of morality and sportsmanship, and whenever two teams are formed both begin clamouring to be called "Los Mormones"'.[62] As a result of his relationship with the Mormons, Forrest published a three-part article on physical exercises in *El Mensajero*, an example of just how enmeshed the Mormons were in the context of Argentine physical culture.[63] Forrest's mother and two sisters would end up joining the Mormon faith, and in 1940, he would become the first South American to enroll at Brigham Young University, where, as a freshman, he tried out for the (American) football team.[64]

Los Mormones in Baseball and Softball

As noted, CALM sponsored professional teams in softball, baseball, and basketball (in that order).[65] The Mormons' choice of which sports to play was not coincidental. Mangan has argued that for the English, 'modern games in Argentina were a means of fashioning a cultural umbilical cord to their mother country'; that they adopted a centripetal focus, playing for and among themselves.[66] By contrast, the Mormons were clearly motivated by what was missing among the English, the 'wider major purpose' of their missionary efforts.[67] Without the success of their teams, the Mormons likely would not have 'broke[n] down prejudice, spread good will, [and] made the Church's name synonymous with good sportsmanship and clean living'.[68] In this sense, Williams's decision to enter teams in the specific sports of softball, baseball, and basketball proved fortuitous for it played to the Mormons' strengths. Not only was Williams's background steeped in these sports, but also the missionaries that served under him happened to have experience and talent in them as well.[69] Trying to compete with Argentines in, say, football (soccer), likely would have led to a different outcome entirely.

Referring to baseball, *Los Mormones* joined what Williams called 'a dying institution'.[70] 'People told us', he recalled, 'If it weren't for the Mormons, baseball would be dead in Argentina'.[71] *Boca Juniors* had the resources to hoard the best players, most of whom were foreigners.[72] The competition provided by *Los Mormones* thus infused the sport with a breath of fresh air. As Davis, one of *Los Mormones*' standout players, would put it, 'the word is out among all the teams, 'beat the Mormons'.[73] The Buenos Aires *Herald* would put it somewhat more diplomatically, 'Phil [Davis] is one of a number of sports-loving young Americans who work for a period of two and a half years with the Mormon organization in Buenos Aires—an organization whose playing and fine sporting example has been one of the causes of the recent revival of interest in local baseball'.[74]

In the case of softball, Mormons were among the original group that founded the league. It was also the sport in which they would prove most dominant, winning four consecutive championships from 1939 to 1942.[75] In his life history, Williams recounts the genesis of the softball league. He and his mission secretary responded to an advertisement in the *Herald* in late 1938, which invited all those interested in forming a softball league to a meeting 'at the famous Boston Bar, on Calle Florida'. Those in attendance included Juan Carlos Noodt, president of the Argentine Baseball League; a Mr Romeo, the baseball league's secretary and representative of the *Boca Junior* club; a Mr West, who represented Goodyear Tire; and Federico Forrest, of *Club Atlético Chacabuco*. Those present at the meeting agreed to a subsequent meeting at Williams's home where they would officially organize the softball league. The next day, however, Noodt met with Williams at Williams's office and proposed that the softball league form part of the extant baseball league. Willliams 'felt there was merit in what he said, and when the time came, his suggestion was put into effect'. Eight to 10 sports clubs sent representatives to the organizational meeting, and those present elected Williams president of the *Liga Argentina de Soft Ball* ('Argentine Softball League'), a position he held for four consecutive years. At a subsequent meeting, he was also elected vice president of the baseball league, a position to which he was re-elected the following three years.[76]

The baseball league had multiple divisions, though the first division tended to comprise no more than four or five teams, including *Los Mormones, Ateneo de la Juventud, Boca Juniors*, YMCA, *Asociación Jóvenes Nipones, Gimnasia y Esgrima*, and *Gimnasia Chacabuco*. The softball league had as many as seven different schools or clubs field a team over the four years Williams was involved, among them Goodyear, Cambridge, Young America, *Unión Deportiva Argentina*, and *Deportivo Central Argentino*.[77] *Los Mormones* became the favorite team for many 'unaligned Argentines', suggesting CALM did not create the same type of *barrio* identity that other clubs did.[78] Games typically took place in public parks or at football stadiums, though *Los Mormones* once played on the British Cricket Club pitch. Citing damage done by the players' cleats, the cricket club never invited them back.[79] *Boca Juniors* had built a moat around their field as a protective measure against rowdy fans, though *Los Mormones* found it to be more of an annoyance than anything, since they had to fish out foul balls before they became waterlogged.[80]

The baseball season followed immediately on the heels of the softball season, with both lasting roughly a month. The softball season typically began in mid to late December and ran through the third week of January. The team with the best record at the end of the season was crowned league champion. At the awards banquet after each baseball season, the champions received the Bill Terry trophy—donated to the league in 1934 by the New York Giants' Hall of Fame first baseman—and members of the winning team received individual medals (see Figures 3 and 4).[81] After the regular season, *Los Mormones* would often participate in various exhibition games. One type involved games between *Los Mormones* and other Americans, either servicemen in the Atlantic fleet or passengers traveling on Moore-McCormack and Delta ship lines.[82] Not wanting to stoke any political tensions, the servicemen would only play against other Americans, and *Los Mormones* were happy to oblige.[83] On occasion, *Los Mormones*' 'nationwide publicity' led teams from the country's interior to invite them to play.[84] For instance, on 12 and 13 May 1939, the team travelled to Rosario at the request of the local baseball association, with all expenses paid. Figure 5 shows Williams standing next to the Rosario Baseball Association president, the Rosario team captain, the club president, and Juan Carlos Noodt, president of the Argentine Baseball League. It was in Rosario where the Mormons would meet Raúl Rovira, secretary of the Rosario Baseball Association. Rovira would convert to Mormonism and even join the leadership ranks of the Church in Argentina.[85] In 1941, Argentina's Ministry of Education (Department of Physical Education) held an all-star game that pitted Foreigners against Argentines.[86] The Ministry even donated a large loving cup. *Los Mormones* typically had four or five players on the Foreigners team for the two years that the all-star game took place. The Foreigners won the 1941 contest, but lost the following year (Figure 6).

As a result of their success, *Los Mormones* attracted the attention of a wide swath of Argentine society. *El Gráfico* included multiple photographs in its write up of *Boca*

Figure 3. Frederick Salem Williams, president of *Club Atlético Los Mormones*, holding the Bill Terry Cup. Image courtesy of the Frederick G. Williams collection.

Figure 4. First place medal issued to Williams by the Argentine Baseball League. Image courtesy of the Frederick G. Williams collection.

Figure 5. The Rosario Baseball Association invited *Los Mormones* to play an exhibition match. From L to R, the Association's president, the Rosario team captain, the club president, Williams, and Juan Carlos Noodt, president of the Argentine Baseball League. Image courtesy of the Frederick G. Williams collection.

Figure 6. The 1942 Foreigners versus Argentines all-star match. J. Torres Viñas, captain of the Argentine squad, accepts the trophy from *Los Mormones*' Williams. Image courtesy of the Frederick G. Williams collection.

Juniors' victory over *Los Mormones* in the championship game of the 1941 season (See Figure 7).[87] After the season, *Los Mormones* played in a charity game to benefit the British Red Cross (See Figure 8). The game pitted *Los Mormones* against a select squad from the league, which included Fred Dickens Jr and his brother, Charles, as well as G. Newbery, members of two of the most prominent families in the Argentine sports

Figure 7. *El Gráfico's* coverage of *Los Mormones'* second place finish to *Boca Juniors* in the 1941 baseball championship.

BASEBALL

SE JUGARA UN PARTIDO DE EXHIBICION DE BASEBALL

EL DIA

19 de Abril

en el

BELGRANO ATHLETIC CLUB

PINO 3456   a las 14 15 horas

Entre los Mormones y un Cuadro seleccionado de la Liga

•

ENTRADA **$ 1.—** mayores
    "   " **0.50** menores

A total beneficio de la CRUZ ROJA BRITANICA

"COMBINADOS" TEAM			"LOS MORMONES" TEAM		
Catcher	: H. Peyrú	(Boca Juniors)	Catcher	:	Davis
Pitcher	: E. Friede	(Boca Juniors)	Pitcher	:	Forrest
1st. Base	: G. Newbery	(Ateneo de la Juventud)	1st. Base	:	Salerno
2nd. Base	: R. Smith	(Ateneo de la Juventud)	2nd. Base	:	Williams (Capt.)
3rd. Base	: A. Seeberg	(Cia. Unión Telefónica)	3rd. Base	:	Beck
Short Stop	: A. Ruch	(Ateneo de la Juventud)	Short Stop	:	Barton
Left Field	: J. Kernath	(West India Oil Co.)	Left Field	:	Jones
Centre Field	: F. Dickens (Jr.)	(Ateneo de la Juventud)	Centre Field	:	Dana
Right Field	: M. Muñoz	(Ateneo de la Juventud)	Right Field	:	Wheeler
Substitutes	: J. Costanzo	(Ateneo de la Juventud)	Substitutes	:	Sorrensen
	Allingham	(Swift Golf Club)			Smith
	A. García	(Ateneo de la Juventud)			
	C. Dickens	(Ateneo de la Juventud)			

★

Organizado por los Sres. L. G. Babb y F. E. Sheehy bajo los auspicios de la Comisión del Distrito de Belgrano del Consejo de la Comunidad Británica

Figure 8. A 1941 charity baseball game between *Los Mormones* and a combined squad from the rest of the league.

world. The network of connections the Mormons established would reach into high offices of the government. After they secured the league championship in 1939, César S. Vásquez, Director General of Physical Education for the Ministry of Education, invited them to play an exhibition game against a group of marines from the USS Quincy.[88] The marines' team had recently been crowned Atlantic fleet champions.

Vásquez arranged to have between 3000 and 5000 schoolboys in attendance, arguing that baseball 'has preference in our school physical education program'.[89]

The relation between *Los Mormones*' success and their popularity is important for two reasons. First, it suggests a fundamental connection between athletic prowess, physical fitness, and modernity. Andrés Horacio Reggiani has argued that in the 1930s and 1940s, 'achieving personal health and a fit body increasingly functioned as a marker of social distinction and modernity' in Argentina.[90] Thus when the *Herald* sang the praises of *Los Mormones*' Phil Davis for going six for six with a homerun in a game—a record-setting feat he accomplished while wearing a cast on his broken right hand (Figure 9)—it was highlighting not only a 'behemoth of the ball diamond', but also a paragon of the modern, fit individual. Second, and in a related sense, *Los Mormones* were popular not just because they were successful, but also because they embodied certain values and ideals on which 'alternative ideas of citizenship were conceived and acted on'.[91] The attention of the Ministry of Education is particularly

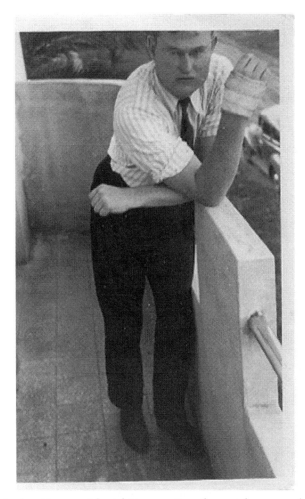

Figure 9. Phil Davis, *Los Mormones*' best hitter, sporting the cast he wore when hitting a record-setting six for six in a game. Image courtesy of Dian D. Shumway.

noteworthy in this regard because modern physical education in Argentina traces its roots to the years leading up to and including those that *Los Mormones* participated in professional sports in the country. The combination of *Los Mormones*' athletic excellence and spiritual values must have struck Vásquez, the Director General of Physical Education, as consistent with the objectives of the Argentine System of Physical Education, which sought to integrate moral values into the rational, scientific foundation of physical education.[92]

Los Mormones in Basketball

Unlike with baseball and softball, the Mormons would play no leadership role in the *Federación Argentina de Basket Ball* ('Argentine Basketball Federation'). Their impact was limited to the success of their team, and especially to a couple of standout players, which, as Williams has noted, brought them more favorable publicity than their success in baseball and softball did.[93] Williams registered *Los Mormones* with the league on 1 November 1938.[94] Typically teams were forced to work their way up to the first division, but the reputation of two of *Los Mormones* players, Rolf Larson and Dale Bergeson, was enough to convince Federation authorities to grant the team a special exemption (on 31 August 1939) (See Figure 10).[95] Bergeson and Larson had both played for *Club Atlético Lanús* the previous year, leading the team to a third place finish in the league championship. That year both were also selected as all-stars to play in the National Championship tournament in Bahía Blanca, though

Figure 10. Members of the 1939 *Los Mormones* basketball team (L to R): Ben Allen, J. Donal Earl, Riley Goodfellow, Rolf Larson, Dale Bergeson, Dwight Dana, Ivan Hatch, Sam Boren, and Max Willis. Boren and his brother Juan (not pictured) were two Argentines who played with *Los Mormones*. Image courtesy of the Frederick G. Williams collection.

'international technicalities' kept them from participating.[96] According to *El Gráfico*, Larson had also played lower division ball with *Quilmes Atlético Club*.[97]

Los Mormones played in Zone A along with 14 other clubs. Each team played the others on one occasion with zone champions earning the right to face each other in a final tournament.[98] *Los Mormones* finished their inaugural season (1939) tied for first place in the zone.[99] After winning the zone in a pair of playoff matches, *Los Mormones* went on to play at the inter-zone championship.[100] Citing the loss of key players and a bit of bad luck, they lost the final two games and ended up in fourth place for the season, the highest finish they would achieve.[101] After the 1939 season, *Los Mormones* 'struggled along for another season or two, with little success'.[102]

Based on their performance in the 1939 season, Larson and Bergeson were selected to play on the national team at the eighth South American Basketball Championship, held in Montevideo, Uruguay from 20 to 28 January 1940. Unfortunately, Bergeson fell one month short of the two-year residency requirement and could not participate, and Larson would be the lone player from *Los Mormones* to play.[103] In Montevideo, the Argentine squad lost the championship match by two points when Larson's shot fell short.[104] The tournament made Larson, who was already a popular player in Argentina, something of a sports celebrity, though here again there are different discourses at play. For the Mormons, Larson's success provided positive exposure for their faith. In a letter to the Church's First Presidency, Williams noted how Larson had endeared himself to Argentines through both his athletic performance and his demeanor: 'He was the sensation of the tournament and has done more to make Mormonism known in South America than any other individual … His name is a by-word in these two countries. He is such a gentleman—a missionary in the best sense of the word, that he has captured the hearts of the people'.[105] For some Argentines Larson no doubt embodied the same ideal of the modern, fit man as his fellow missionary, Davis. For its part, *El Gráfico* took issue with what it felt was the disproportionate amount of media attention Larson was receiving. After Argentina's first victory in the tournament, the magazine wrote: 'To praise the "North American" supposing that Argentina won because of his inclusion seems to detract from our triumph, attributing it almost exclusively to the foreign player'.[106]

As sweet as the South American Basketball Championship would be for the Mormons, their participation at major tournaments would end on something of a sour note, one in which regionalism/nationalism and religion seemed to play a part. Larson and Bergeson were both selected to play at the XII National Championship in Santiago del Estero, representing the *Capital* team. The tournament was scheduled for 16–23 March 1940, though authorities were forced to suspend it when the game between *Capital* and *Santiago* turned riotous. More than 1,000 fans had been turned away from a packed stadium, and the game proved to be intense, with neither team able to pull away from the other.[107] When the referee whistled 'Chango' Jiménez, one of *Santiago*'s main goal scorers, for his third foul (one short of the limit), 'the stadium was boiling'.[108] Bournaud writes: 'At halftime the imminence of the storm that was going to be unleashed was already evident'.[109] Seven minutes into the second half, with *Capital* leading 13–10, Jiménez fouled out and pandemonium ensued. Fans began throwing rocks onto the court, tearing up the wooden stands for more ammunition, and trying to rush the court. The referee halted the match and team delegates convened an impromptu meeting to determine what to do. Some of the delegates turned to the Chief of Police, hoping he could restore order so the game could continue, but 'with his vintage provincial intonation' he merely replied, 'And what are we supposed to do to contain those beasts? ... The few men I have would easily be overpowered by the crowd ... and I doubt they'd be very helpful anyway, since they're as ardent as any fans here'.[110]

When the match was scheduled to resume at 11.00 am the next morning, Frank Chevallier Boutell, *Capital*'s delegate, instructed his team not to leave their hotel, citing concerns over what Bournaud euphemistically called 'other consequences'.[111] An hour later, the team was supposedly on a train to Tucumán.[112] Williams's life history fills in the missing details. Chevallier had called Larson because rumors began to circulate that the *Capital* team would be mobbed. Speaking in English so that no one would understand him, Chevallier instructed Larson to have the team gather at the back door of the hotel at a certain time, where Chevallier would have a bus waiting.[113] With *Capital* safely out of town, the match with *Santiago* was never completed. However, *Capital* was apparently declared the winner, for in the appendix to his book Bournaud lists *Santa Fe* as tournament champions in the final match over a presumably absent *Capital*, with the unusual score of 2–0.[114]

Before the tournament even began, a local paper in Santiago caused a bit of controversy when it implicitly called into question the eligibility of *Capital*'s Mormon players.[115] The claim was misguided, says Bournaud, since Bergeson and Larson represented *Los Mormones*, a team officially affiliated with the Argentine Basketball Federation; however, the inflammatory article seemed to presage the direction the tournament would take. Bergson and Larson's team hailed from the Federal capital, while *Santiago* represented an interior region of the country. The two missionaries thus found themselves caught in the middle of a regional grudge match. For the *Santiago* supporters, criticizing the missionaries' faith was simply an excuse to try and garner their team an advantage. For their part, the Mormons suspected religious discrimination. The *Argentine Mission History* mentions a bulletin published by the basketball association of the city: 'It was very bitter toward the two missionaries expressing that they had gone to Santiago del Estero to spread tracts about a doctrine contrary to their state religion (Catholicism)'.[116] Whether discriminatory or not, the bulletin does suggest that *Los Mormones* can only be considered 'evangelical athletes of the empire' if by 'empire' we mean something radically different from what the concept has come to mean in the scholarly literature.[117]

Concluding Remarks

It seems logical to ask what lasting impact *Los Mormones* had on modern Argentine sport. It is true that in the case of baseball and, especially, softball, they proved instrumental in the foundation (softball) and early organization (softball and baseball) of the respective sports leagues. Unlike other groups or organizations, however, including religious organizations like the YMCA, the Mormons did not establish a substantial institutional footprint in the country, at least in sports. With the end of

Williams's tenure as mission president (in August 1942) and the escalation of war time complications, which forced all North American missionaries to abandon the country by the end of 1944, any momentum they had achieved was lost. Williams's successor did not pursue sports with the same zeal as Williams. In fact, during his subsequent time as mission president of Uruguay, Williams himself would abandon the model of using sports as a proselytizing tool, which had proved so instrumental in Argentina. Argentina had taught him that *Los Mormones*' success at sports did not come without its downside, as the national pride that invariably suffused the competition between Argentines and the North American missionaries at times led to 'hard feelings'. Hoping to avoid a similar problem in Uruguay, Williams turned instead to music. With music, 'no one loses, everyone wins'.[118]

Los Mormones place in Argentine sports history was largely a function of the temporary efforts and success of Williams and his missionary sportsmen. They did not shape the trajectory of the evolution of modern Argentine sport (again, with the exception of softball and possibly baseball) so much as they contributed to a trajectory that was already underway, and which would continue long after *Los Mormones* faded from the public's eye. They were, to use a sports metaphor, something of a rag-tag group that punched above its weight.[119] What is more, the sports they played paled in popularity compared to soccer. The large crowds they attracted at select games were rather the exception than the norm. Nor did they leave a lasting legacy the way other North Americans like the Newbery or Dickens families did. And yet despite all of these qualifications, *Los Mormones* can rightly claim their place alongside a myriad of other 'carriers' of North American sports to Latin America.[120] They became for a few years bona fide sports celebrities, and their story adds a unique thread to the truly international tapestry that is modern Argentine sports.

Notes

1. Phil E. Davis and Velma Peterson Davis, *Pre-Mission and Mission Years, 1937–1943: Diaries and Letter Excerpts*, 195 (entry for 1 March 1941).
2. Héctor Pastrian, *Beisbol: Reseña histórica internacional y argentina* (Federación Argentina de Beisbol, 1977), 48. My translation.
3. Frederick Salem Williams, *The History of My Life*, 1971, Church History Library, The Church of Jesus Christ of Latter-Day Saints, Salt Lake City, Utah.
4. Joseph L. Arbena, 'American Sports Across the Americas', *The International Journal of the History of Sport* 28, no. 17 (2011), 2527–46.
5. Robert M. Levine, 'Sport as Dramaturgy—for Society: A Concluding Chapter,' in Joseph L. Arbena (ed.), *Sport and Society in Latin America: Diffusion Dependency and the Rise of Mass Culture* (New York: Greenwood Press, 1988), 145. See also J.A. Mangan, 'The Early Evolution of Modern Sport in Latin America: A Mainly English Middle-Class Inspiration?', *The International Journal of the History of Sport* 18, no. 3 (2001), 21.
6. Mangan, 'The Early Evolution of Modern Sport in Latin America', 37.
7. The few authors to treat the role of Mormon missionaries in Argentine sports are Jessie L. Embry and John H. Brambaugh, 'Preaching Through Playing: Sports and Recreation in Missionary Work, 1911–64', *Journal of Mormon History* 35, no. 4 (Fall 2009), 53–84; and Frederick Salem Williams and Frederick Granger Williams, *From Acorn to Oak Tree: A Personal History of the Establishment and First Quarter Development of the South American Missions* (Fullerton, CA: Et Cetera, Et Cetera Graphics, 1987).

8. Joel Horowitz, 'Football Clubs and Neighbourhoods in Buenos Aires Before 1943: The Role of Political Linkages and Personal Influence', *Journal of Latin American Studies*, 46 (2014), 567.
9. On the 1942 Pan-American games, see Cesar R. Torres, 'The Limits of Pan-Americanism: The Case of the Failed 1942 Pan-American Games', *The International Journal of the History of Sport* 28, no. 17 (2011), 2547–74.
10. Williams and Williams, *From Acorn to Oak Tree*, 149, note 10.
11. Williams and Williams, *From Acorn to Oak Tree*, 140.
12. Ibid., 149, note 10. M-Men teams were basketball teams organized by the Church's youth program for young men between the ages of 17 and 24. They became so popular that a Church-wide tournament was organized, which by the 1950s was considered 'the largest basketball tournament in the world', outstripping both the NIT and NCAA tournaments. See Darrell Lloyd Parkin, 'The Athletic Program of the Mormon Church: Its Growth and Development' (Master's diss., University of Illinois, 1964), 38; Jessie L. Embry, *Spiritualized Recreation: Mormon All-Church Athletic Tournaments and Dance Festivals* (Provo, UT: Brigham Young University, 2008), 54–93; and Rex A. Skidmore, 'Mormon Recreation in Theory and Practice: A Study of Social Change' (PhD diss., University of Pennsylvania, 1941), 103–4.
13. Williams and Williams, *From Acorn to Oak Tree*, 195.
14. Ibid., 141.
15. Ibid., 138.
16. Quoted in ibid., 137. The translation appears to be Williams's.
17. Cited in ibid., 139–40. The quotation appears to be Williams's English language recollection of the conversation.
18. Ibid., 139, 140.
19. See Kimball, *Sports in Zion*, 21–56; Skidmore, 'Mormon Recreation in Theory and Practice', 91–105; and Parkin, 'The Athletic Program of the Mormon Church', 32–59.
20. See Kimball, *Sports in Zion*, 4; and Richard Ian Kimball, 'Muscular Mormonism', *The International Journal of the History of Sport* 25, no. 5 (2008), 549–78.
21. The journal entry above from Phil Davis captures a sense of what muscular Mormonism looked like in practice among Mormon missionaries in Argentina, especially the idea of physical strength (Phil knocking out the players who slid into home) tempered by missionary spirit, respect, and playing clean ball.
22. Williams and Williams, *From Acorn to Oak Tree*, 137. The question of just how coordinated these missionary efforts were among the Mormons remains open. For their part, Embry and Brambaugh found no evidence that LDS Church headquarters provided instructions to mission presidents to get involved in sports, or that mission presidents in some areas jumped on the sports bandwagon after hearing of their counterparts' success elsewhere. However, they also note that LDS archives that could shed light on the issue remain closed to researchers. Embry and Brambaugh, 'Preaching Through Playing', 58–9. In perusing Williams's personal files, I discovered various copies of a 'Mission President's Personal Report to the First Presidency for the Month of _____, 194__'. Under the section 'Special Missionary Activities' is the following line: 'Number of missionary organized athletic groups___ No. of Appearances_____'. Photocopy in my possession.
23. See Embry and Brambaugh, 'Preaching Through Playing', 63–79; Richard Ian Kimball, *Sports in Zion: Mormon Recreation, 1890-1940* (Urbana, IL: University of Illinois Press, 2003), 100–1; and Booker T. Alston, 'The Cumorah Baseball Club: Mormon Missionaries and Baseball in South Africa', *Journal of Mormon History* 40, no. 3 (2014), 93–126.
24. Embry and Brambaugh, 'Preaching Through Playing', 64.
25. Glynn Bennion, 'New Ways of Proselyting and the Reason Therefor', *Deseret News*, 25 January 1936, 6.
26. *Spirit of the Game*, DVD, directed by Darran Scott (Chippendale. NSW: Steve Jaggi Company, 2016).

27. On the role of non-Mormon Christians, see Claudia Guedes, '"Changing the Cultural Landscape": English Engineers, American Missionaries, and the YMCA Bring Sports to Brazil—the 1870s to the 1930s', *The International Journal of the History of Sport* 28, no. 17 (2011), 2596–605; Patrick Scott, 'Cricket and the Religious World in the Victorian Period', *Church Quarterly*, 3 (July 1970), 134–44.
28. J.A. Mangan, *The Games Ethic and Imperialism: Aspects of the Diffusion of an Ideal* (New York: Viking, 1986), 168.
29. See Craig L. Blomberg and Stephen E. Robinson, *How Wide the Divide?: A Mormon and an Evangelical in Conversation* (Downers Grove, IL: InterVarsity Press, 1997).
30. See Sarah Barringer Gordon, *The Mormon Question: Polygamy and Constitutional Conflict in Nineteenth-Century America* (Chapel Hill, NC: University of North Carolina Press, 2002); Christine Talbot, *A Foreign Kingdom: Mormons and Polygamy in American Political Culture, 1852–1890* (Urbana, IL: University of Illinois Press, 2013); J. Spencer Fluhman, *"A Peculiar People": Anti-Mormonism and the Making of Religion in Nineteenth-Century America* (Chapel Hill, NC: University of North Carolina Press, 2012).
31. See Davis and Peterson Davis, *Pre-Mission and Mission Years*, 244 (8 July 1941), 198 (6 March 1941). On the dissolution of the German-language congregation, see Williams and Williams, *From Acorn to Oak Tree*, 127.
32. Williams and Williams, *From Acorn to Oak Tree*, 141.
33. Ibid., 144. Williams's approach resembles that of Don Mack Dalton, mission president in South Africa in 1932. See Alston, 'The Cumorah Baseball Club', 95–6, 98.
34. Andrés Horacio Reggiani, 'Fitness and the National Body: Modernity, Physical Culture, and Gender, 1930–1945', in Benjamin Price and David M.K. Sheinin (eds), *Making Citizens in Argentina* (Pittsburgh, PA: University of Pittsburgh Press, 2017), 83. On the lack of coordination of athletic efforts in Mormon missions, see Embry and Brambaugh, 'Preaching Through Playing', 58–9.
35. *Gaucho Gazette* 1, no. 2 (1939), 11.
36. *Gaucho Gazette* 1, no. 2 (1939), 11.
37. *Gaucho Gazette* 1, no. 2 (1939), 11. See also the *Argentine Mission History*, 16 August 1938, Church History Library.
38. *Gaucho Gazette* 1, no. 2 (1939), 11. Mormons were not alone in their concerns for the well-being of young people. See Roddrigo Daskal, 'Clubes, deporte y política en el Honorable Concejo Deliberante de la Ciudad de Buenos Aires (1895–1920)', in Julio Frydenberg and Roddrigo Daskal (eds), *Fútbol, historia y política* (Buenos Aires: Aurelia Rivera, 2010), 213, 230.
39. Julio Frydenberg, Rodrigo Daskal, and Cesar R. Torres, 'Sports Clubs with Football in Argentina: Conflicts, Debates and Continuities' *The International Journal of the History of Sport* 30, no. 14 (2013), 1677. See also Horowitz, 'Football Clubs and Neighbourhoods in Buenos Aires Before 1943', 564.
40. *El Mensajero* 4, no. 8 (1940), 141, 156. All translations from *El Mensajero* are mine.
41. *Gaucho Gazette* 2, no. 1 (1940), 9.
42. *El Gráfico* 20, no. 1066 (1939), 40. The article of faith states: 'We believe in being honest, true, chaste, benevolent, virtuous, and in doing good to all men; indeed, we may say that we follow the admonition of Paul: "We believe all things, we hope all things"; we have endured many things and hope to be able to endure all things. If there is anything virtuous, lovely, or of good report or praiseworthy, we seek after these things'. On the place of *El Gráfico* in Argentine culture, see Martín Bergel and Pablo Palomino, 'La revista El Gráfico en sus inicios: una pedagogía deportiva para la ciudad moderna', *Prismas: Revista de historia intelectual*, 4 (2000).
43. *El Tribuno*, 29 October 1938, cited in Williams and Williams, *From Acorn to Oak Tree*, 138. The translation seems to be Williams and Williams's.
44. Frydenberg, Daskal and Torres, 'Sports Clubs with Football in Argentina', 1676. On sports clubs in Argentina, see Rodrigo Daskal and Mariano Gruschetsky, 'Clubes de fútbol: su dimension social. El Club Atlético River Plate a comienzos del siglo XX',

EFDeportes.com 17, no. 176 (2013); Rodrigo Daskal, *Los clubes en la Ciudad de Buenos Aires (1932–1945)* (Buenos Aires: Teseo, 2013); Daskal, 'Clubes, deporte y política', 203–39; and Horowitz, 'Football Clubs and Neighbourhoods in Buenos Aires Before 1943', 557–85'; Frydenberg, Daskal and Torres, 'Sports Clubs with Football in Argentina', 1670–86; Julio D. Frydenberg, 'Los clubes de fútbol de Buenos Aires en los años veinte', in Julio Frydenberg and Rodrigo Daskal (eds), *Fútbol, historia y política* (Buenos Aires: Aurelia Rivera, 2010), 23–81.

45. *El Mensajero* 3, no. 6 (1939), 31. My translation. The Church's young men were encouraged to memorize the following promise: 'So that I may render the highest service to humanity, I commit myself before God and my companions to keep myself morally clean, to defend the truth without fear, to learn modesty and courage, and to obey the laws of morality and good intention in sports'. *El Mensajero* 3, no. 5 (1939), 15. My translation.
46. Frydenberg, Daskal and Torres, 'Sports Clubs with Football in Argentina', 1672.
47. See Eduardo Lautaro Galak, 'Educación del cuerpo y política: Concepciones de raza, higienismo y eugenesia en la Educación Física Argentina', *Movimiento, Porto Alegre* 20, no. 4 (2014), 1555; Eduardo Lautaro Galak, '"La educación física persigue el perfeccionamiento de la raza": Políticas públicas, salud, eugenesia y educación de cuerpos', in Alex Branco Fraga, Ivan Marcelo Gomes, and Yara Maria de Carvalho (eds), *As prácticas corporais no campo da saúde* (Porto Alegre: Rede UNIDA, 2015). I explore the connection between the spiritual underpinnings of *Los Mormones*' ideas about sports and those of Enrique Romero Brest in an unpublished essay, 'The Spirituality of Sport: *Los Mormones* in Argentina, 1938–42'.
48. Williams, *History*, IV–151. The organization of the club included two advisors (including Williams); a secretary; an executive committee; and committees that oversaw new memberships, the club's programs, and the facilities. The program committee had four subcommittees: athletics, music, drama, and the art of speaking. *El Mensajero* 2, no. 12 (1938), 27.
49. See the following entries in the *Argentine Mission History*: 31 October 1940, 30 August 1941, and 31 December 1941.
50. The plans for the cement basketball standards came from Federico Forrest. Williams, *History*, IV–148. It is unclear whether badminton was played on the same court as basketball and volleyball; however, the language of different sources suggests there were different courts. See the *Gaucho Gazette* 1, no. 3 (1939), 4.
51. To celebrate the Club's inauguration, the Mormons had invited *Ateneo de la Juventud* to play a friendly basketball game. Williams recalled the good-naturedness of the *Ateneo* players despite the cold weather, noting that *Ateneo*'s facilities included an indoor gymnasium. See *History*, IV–149.
52. *El Mensajero* 4, no. 7 (1940), 137.
53. 'Club Atlético "*Los Mormones*": Reglamentos', 13 July 1940. The regulations I consulted were printed on the reverse of a membership application for CALM. My translation.
54. *Gaucho Gazette* 2, no. 1 (1940), 9.
55. To encourage new members to sign up, Club members received invitation-cards that granted entrance into certain events, typically dances, free of charge. Fearing the measure was being abused, the Club approved a resolution stipulating that after three invitations, a person was expected to pay for a Club membership. *El Mensajero* 3, no. 9 (1939), 31.
56. The figure for *Boca Juniors* comes from Frydenberg, 'Los clubes de fútbol de Buenos Aires en los años veinte', 78. The figure for CALM, which is likely underestimated, given the complaint that some religious units had not sent in their reports, is found in *El Mensajero* 3, no. 2 (1939), 30.
57. Horowitz, 'Football Clubs and Neighbourhoods in Buenos Aires Before 1943', 563.
58. Jorge Saraví Riviere, *Aportes para una historia de la Educación Física, 1900 a 1945* (IEF No. 1 'Dr. Enrique Romero Brest', 1998), 69.
59. Riviere, *Aportes*, 67, 68.

60. *El Mensajero* 4, no. 6 (1940), 117.
61. Williams, *History*, IV–148. Another prominent contact who helped secure facilities for games was a Mr Newburg, whom Williams refers to as 'the Government's official inspector of all "shows, spectacles and events"'. Ibid., IV–128.
62. *El Mensajero* 1, no. 3 (1939), 12. Williams calls Forrest's club *Club Atlético Chacabuco*. Williams, *History*, IV–123.
63. *El Mensajero* 3, no. 4 (1939), 30–1; *El Mensajero* 3, no. 6 (1939), 27, 30; *El Mensajero* 3, no. 8 (1939), 26–7.
64. Williams, *History*, IV–123; *Deseret News*, 23 January 1940, 12; *The Y News*, XIX, no. 29 (1940), 4.
65. Williams, *History*, IV–121.
66. Mangan, 'The Early Evolution of Modern Sport in Latin America', 13.
67. Ibid., 13.
68. Williams and Williams, *From Acorn to Oak Tree*, 148.
69. Williams, *History*, IV–125–6.
70. Ibid., IV–124.
71. Williams and Williams, *From Acorn to Oak Tree*, 144.
72. Davis recalls the *Boca* team of 1942 comprising 'Cubans, Puerto Ricans, French, German, San Salvadorans and others that had played baseball in their countries'. Davis and Peterson Davis, *Pre-Mission and Mission Years*, 289 (7 April 1942).
73. Davis and Peterson Davis, *Pre-Mission and Mission Years*, 277 (22 January 1942).
74. *Herald*, 14 March 1942.
75. After Williams left Argentina in August 1942, *Los Mormones* fielded their last softball team in 1943 under the new mission president, James Barker. In a letter home to his fiancée dated 11 January 1943, Davis wrote, 'We lost the softball championship this year. Some of the boys are not serious about it as we were last year. Then again, you can't be a winner all the time'. Davis also mentions that the Mormons had not at that point decided whether to field a baseball team for the 1943 season. Davis and Peterson Davis, *Pre-Mission and Mission Years*, 321–2. Pastrian suggests they did play. Pastrian, *Béisbol*, 51.
76. Williams, *History*, IV–123–4. Pastrian suggests the two sports were combined as part of the same league (the *Liga Argentina de Béisbol y Sóftbol*) at least as early as 1937. Pastrian, *Beisbol*, 40.
77. Williams and Williams, *From Acorn to Oak Tree*, 141.
78. Ibid., 144. On the relation between clubs and *barrio* identity, see Horowitz, 'Football Clubs and Neighbourhoods in Buenos Aires Before 1943', 558–9, 564.
79. Williams, *History*, IV–141.
80. Ibid., IV–141.
81. *El Mensajero* 4, no. 7 (1940), 139.
82. Williams, *History*, IV–130.
83. Ibid., IV–132–3.
84. Williams and Williams, *From Acorn to Oak Tree*, 145.
85. Williams, *History*, IV–142.
86. See Pastrian, *Béisbol*, 49–50; and Williams, *History*, IV–140.
87. The *Boca* victory was apparently not without its asterisk in the history books. Williams notes in his life history that *Boca* had failed to show up for the final match with *Los Mormones*, and that *Los Mormones* should have won the game by forfeit. Given that the game would also decide the league championship, however, and not wanting to claim the championship by virtue of a forfeit, Williams decided to reschedule. Williams, *History*, IV–139. When the two teams played, *Los Mormones*' pitcher, one of the few non-missionaries occasionally to play with the team (he was a North American who worked for Swift and who had played semi-pro ball in the US) was unable to play. Davis and Peterson Davis, *Pre-Mission and Mission Years*, 198 (6 March 1941).
88. Williams and Williams, *From Acorn to Oak Tree*, 144.

89. Cited in ibid., 144.
90. Reggiani, 'Fitness and the National Body', 83. See also Eduardo P. Archetti, *El potrero, la pista y el ring: Las patrias del deporte argentino* (Buenos Aires: Fondo de Cultura Económica, 2001), 12.
91. Reggiani, 'Fitness and the National Body', 82.
92. See Pablo Ariel Scharagrodsky, 'El Sistema Argentino de Educación Física. Entre el cientificismo, la higienización, el eclecticismo y la argentinidad', *Revista Brasileira de Ciências do Esporte* 37, no. 2 (2015), 159–64; Abel Luis Agüero, Silvia Beatriz Iglesias and Milanino del Valle, 'Enrique Romero Brest, el creador de la educación física escolar. Comentarios a su obra', *Res Gesta*, 48 (2010); Ángela Aisenstein and Pablo Scharagrodsky (eds), *Tras las huellas de la Educación Física Argentina: Cuerpo, género y pedagogía. 1880-1950* (Buenos Aires: Prometeo Libros, 2006).
93. Williams and Williams, *From Acorn to Oak Tree*, 146.
94. Ibid., 141.
95. *El Mensajero* 3, no. 10 (1939), 31; Williams, *History*, IV–152.
96. *Argentine Mission History*, 31 January 1939.
97. *El Gráfico* 21, no. 1072 (1940), 11.
98. Williams, *History*, IV–152. This final tournament appears to have been limited to the capital city. See Abel A. Bournaud, *Bahía Blanca: Capital del basquetbol argentino* (Bahía Blanca, Argentina: Martínez y Rodríguez S.R.L., 1972), 48.
99. *El Mensajero* 3, no. 11 (1939), 32.
100. *El Mensajero* 3, no. 12 (1939), 31.
101. *Argentine Mission History*, 22 December 1939; *El Mensajero* 4, no. 1 (1940), 18.
102. Williams, *History*, IV–146.
103. Ibid., 156–7.
104. *El bien público* (Uruguay), 29 January 1940, 8. Williams, *History*, IV–158.
105. Williams, *History*, IV–158.
106. *El Gráfico* 21, no. 1072 (1940), 12. My translation.
107. Bournaud, *Bahía Blanca*, 48.
108. Ibid., 49. All translations from Bournaud are mine.
109. Ibid., 49.
110. Ibid., 49.
111. Ibid., 50.
112. Ibid., 50.
113. Williams, *History*, IV–161.
114. Bournaud, *Bahía Blanca*, 159.
115. Ibid., 48. Bournaud mentions three missionaries—Bergeson, Larson, and a Mac Laren—though I have found no references to Mac Laren in any of the Mormon sources consulted.
116. *Argentine Mission History*, 29 March 1940.
117. Mangan, *The Games Ethic*, 168. See also Allen Guttmann, *Games and Empires: Modern Sports and Cultural Imperialism* (New York: Columbia University Press, 1994); Mark Dyreson, 'Imperial "Deep Play": Reading Sport and Visions of the Five Empires of the "New World", 1919-1941', *The International Journal of the History of Sport* 28, no. 17 (2011), 2421–47; and Dyreson, 'Mapping an Empire of Baseball: American Visions of National Pastimes and Global Influence, 1919-1941', in Donald G. Kyle and Robert B. Fairbanks (eds), *Baseball in America and America in Baseball* (College Station: Texas A&M University Press, 2008), 143–88.
118. Williams and Williams, *From Acorn to Oak Tree*, 261.
119. Williams recalls that were it not for the Moore-McCormack ship line, which 'kept us in balls and bats', *Los Mormones* would have lacked the minimum equipment to even play. Williams, *History*, IV–133.
120. Arbena, 'American Sports Across the Americas', 2538.

Acknowledgments

I would like to offer my sincere thanks to a number of people for supporting this project. Drex Davis and Dian Shumway allowed me to consult Phil Davis's journal and memorabilia from his time in Argentina. Frederick Salem Williams's son, Frederick G. Williams, opened his home, his office, and his father's personal files, providing me unparalleled access to various documents, photographs, medals, a *Los Mormones* jersey, and copies of *El Mensajero* and the *Gaucho Gazette*. Dian and Fred also granted permission to reproduce a number of images. The archivists and librarians at the LDS Church's Church History Library facilitated archival research, as did Brigham Young University's special collections department. David Golding offered useful historical perspective on Mormon missionary baseball. Joe Blaney provided funds from the Illinois State University Research Grants-Faculty Research Awards. BYU's Department of Spanish and Portuguese hosted an invited lecture, allowing me to present my research for the first time. Cesar R. Torres graciously shared his article on the Pan-American games.

Disclosure Statement

No potential conflict of interest was reported by the author.

'Necessary Cessation from Toil and Work': Young Christian Workers and the Question of Sport on Sundays in Post-War Melbourne

Melissa Jean Walsh and Nicholas Thomas Shaw Marshall

ABSTRACT
The Young Christian Workers (YCW) is an international movement for young Catholics, engaged through a method of education called 'See, Judge, and Act'. From the 1950s to the 1980s, the Australian YCW became known for running campaigns on a range of social issues and the provision of services – including sporting events and competitions. In this paper, the development of the Australian YCW Football Association during the 1950s is explored, and the history of YCW members' participation in public debates about the morality of Sunday sport, which culminated in a local referendum in the Melbourne suburb of Camberwell in 1959, is traced. Drawing on archival materials and interviews conducted with former young workers, the paper explores tensions within Christianity around the meaning of 'leisure', 'idleness', and Sunday as a day of observance and rest. This examination of the Melbourne debate of 1959 will show how religious tensions around Sunday sport were shaped by class, youth, and masculine identities.

Introduction

The impetus for this paper came from the discovery of a seemingly inconsequential manila folder, unpacked from a dusty cardboard box in late 2013. Tasked with sorting through hundreds of files collected over 70 years by the Australian Young Christian Workers (YCW) movement, the team at the newly established YCW Archive in Melbourne began to shape a research collection of manuscripts, photographs and ephemera, which in the following months would be supplemented by life-story interviews with former members of the YCW. There were many exceptional finds in those early days, but for the sport historian the folder eventually numbered '24' was of particular interest. It contained 100 articles, dutifully clipped from newspapers by an unknown hand, tracing debates in Melbourne between 1959 and 1967 about the playing of competitive sports in local areas on a Sunday. Often undated and unattributed, the clippings illuminated how the post-war decades were a period of change in urban Australia. The debate about sport, articulated in letters to the editor, news articles and editorials in the Melbourne press, gave an opportunity for people to express their joy or articulate their anxieties about changes they perceived in Australian society – increasing secularization, modern entertainment culture, and the rise of the 'teenager'.

Drawing on these sources, a case study of the debate conducted in the Melbourne suburb of Camberwell in 1959 is presented. At the time, local government by-laws prohibited the playing of sports on council reserves, courts, and greens on Sundays. Lobbying by a coalition of tennis clubs to relax the restrictions saw the Council call a referendum to gauge ratepayers' opinion on the question. Members of the YCW – a Catholic youth movement – were active in the Camberwell campaign, making the case that sports – particularly Australian Rules football – should be permitted on the Sabbath. The significance of this intervention is understood when the demography of Camberwell is taken into account, as no other suburb in the city of Melbourne had such a concentration of Protestant adherents, far outnumbering Catholic and followers of other Christian and non-Christian faiths. In contrast to other studies of Catholic and Protestant sporting rivalries, however, the sides of the debate in 1959 were not drawn on simple sectarian lines.[1] The case for 'Yes' – freedom to play on a Sunday – was not only made by the Catholic YCW, but representatives of Protestant sporting clubs, churches, and individuals. The heat of the debate was fired by a desire to (re)define the meaning and sanctity of Sunday to Christians in post-war Australia.

The foundations for Melbourne's 'austere Sunday' – where shops and entertainments were closed and sports banned – were laid in the 1860s. During the nineteenth century, both Protestants and Catholics – the latter a minority of the population – accepted and enacted the obligations of Sunday observance, however as Moore suggests, its manner varied between denominations.[2] The debate of 1959 was by no means the first time Sabbatarianism had been critiqued by citizens, lawmakers, and the clergy.[3] The success of the Camberwell 'Yes' campaign does, however, intimate the changes that were to come in the 1960s and 1970s, as laws and mores increasingly shifted, giving greater license for recreational pursuits on a Sunday.

The file of clippings held by the YCW Archive attests to the interest its members and mentors had in the debate at the time, and the following discussion will draw on this material. Yet in addition to these public and published interventions from the period, five interviews gathered with former YCW members who were active in the boys' movement in Melbourne during the 1950s and 1960s are drawn upon. Conducted between 2013 and 2015 as part of the YCW Oral History Project, these interviews followed a 'life story approach', a methodology which enabled the interviewee to reflect on life before, during, and after participation in the YCW movement.[4] The question of Sunday sport was not, therefore, a specific area of enquiry during the interviews, so the manner in which stories of this particular campaign emerged are telling. The tenacity of memories suggests the quest to allow Sunday sport was deeply felt and hard fought. Yet these narratives 'composed' in the twenty-first century, also illuminate how aspects of daily life in post-war Melbourne, were remembered as being shaped by age, class, and religious identity.[5] These memories enrich understanding of the context in which the Sunday sport debate took place.

Following a brief description of how the YCW in Australia understood sports' role in engaging youth, the paper traces the YCW's involvement in the Camberwell referendum, and how the campaign was shaped by the particular religious – namely Christian – 'flavour' of the suburb. By tracing the key rhetorical touchpoints employed by both sides of the issue and the denominational and generational differences in understanding sport, the reshaping of old sectarian divisions between Australian Catholics and Protestants in the 1950s is revealed.

Home, Work, and Leisure: The Methodology of YCW

The YCW was established by Catholic priest – later Cardinal – Joseph Cardijn in Belgium in 1925.[6] The impetus for the YCW – known in French as the *Jeunesse Ouvrière Chrétienne* (JOC), – was twofold, namely to counteract the de-humanizing and de-Christianizing effects of industrialization, and to bring 'religion back to the surroundings of real life and the problems these raise'.[7]

The instrument Cardijn developed to foster this movement was the parish study group comprising young working people, usually 14–20 year olds. His first experiment with the study-group method occurred in 1912 in the Belgian town of Laeken, where as curate, he was given charge of the local Girls' Club, which had around 30 members.[8] There, Cardijn synthesized the approach to social research, thought and action embodied in the work of Victor Brants, the study circles of Le Sillon, and the rules of individual action in Ben Tillet's Dock, Wharf, Riverside, and General Workers' Union.[9] Cardijn described this method of enquiry as 'See, Judge, Act'. Writing in 1960, John Molony, chaplain to the YCW in the Australian regional town of Ballarat described the method as follows:

1. To SEE himself [sic] in the whole of his life, in his relations with God, with others, with his surroundings in his home, his work and his leisure.
2. To JUDGE what he has seen, to judge it with the mind of Christ.
3. To take ACTION, either personally or in conjunction with others; action which is formative, educative, of service to others, representative on behalf of those for whom he knows he has responsibility.[10]

Through this process, young workers would experience *formation*, a personal transformation enabling the 'the young worker to recognize and fulfil his destiny'.[11] To be a YCW meant understanding oneself as an agent of change in the home, neighbourhood, workplace, and beyond. Indeed YCWs were encouraged to develop a sense of solidarity with young people around the globe, and to imagine that through the universal application of see-judge-act, they would be able to meet the challenges of a world often indifferent to their fate. This required more than simply attending a weekly parish meeting. To be a YCW was a 'personal vocation':

> ... to be fulfilled first in the ordinary acts of his daily life. It is in his daily acts, whether at home, work or leisure, that he fulfils his vocation. It is not something abstract or apart from his life. It is his life.[12]

Ideally, this formational movement was to be organized and led by and with young workers for young workers, with the clergy acting as chaplains and advisors to the young leaders. To this extent the YCW was an exemplar of French-Belgian Catholic Action, differing from the cleric-centric, party political *Azzione Cattolica* favoured in Italy.[13] In 1925, Cardijn travelled to the Vatican and Pope Pius XI gave his imprimatur to the 'aim, method, and organization' of the YCW.[14] The year 1925 is therefore considered as the founding year of the YCW/JOC.

During the 1930s, Australian Catholic intellectuals began to receive news of this 'Jocism', whilst the arrival of the Women of Nazareth (also known as Ladies of the Grail) in Sydney in 1936 improved local understanding of European methods of enquiry.[15] In 1941 and despite the dramatic interruption of war,[16] the YCW, the National Catholic Girls' Movement (NCGM), and the Young Christian Students (YCS) were established with the imprimatur of the Australian Archbishops who viewed the movements as specialized and appropriate forms of Catholic Action.[17] In that year, the first Australian YCW boys' group was established by Father Frank Lombard in the working class suburb of Northcote in Melbourne.[18]

The Service of Sport

After the Second World War, the YCW developed into a popular social movement with thousands of members based in parishes around Australia. By 1950, the NCGM had 168 groups around the country.[19] In 1960, the boys' movement reported that it had 255 branches operating with 5,152 general members.[20] Through the provision of services such as sports, camps, and cooperatives, the NCGM and YCW sought to reach many more thousands of young people, most of whom were Catholic.[21] In the last year of the decade, YCW (Boys) claimed that nearly 13,500 young people had been catered for in services, including sporting teams.[22]

Sport did not have a distinct and particular place in Joseph Cardijn's methodology of education. The founder's thinking, therefore, contrasts to that underpinning other Christian youth movements such as the Young Men's Christian Association and the Young Women's Christian Association. Whilst Cardijn was silent on the use of sports as a proselytizing instrument, during the 1940s and 1950s the Australian YCW and NCGM did include sports among the services the movement offered to young people, creating opportunities to make contact with potential members.[23]

The extent to which local groups channelled their efforts into providing organized sporting service differed between the YCW and NCGM, and according to location. Whilst the women in the NCGM did engage in sports teams and competitions, the men's movement placed more emphasis on sport as a means of engaging youth compared to their counterparts, reflecting the perceived interests of the target group. This gendered difference is intersected, however, with regional distinctions, which were shaped in part by the theological understandings of the local YCW chaplain. Across Australia there were differences in the degree to which local groups embraced the idea that involvement in a local YCW sporting club would contribute to the formation of young Australians in the way Cardijn envisaged. In Melbourne, large scale sporting competition *was* understood by chaplains such as Lombard and, later, Fr

Kevin Toomey, as a mechanism for building a mass movement of young working men. It is likely Lombard's keenness stemmed from his own experience as a student and 'splendid sportsman' at Melbourne's St Kevin's College, established in 1918 by the Christian Brothers.[24] Attempting to bring together boys and young men without the ready scaffold of a school's corporate identity, sports, particularly team sports, must have seemed an excellent means to foster solidarity and organizational identity amongst members in the YCW's early years.

Having adopted the motto 'A Service for Every Need' in 1942, the Melbourne YCW proclaimed its ambition to provide services which would assist a young worker 'to recognize and fulfil his destiny'.[25] Over the next four decades these included housing, credit, and building cooperatives, an accommodation service which arranged suitable board for young people moving to the city for work, education programmes on a range of matters including preparation for marriage, unionism in the workplace and money management. Another form of service were the 'enquiries' the YCW conducted to identify and understand issues facing young workers. Sometimes a 'campaign' would follow. Coordinated by the YCW leaders at a diocesan, state, or national level, campaigns would aim to raise awareness and, if thought necessary, agitate for changes in government policy.

To what extent Lombard, Toomey, and the Melbourne chaplains were motivated by 'manly Catholicism' is unclear from the available evidence.[26] It would seem they were in part driven by prosaic considerations: in a city where Australian Rules football was the preeminent winter sport for men, establishing local YCW football teams offered a particularly good opportunity to increase the reach and recognition of the YCW across the city. Politics between the local Catholic youth movements may have also played a role. Providing sport was a key function of Catholic Boys' Legion (CBL) and Catholic Young Men's Society (CYMS) who in the 1940s and 1950s were vying with the YCW for members. In his unpublished manuscript of the history of the Melbourne YCW, David Kehoe suggests the Jocist priests 'simply appropriated' the existing junior football competition run by the CBL and persistently challenged the CYMS' maintenance of football, cricket, and basketball competitions on the basis that the YCW was the official Catholic Action movement for young men in the city.[27]

Whilst Kehoe argues that the YCW chaplains simply used football as a method of recruiting members and gaining notoriety in the parishes, the sporting services were not simply a utilitarian device. Whilst members of the YCW were by definition *working* boys and men, the movement's mission was to elevate youth beyond their 'forsaken, neglected, and demoralized' condition as workers.[28] Sport was play, the antithesis of work.[29] In this light football, and other sports, offered moments of freedom and transcendence, as well as the opportunity to identify with one another and as something 'other' than working youth.

In 1941, there were 36 teams in the YCW Football Association (YCWFA), which ran Under 18 and Under 16 divisions.[30] In 1943, this had grown to 51 teams. When the age limit for belonging to the YCW was raised to 25 in 1943, an uneasy power sharing arrangement was struck between the CYMS and YCW. It was agreed that if a CYMS – which was for Catholic men aged 18–30 – already existed in the local parish, the YCW would not attempt to field their own open age team.[31] Yet during the

1950s, as Melbourne accelerated its suburban expansion, new parishes were ripe for establishing YCW branches and, by extension, football teams. Due to growth of the YCW and the associated collapse of the CYMS, by 1966 the YCWFA stood as the 'largest single football organization in Australia with 140 teams and 3,000 registered players'.[32] As a consequence, the YCWFA occupies an important place in the collective memory of football followers – Catholic and non-Catholic – who came of age in the post-war decades, despite the folding of the Association's operations in 1986.

There is a lack of evidence to support the idea that all the young people who engaged with the YCW sporting teams were also soundly formed in the methodology of see, judge and act, and this is a source of tension for many former YCWs when reflecting on the long-term impact of the movement as an agent of social change. Brian Marshall joined the Oakleigh branch of the YCW in 1954 as a 14-year-old, and his memories illustrate some of the complexities surrounding this question. Interviewed in 2015, Marshall remembers that his first impression of the YCW was that 'just like any other youth club I suppose. You just came along to a meeting and just got through the business, then played your table tennis and had a chat'.[33] But when he was invited to join the leaders' group he remembers that his understanding deepened:

> Oh well, from just being a youth group like any other youth group, the leaders' group, suddenly, you've got vision and direction and perspective. You're on a mission. Once you get introduction to the see, judge, act it just … all of a sudden all the other things started to gain purpose. Yeah, that this is not just a youth group, this is a chance to get kids off the street, to provide community, to give them support, to provide development and education.[34]

Marshall went on to become a leader and then a full timer for the movement, working in central Victoria to help establish new branches in regional areas. Yet for many young men, their involvement would have begun and ended with the YCW football, cricket, soccer, or basketball team. They may not have had the opportunity to join a leaders' group, or decided the 'vocational' aspirations underpinning the movement were not for them. Former YCWs now in their 60s, 70s, and 80s, express ambivalence around the importance they and the chaplains placed on sporting service in their youth, and the extent it transformed the lives of young workers. The Sunday sport campaign is, however, remembered by some former YCW members as a moment where activism and service intersected. John Finlayson recalls the campaign around Sunday sport as a moment of political awakening:

> I was about 16 or 17, and I couldn't understand it fully, but I knew we had a right [to play football on a Sunday]. And we fought it. Now that was the first time I'd ever experienced doing a political campaign of any nature.[35]

'Suburbia Perfected'

In 1959, Melbourne's city and suburbs boasted a population of just over 1.7 million people. Whilst Sydney held claim to being Australia's largest city, it was Melbourne that had hosted the Olympics just three years earlier – the 'Friendly Games' – the first in the southern hemisphere. The city was the home of Australian Rules football, a game that over a century had spread from Melbourne across the country. The Victorian Football League (VFL) was the premier competition in the land, comprising 11 clubs in Melbourne and a 12th in the nearby seaside city of Geelong. During the winter months, football was the 'king' of spectator sports in Melbourne, and whilst women were not actively encouraged to participate as players, thousands of boys and men ran out for their local footy team each week.[36]

Camberwell did not have a team in the VFL, although they did field a team in Melbourne's other prominent suburban football competition, the Victorian Football Association (VFA). Ten kilometres (six miles) by train to the east of the city centre, Camberwell was one of Melbourne's most populous suburbs by the 1950s. Yet it was different to the crowded, inner suburbs that ringed the city centre, with their nineteenth century terrace housing and factories. This was 'suburbia perfected' the 'carefully managed middle-class frontier', comprising detached brick homes set in private gardens on 'comfortable, cosy, deciduously leafy crescents, and avenues'.[37]

Bob Maybury, who joined the YCW in 1944 as a 16-year-old, grew up in Deepdene, a small pocket of streets nestled between Camberwell and neighbouring Balwyn. He described his family as being 'fairly typical' of others in the area – 'you'd class them as lower middle class I suppose these days'.[38] The men on the street were employed – 'we would have had policemen, we would've had salesmen, public servants' – and all the homes were 'owner occupied', the Mayburys included.

Yet the Maybury family *were* different, in that they were Catholics living in a suburb historian Janet McCalman has described as the 'showpiece of the Protestant middle class'.[39] In Camberwell the number of people identifying themselves as Protestant far outnumbered adherents of other Christian and non-Christian faiths. This was a feature of Camberwell as early as the 1880s,[40] and the census of 1954, the last before the referendum of 1959, illustrates how the suburb housed a concentration of conforming and non-conforming worshippers. Just over 90,000 people lived in Camberwell that year. Of those, 82,500 identified as Christian, with 68,836 belonging to one of the Protestant churches. Indeed more followers of the Church of England and Methodism resided in Camberwell than any other suburb of Melbourne.[41] This, the historian Geoffrey Blainey suggests, contributed a particular religious flavour to the area which, in turn, shaped local law making around social issues such as the sale of alcohol and Sunday sport.[42] In 1919, the citizens of Camberwell and neighbouring Box Hill voted for tighter liquor licensing laws, resulting in the closure of all hotels in the suburbs, thus becoming the only two 'dry' council areas in suburban Melbourne.[43] And in 1936, Sunday sport at Camberwell's council facilities was banned.[44]

In his study of sectarianism in Australia, Michael Hogan argues that:

> For almost all of the 200 years [since European settlement], the majority of Australians have not been particularly religious or irreligious. As far as individuals are concerned the norm has been a nominal adherence to one of the main denominations and a studied indifference to all but the most private aspects of religion.[45]

Even so, Hogan goes on, religion has played a role in shaping Australian history because faith often intersected with ethnicity and class. Maybury's memory of joining Shell as a junior clerk in 1945 illustrates how religious identity did infuse interactions between Catholic and Protestant Melburnians in their daily lives. After going to the local parish primary school, Maybury was awarded a scholarship to Parade College, a boys' secondary school run by the Christian Brothers.[46] On matriculating, Maybury entered the workforce:

> ... everything had been Catholic up 'til then, you know, you never had any contact with non-Catholics at all. Others, perhaps in your street, you know, but you suddenly found a different attitude to all sorts of things ... Shell only recruited from public schools basically. I was the only Catholic in the group that started. They usually started around eight or 10 lads every year, and I was the only Catholic in that group, and they were all well-educated groups so they weren't larrikins but they were, you know, they had a different set of standards to what I'd been used to.[47]

Whilst Maybury's employment at Shell suggests that sectarian divisions were not always rigidly adhered to, the resilience of his memory that religious distinction shaped employment options and social discourse affirms Hogan's argument that from the late nineteenth century, Australian Protestants and Catholics were understood to have different standards on social issues, particularly the consumption of alcohol, gambling, and the keeping of the Sabbath. Whilst 'wowsers' – often understood as drawing from a Protestant tradition – were 'the typical religious do-gooder who was determined to deprive the ordinary Australian of his Sunday sport, his drink with his mates and his flutter on the races', Protestant clerics often characterized working-class urban culture as having 'a disregard of traditional Sunday observance, an impoverishing devotion to gambling, a debasement of womanhood, a network of political cronyism and corruption and a contempt for Empire'.[48]

One should not, however, be drawn into a simplistic sectarian reading of Australian society. Differences within denominations had impacted on Australian political, social, and religious life in the 1950s.[49] Leon Daphne, who was involved with the East Camberwell and Wattle Park YCW as a teenager in this period, remembered how some Catholic families were 'ostracized' in the parish for remaining loyal to the Australian Labor Party (ALP) after 1955, resisting calls from the pulpit to join the new anti-Communist, staunchly Catholic, Democratic Labor Party (DLP).[50] So too, within Protestantism, differences in class, outlook and age shaped attitudes on social questions in the post-war years. The debate around Sunday sport in Camberwell therefore illuminates the problematic history of sectarianism in Melbourne society in the 1950s.[51]

Not a Day for 'Voluptuous Pleasures'

The practise of setting aside a day for godly worship can be traced back to the Romans, and over the centuries this custom became enshrined in commandment and law. Sabbath observance was the fourth of the 10 Commandments and helped shape patterns of worship in both Judaism and Christian sects.[52] It was in the fifth century AD that Roman law recognized Sunday as the 'Lord's Day', a day to be held in 'honour and veneration' and one: 'Dedicated to the Majesty Most High, to be employed in no voluptuous pleasures, and profaned by no vexatious exactions'.[53]

This idea of Sunday being a day of dedication (worship), rest from toil ('exactions'), and the avoidance of 'impure pleasure', influenced the setting of Sunday laws in England (and therefore in Australia), and framed the moral valuation of the Sabbath.

In the 1940s and 1950s these Sabbatarian values were enforced by state law in Victoria and these structures heavily restricted what Melburnians could do on Sunday. The *Sunday Observance Act* stood firmly in the way of commercial activities on a Sunday and discouraged people from engaging in many activities outside the household, leading to what some derided as a 'closed Sunday'. Shopping and public transport were limited and theatres and hotel bars were completely prohibited from opening.[54] Even if many Melburnians did not consider themselves devout Christians, custom suggested that competitive sport played on a Sunday signalled a 'deterioration in moral standards', and organizations such as the Sunday Christian Observance Council (SCOC) were at the forefront of arguments against activities other than worship and rest.[55] The big football leagues, which charged admission – the VFL and VFA – played on a Saturday afternoon, and from the 1930s until the mid-1950s limiting laws extended to the playing of local sports in some council areas. Not all sporting activities were banned, however. Whilst Camberwell forbid the use of tennis courts and cricket and football ovals, it did permit the local swimming pool to open its doors. This anomaly suggests that the moral injunction was against organized, public, competitive endeavours that might draw a spectating crowd.[56]

The call to hold a referendum in the suburb was made most loudly by the eight Camberwell tennis clubs. They were a diverse coalition of Protestant, Catholic, and non-denominational groups and they linked the ban on Sunday games to lengthening waiting lists for membership. Given the population boom in the suburb, they argued, this situation would simply get worse and that it was unconscionable to allow facilities funded by the taxpayer to remain unused one day of the week.[57]

Interestingly, the other clubs associated with other sports in the area – particularly the YCW football clubs – were publicly silent on the issue. This is not to suggest the ban did not inconvenience them, or that they were disinterested in the outcome. Given that singles and doubles tennis, played by men and women, could be regarded as one of the less boisterous games, it was hoped arguments that Sunday sports would lead to rowdiness, crowd barracking, and disturbance of the peace would be less convincing. In fact, the banning of football on council ovals created practical problems for sporting associations such as the YCWFA. In Melbourne, senior football and school football were played on a Saturday, therefore many ovals were only available to the YCW on a Sunday. Many local councils did not prohibit the use of facilities on the Sabbath, and where bans prevailed such as Brunswick and St. Kilda, the YCW was successfully able to lobby for the laws to be rescinded in the 1940s. Camberwell, however, with its strong Protestant 'flavour' resisted: in 1947 a local referendum on the question soundly rejected the idea.[58]

The Camberwell and East Camberwell YCW branches therefore had to play their 'home' games outside the suburb. Leon Magree, who was a member of the East Camberwell YCW, remembers that they found a ground to play on in Richmond, but the club needed to take their own goalposts, and 'they had some arrangement with the Tramways Board that they could carry the posts on the running boards of trams'.[59]

In many respects, the prohibition on Sunday sport put young people at a particular disadvantage. Either too young to drive or not yet able to afford a car, journeying beyond the suburb to compete posed real challenges. Discussions had by the Methodist Youth Fellowship in 1947 hints at how the solidarity of youth could become a more powerful force than intergenerational religious identification in the coming years:

> The [Methodist] church still suffered the unfortunate legacy of excessive Puritanism inherited from Cromwell, Knox and Calvin ... surely the question of having games or sport on Sunday can no longer be considered a matter of immutable principle.[60]

Despite the failure at the poll in 1947, in the following decade a shifting of attitudes was reflected in decisions by Heidlberg Council (1951), Kew Council (1956), and Doncaster-Templestowe Council (April 1959) to allow sport to be played on Sundays in their municipalities.[61] By 1959, Camberwell Council's position on Sunday sport seemed increasingly incongruous. Declining to hold another referendum in 1951, the pressure had mounted sufficiently to conduct another ballot at the end of the decade.

'The Power to be at Leisure'

In April 1959, Camberwell's councillors agreed (nine votes to three) to hold a referendum to assess public opinion on by-law 65, which to date prevented the use of council controlled sporting facilities for the use of play, practice, or any game of sport.[62] The Camberwell tennis clubs were heavily restricted by the policy and had made deputations to council to amend the by-law, arguing that Sunday tennis matches would be 'quiet, recreational, and non-commercialized', producing very little noise or disturbance to the Camberwell public.[63] The opening of the Council swimming pool on a Sunday simply highlighted the absence of sports on courts and ovals around the suburb. Councillor Cooper, who openly opposed Sunday Sport, moved in favour of a referendum in Camberwell, reasoning that after dealings with the tennis clubs the council was 'obliged to hold a referendum'.[64] It is important to note that the Council did not consider itself bound by the result, nor would a 'Yes' vote guarantee unfettered access to facilities, with Council explaining they would consider applications by clubs on a case-by-case basis.

The question, therefore, was on whether the blanket ban on Sunday sports should be lifted, and Councillor Cooper may have felt confident that the local community would return a 'No' vote just as they had in 1947. In that year only 9,553 ratepayers from an eligible 27,000 made the effort to cast a ballot, and the 'No' vote won by 1,771 votes.[65] Whilst the low return may have indicated apathy amongst voters in 1947, the debate in 1959 was vigorous and lively. Asked 'Are you in favour of non-commercialized games approved by the Camberwell City Council being played on municipal reserves on Sundays?',[66] the 37,762 rate paying citizens of Camberwell were exposed to a range of perspectives before the polls closed on 1 June.[67]

The Sunday Christian Observance Council was at the forefront of the 'No' Campaign. Backed primarily by local Protestant churches they argued that Sunday was the Lord's Day and should be dedicated to worship and rest. Sunday sport would encroach on Sunday's sanctity and in doing so 'tarnish' the reputation of Camberwell as 'a premier place in Melbourne municipal life and affairs'.[68] The Camberwell tennis clubs led the campaign for 'Yes', with the YCW, and the Anti-Delinquency Council (ADC) in support. The ADC was, in fact, a moniker adopted by the YCW. Leon Magree recalls that a number of YCWs from Camberwell, East Camberwell, Deepdene, and Surrey Hills:

> Got themselves together and with the help of some ex-YCW's and some parents we came up with a campaign which culminated in the printing of dodgers, you know, leaflets, and we letterboxed the area ... with these dodgers saying Vote Yes ... and we even dreamt up the name of [laughs] a non-existent body to put on it, like it was authorized by the Committee to Prevent Juvenile Delinquency [laughs] or something.[69]

Whether the ADC was developed to give credence to the delinquency issue, or was a ploy to give the YCW another voice disassociated from any religious grouping is unclear. The leaflet did, however, seem to make a difference. In a hand-written letter of thanks sent to Magree after the vote, the Parish Priest of Our Lady of Victories Church in Camberwell – also one of the tennis clubs in the 'Yes' coalition – commended the YCW for their leaflet drop, admitting he was surprised the young men were able to distribute 30,000 handbills: 'I really thought it was beyond the capacity of the YCW'.[70]

The Sunday sport debate conducted in Camberwell in 1959 was clearly set inside a framework of 'Christian values'. There was universal acceptance on both sides that Sunday was customarily a day different from the others of the week, and that the morning at least should be given over to formal services of worship. Where the sides, differed, however was how the rest of the day should be spent. In the four weeks between the announcement of the referendum and the closing of the postal ballot, the arguments both for and against teased out concepts of 'rest' and 'quiet', 'idleness' and 'entertainment', and revealed underlying concerns around unruly youth.

In his letter to the editor, Sabbath defender and Salvation Army member Cyril Brimblecombe argued that:

> Man is a spiritual being and for him to enjoy life in rich completeness he must be linked with God in Christ ... Now there must be time to foster this all satisfying experience and a quiet restful worshipful Sunday is admirably suited and, indeed, ordained for this very purpose.[71]

For Brimblecombe, the act of worship was not demarcated in time and space through service attendance. The whole day was an opportunity for reverence, and that reverence was 'quiet' and 'restful'. In both its handbill and letters published in the local and city papers, the YCW also affirmed that Sunday morning was a time for formal worship, and Catholics should give 'Him the first-fruits of the day'.[72] Afterwards, however, people should be free to honour God as they pleased, including participation in 'innocent recreational activities'. For the YCW, Brimblecombe's restful Sunday was one of 'gloom and sloth'.[73] In contrast, the young workers and their allies interpreted Sunday 'rest' as a break from the routine of work: '... from the type of work we do throughout the week, a rest from servile work in order to more effectively worship God and honour him in all our activities of the day'.[74]

Neither Cardinal Newman, nor German theologian Josef Pieper were cited by the YCW as they built their case. Yet the arguments of the YCW/ADC echoed a philosophy in which active leisure was understood as a deeply human act of resistance against utilitarianism embedded in the Protestant 'work ethic' and 'servile work':

> ... the ability to be 'at leisure' is one of the basic powers of the human soul. Like the gift of contemplative self-immersion in Being, and the ability to uplift one's spirits in festivity, the power to be at leisure is the power to step beyond the working world and win contact with those superhuman, life-giving forces that can send us, renewed and alive again, into the busy world of work.[75]

The YCW framed this in the Australian vernacular, as a dichotomy between the 'wowser' and the joyful youth:

> Sunday is in a very special sense God's day, and we all realize our obligation of His commandment, which commands us to keep holy His Sabbath ... To turn His Day into a day of gloom and pharisaical piety constitutes a poor idea of God ... the wowser makes it a day of gloom and sloth; we make it a day of worship and joy in action.[76]

The YCW's interpretation of Sunday observance raised the ire of some Camberwell Catholics. Disputing the YCW's urging of all Catholics in Camberwell to vote 'Yes', Kenneth Hince – also a Catholic – wrote an impassioned letter to the *Tribune* criticising the young workers for being 'chauvinistic' and clannish:

> They promulgate a view of the Church as a sort of minor masonry, in which Catholics hang together for the sake of signs and shibboleths, and for the sake of hanging together on issues small and large – because they are different from those outside, or maybe because they feel persecuted and unsafe. I did have the impression that this type of attitude towards the Church, which we used once to see labelled the 'ghetto mentality' of Catholics, was fading rapidly out of the Australian scene.[77]

Hince's critique of the YCW for feeding sectarian suspicion hints at how the debate was, in part, fuelled by old, perceived differences between Protestants and Catholics. In his study of sectarianism in Australia, Ben Edwards noted that during the 1950s it was not uncommon for Protestant denominations to support and cooperate with one another in order to oppose Catholic influence in society,[78] and in launching their 'No' campaign, SCOC stated that 'the united churches throughout the municipality numbering 45 in all (non-Roman Catholic), are actively engaged organizing their forces in order to contest the issue effectively'.[79] Michael Hogan contends, however, that for the most part 'frictions between Catholics and Protestants, were merely relics of an earlier and more sectarian age'.[80] The debate over Sunday sport in Camberwell can be read as an example of this archaic 'friction', however it should not be only interpreted through this lens.[81] Just as in the broader political machinations shaping Australia during this time, intra-denominational differences abounded in Camberwell. While Baptist Gordon Sprigg of SCOC and Brimblecombe of the Salvation Army drew on their Protestant faith to argue against Sunday sport, other ministers in the suburb – the Brotherhood of St Laurence's Father Tucker and St Silas' Reverend Stevenson – supported the tennis clubs' quest to loosen restrictions. Other factors, aside from religious affiliation were, therefore, at play.

Both Catholics and Protestants who supported the playing of sport on a Sunday argued that the current ban created inconvenience for many which could lead to anti-social behaviour in the few, particularly the young. The ADC fashioned their case around issues of idleness and delinquency, as well as appealing to ratepayers' sense of economic value and common sense. Given that the voting age was 21, the YCW/ADC perhaps thought it strategic to appeal to the 'adult' sensibilities of the decision makers on their campaign flyers:

1. Vandalism and Delinquency are at their worst on Sunday afternoons. In Camberwell, youth are not permitted to use their energy for healthy recreation.
2. The Council opens the Municipal Baths on Sundays but denies other sports the same opportunity.
3. Present facilities are inadequate to cater for those wanting to use them. Therefore, certain ratepayers are denied the use of amenities for which they have paid.
4. Well conducted and wholesome sport is preferable to idleness and street corner rowdiness.
5. The majority of Australian Christians do not consider playing sport is violating the sanctity of the day.[82]

The very activeness of sports and the togetherness offered by team games was celebrated by the YCW, and any qualms around competitiveness and the presence of spectators were not addressed explicitly. The YCW did imply, however, that competitive sports were particularly attractive to young men. Representing itself as an authority on the needs of young working people, the YCW suggested that while adults might find solace in gardening or golf or reading, young men preferred more active pursuits such as football, cricket, or tennis to satisfy. An absence of vigorous sports would, therefore, increase opportunities for delinquency. This appeal to public safety was supported by 'evidence' drawn from a YCW enquiry into the behaviours of youths in different suburbs, and these examples were picked up by the press:

BOX HILL: Between 30 and 40 youths wandering aimlessly near the station. Smaller groups standing idly about.

ESSENDON: More than 25 groups, ranging from 4 to 10 in number, mainly loitering around milk bars and shopping centers.

COBURG: More than 100 youths in vicinity of Coburg Lake and Sydney Road milk bars. Brawls not uncommon. A youth lost an eye in an incident recently.

MULGRAVE: Mobs are already a reality and violence has been used.

SANDRINGHAM: In newer areas police have to move on mobs.[83]

Simplifying – or ignoring – the complexities of 'gang' identification, this evidence was widely reported by the media. It was a line of argument which struck a chord with some voters, who wrote letters to the press agreeing that non-commercial sport was a healthy alternative to hanging around street corners, 'joy-riding in stolen cars, larceny, wilful damage to property, and street larrikinism'.[84] The local branch president of the ALP made a small contribution to the debate by suggesting that wholesome sport was a good distraction from the 'bodgie–widgie cult'.[85] Others, however, were aghast at the idea that the community would accept that sports clubs rather than parents should be the agents of discipline. 'A. Parent' writing to the paper countered that delinquency was the result of poor parenting, and 'at the first sign of larrikinism I knock it out them [own children] – by various methods'.[86]

The voiced concerns around youth crime – real or perceived – and the evocative images of teenagers hanging around 'milk bars' and causing disturbances in 'genteel' spaces such as the art gallery revealed a growing anxiety around 'modern teenagers' who were growing in number as a consequence of the post-war baby boom.[87] The YCW, speaking on behalf of young men, tapped into the fears of adults and echoed the values embedded in muscular Christian conceptions of active sports, that they were an ideal 'safety valve' for youth.[88]

Intersecting with this discussion about youthful behaviour was the question of noise, and some used the debate as an opportunity to rail against all forms of aural disturbances, not only the sound of raucous youths playing sports on council ovals. Lawn mowers, car engines being tuned, hammers, even church bells were blamed for noise pollution throughout the suburb, and some writers suggested – possibly tongue in cheek – that all these practises should be banned if the Council was seriously concerned about disturbing the quietness of Sunday:

> Our own quiet suburban backwater is now made hideous from dawn till dark on Sunday by the do-it-yourself brigade, banging, swinging, hammering and using power tools as well as lawn mowers, with complete selfishness as regards the feelings or rights of others.[89]

The lawn mower was just one symbol of the more disagreeable aspects of modern life. In his letter to the editor, Rick Winston claimed that the sanctity of Sunday was already being lost to modern secular activities, that churches were not as popular as they once were on Sundays and if those that supported a ban on Sunday sport were legitimate about their view then they too should attempt to promote a ban on television or radio and other non-religious activities.[90] By implication, Sabbatarianism is cast as anti-modern, with defenders offering an 'Elizabethan' understanding of the Lord's Day. Ewan Tucker of Sandringham observed that 'the churches are addressing themselves in a dead language to situations and issues that no longer exist … playing a kind of word game … the result being that the plain man is bewildered and does not know what to believe'.[91]

It is not possible to know if Winston and Tucker were themselves observant Christians and, if so, to which denomination they belonged. Therefore rather than simply construing the debate as one between Protestants and Catholics, it can also be framed as one between modernists and conservatives. If the former were more inclined to accept changing leisure patterns and attitudes, the latter saw these shifts as something to be defended against the 'traditions' maintained. Brimblecombe, was 'prompted by a sincere desire to maintain Sunday as a day of rest and worship in keeping with scriptural standards and the highest traditions, the spiritual faith and practice of British peoples'.[92] For the devout Protestant, Sunday was to be spent 'studying the will of God'.[93]

Traditional British sentiments that were propagated by the Protestant churches were inherently linked to the middle class of Melbourne suburban life. Church and Sunday school were the primary locations for religious education and moral development in Camberwell's Protestant youth.[94] Therefore, sport or any other form of non-worship based activity could be seen as only detrimental to the traditional religious practice and harmful to the middle class areas of Melbourne. The fear was Melbourne would slide towards a 'Continental Sunday', an ambiguous reference to the social life brought to Australia by the increasing numbers of southern European migrants.[95]

The results of the referendum in 1959 showed that Camberwellians were strongly in favour of Sunday sport. Of the 37,762 voting slips mailed out, nearly 26,000 votes were returned, the final tally showing 18,670 'Yes' and 6,560 'No'.[96] The result was so emphatic that councillors were convinced that an amendment to the by-law was the only suitable response. They did so, but with the condition that those wishing to participate in organized Sunday sport would first need the permission of the Council.[97] The amendment to the law did not completely open the door to sport on a Sunday, but it did create the possibility for a society that was becoming increasingly secular and materialistic.[98]

The result was in striking contrast to the referendum undertaken on the same question in 1947. In that year only one-third of eligible voters cast a ballot, compared to two-thirds in 1959. With war such a recent memory and wartime shortages a continuing, fatiguing, reality, the lack of engagement in the ballot in 1947 is understandable, and Camberwellians possibly thought they had more pressing matters to deal with. By 1959, however, population growth and a rising number of teenagers in the municipality created a new reality.

The tennis clubs were the first to capitalize on the change in 1959, however it is unclear whether the YCWFA was immediately successful in shifting its Sunday home games to Camberwell's grounds. The successful result was, however, perceived as a victory for the YCW. As Finlayson's recollection above suggests, the activism inspired branches in other suburbs where the ban remained to mobilize, and gave some young workers their first experience of political action.

During the 1960s, the pressure to provide entertainment – sporting and otherwise – on a Sunday increased around Melbourne and remained a source of disagreement. In 1955, it was observed by Melbourne newspapers that VFA crowds had dropped significantly and in order to differentiate itself from the more popular VFL, suggestions were made to regularly schedule matches on Sundays.[99] The first VFA match for premiership points played on a Sunday took place on 24 April 1960 between Coburg and Brunswick and attracted a crowd of approximately 17,000 spectators and gate receipts in the vicinity of £2000.[100] According to reports the gate figures were the best for any regular season match since before World War II. The *Sunday Observance Act* at the time prevented charging admission to games on Sundays, so in order to subvert this law spectators were encouraged to 'offer a donation' upon entrance to the ground.[101] By April of 1963, debate surrounding Sunday sport in Camberwell was again aroused when the Camberwell Football Club made an application to the council to play four Sunday matches during the 1963 VFA season.[102] The ADC and YCW had pushed for Sunday sport as a means to provide young people with socially constructive and wholesome physical pursuits, while commercial sporting organizations such as the VFA saw Sunday matches as an opportunity for profit and a means of engaging and maintaining a strong supporter base.

Conclusions

The story of the Camberwell referendum of 1959 hints at the ways Australian society was to change over the next three decades. The debate around organized sport on the Sabbath tested the strength of sectarian distinction in the suburb. Whilst the 'religious flavour' of Camberwell was anomalous compared to Melbourne's other suburbs, it was not the only suburb to become embroiled in a debate over Sunday sport in the period. Nor were its citizens isolated from the broader social and cultural shifts occurring in the city – and world – around them. Into this sporting issue, Camberwellians poured their anxieties and aspirations about a world in seeming flux and change.

The Camberwell case study illuminates tensions between a generation coming of age in the 1950s, and their parents and grandparents who had experienced the deprivations of two world wars and the economic depression of the 1930s. The argument that the provision of sports on a Sunday would offer a healthy alternative to delinquent behaviours tapped into contemporary concerns about wayward youth which, Moore suggests, reached a 'fever-pitch of irrationality' in the late 1950s.[103] The YCW, speaking a language of faith and action, successfully positioned themselves as intermediaries between young and old.

The Camberwell campaign was a success for a movement enjoying its golden age. Yet the shifts toward secularism which helped the 'Yes' vote succeed would also contribute to the undoing of the YCW in Australia. From the mid-1970s, a range of factors, including changes to the role and importance of the Parish church in social life, led to a sharp decline in YCW membership, impacting on its sporting services. In 1986, the YCWFA, once the largest junior football competition, folded, and whilst there remain YCW football and cricket clubs in some suburbs of Melbourne, they are YCW in name rather than reflecting any active engagement with the methodology of Joseph Cardijn.

The motif of the noisy lawn-mower, used by letter writers to good effect in 1959, suggested that in practise, the quiet, reverent, 'austere Sunday' no longer existed – even in Camberwell. The referendum to allow sport on municipal ovals was, to some, simply an official recognition that Sabbatarianism – which had underpinned Sunday restrictions in Melbourne for a century – had lost its moral hold. The mobilization and attendant increase in the 'Yes' vote in 1959 from 1947 was a sign that the population had grown tired of the Sabbath restrictions and sought greater freedoms to 'rest' from work as they saw fit.

The subsequent 50 years has seen almost all of the restrictions on Sunday entertainments relaxed in Melbourne. In twenty-first century Australia, shops, theatres and galleries, cafes and bars, are open for business, while the public is welcome to participate in and attend sporting fixtures without fear of prosecution. Reflecting the further secularization of Australian society, in 2017 the Australian Football League (AFL) scheduled a match on Good Friday, the most solemn day on the Christian calendar.

To avoid the criticism of rampant commercialization and in a nod to the day's religious significance, the AFL assured the public a proportion of gate receipts would be donated to the annual Royal Children's Hospital Good Friday Appeal.[104]

The YCW's participation in the 1959 referendum gave members an opportunity to practise political action, to assert their status as representatives of youth, and to explore the meaning of rest and leisure as a counterpoint to labour. The YCW never questioned the axiom that Sunday was different to other days of the week, and celebrated it as a day free from paid toil. The success of the campaign and the liberalization of Sabbath restrictions over the following decades has, however, contributed to the gradual diminution of Sunday as a day of leisure for working people – because someone is needed to operate the turnstiles.

Notes

1. See for example, Bill Murray, *The Old Firm: Sectarianism, Sport and Society in Scotland* (Edinburgh: John Donald Publishers, 1984); Timothy J. L. Chandler, 'Making Men in Catholic Public Schools, 1945–1980', in Tara Magdalinski and Timothy J. L. Chandler (eds), *With God on Their Side: Sport in the Service of Religion* (London: Routledge, 2002), 99–112; Mike Cronin, 'Catholics and Sport in Northern Ireland: Exclusiveness or Inclusiveness?', *International Sports Studies* 21, no. 1 (2001), 25–41.
2. Laurence Moore, 'Never on a Sunday: A Study of Sunday Observance and Sunday Public Musical Entertainment in Theatres in Melbourne, 1890–1895' (Masters diss., Australian Catholic University, 2009), 4–5.
3. F. B. Smith, 'Sabbatarianism (Sunday Observance)', in Andrew Brown-May and Shurlee Swain (eds), *The Encyclopedia of Melbourne* (Port Melbourne: Cambridge University Press, 2005), 629; Keith Dunstan, *Wowsers* (Melbourne: Cassell Australia, 1968).
4. Valerie Yow, *Recording Oral History: A Guide for the Humanities and Social Sciences*, 2nd ed. (Walnut Creek, CA: Altamira Press, 2005), 225–7.
5. The key text exploring memory composition in the context of oral history is Alistair Thomson, *Anzac Memories: Living with the Legend* (Melbourne: Oxford University Press, 1994).
6. Pronounced 'Cardine'.
7. Joseph Cardijn, *Laymen into Action*, trans. Anne Heggie (London: Chapman, 1964).
8. Michael De La Bedoyere, *The Cardijn Story* (London: The Catholic Book Club, 1958), 42.
9. Joseph Cardijn, 'Worker Organisation in England', *Revue Sociale Catholique* (November–December 1911) and Stefan Gigacz, 'The Sillon and the YCW: Towards an Understanding of the Origins of the YCW', in *First Steps Towards a History of the IYCW: Acts of the Mini-Colloquy on IYCW History 5–6 September 1997* (Brussels: International Cardijn Foundation, 1997), 3–45.
10. John Molony, *Towards an Apostolic Laity* (Melbourne: YCW Australia, 1960), 115–6.
11. *Fundamentals of the Australian Young Christian Workers* (Melbourne: YCW, c. 1959), 4–5.
12. Ibid., 5.
13. For readers familiar with the history of twentieth century Australian politics this distinction will have particular relevance. Santamaria, who is rightly understood as a key antagonist in the split in the Catholic constituency of the ALP – which contributed to the ALP's failure to win government federally between 1955 and 1972 – was a devoted Catholic Actionist, inspired by the example set by his Italian counterparts. See Gerard Henderson, *Santamaria: A Most Unusual Man* (Melbourne: Miegunyah Press, 2015); Bruce Duncan, *Crusade or Conspiracy? Catholics and the Anti-Communist Struggle in Australia* (Sydney: UNSW Press, 2001).

14. Cardijn, *Laymen into Action*, 35.
15. Whilst The Grail was not a 'Cardijn movement' as such, their focus on personal formation and education held many similarities to those developed by the Belgian. Therefore, when the YCW movement for young women – known as the National Catholic Girls' Movement – was established for 14–25-year olds in 1941, it built upon the work of Dr Lydwine van Kersbergen and her team.
16. Not only was communication between Australian and the continental Jocists interrupted. As had occurred during WWI, Cardijn was imprisoned for political activities, this time with his two key lay leaders Fernand Tonnet and Paul Garcet. All three were arrested by the Nazis in June 1942. Whilst Cardijn was later released, Tonnet and Garcet were sent to Dachau concentration camp. Both men reportedly died there, with records showing Garcet died in January 1945.
17. In 1959, the NCGM changed its name to YCW (Girls). Both YCW (Girls) and YCW (Boys) operated separately but co-operatively with separate leadership structures, publications, and chaplains. The two arms merged in 1971 to become the YCW. In this paper, 'YCW' and 'Young Christian Workers' will be used in discussion of the boys' movement to 1959, whilst 'YCW (Boys)' will be used to describe the examination of the period between 1959 and 1971.
18. There is some contestation over this narrative.
19. Geraldine Crane, *Ordinary Young Women Doing Extraordinary Things: The Brisbane NCGM/YCW (Girls) Story 1945–1970* (Brisbane: YCW Past Members Association, 1999), 32.
20. *National Report of the Australian YCW (Boys) 1959–1960*, 26–7.
21. The Australian YCW co-ops were inspired by the Antigonish movement in Nova Scotia and were very successful. By 1958, there were 18 YCW Housing Societies around Australia, a Credit Society as well as a Trading and Insurance co-op. *National Report of the Australian YCW 1956–1958*, 11.
22. *National Report of the Australian YCW (Boys) 1959–1960*, 26–7.
23. Crane, *Ordinary Women Doing Extraordinary Things*, 43.
24. Bruce Duncan, 'Lombard, Francis William (1911–1967)', *Australian Dictionary of Biography*, National Centre of Biography, Australian National University, http://adb.anu.edu.au/biography/lombard-francis-william-10854/text19265, published first in hardcopy 2000 (accessed 1 November 2017).
25. *Fundamentals of the Australian Young Catholic Workers*, 4.
26. Chandler, 'Making Men in Catholic Public Schools', 99–119.
27. David Kehoe, 'Draft History of the Melbourne YCW 1932–58', Unpublished Manuscript (Melbourne: YCW Holdings, 1984), Chapter 9, 6–7.
28. Cardijn, *Laymen into Action*, 28.
29. N. J. Watson and Andrew Parker, 'Sports and Christianity: Mapping the Field', in N. J. Watson and Andrew Parker (eds), *Sports and Christianity: Historical and Contemporary Perspectives* (London: Routledge, 2012), 15–20.
30. *Advocate*, 2 October 1941, 29.
31. Kehoe, 'Draft History of the Melbourne YCW 1932–58', 7, 11–20.
32. Ibid., 19, citing the *Silver Jubilee 1941–1966* booklet, 7.
33. Brian Marshall, interview by Melissa Walsh, 2015, transcript, 19.
34. Ibid., 21.
35. John Finlayson, interview by Melissa Walsh, 2014, transcript, 10.
36. For further details on the popularity of Australian Rules football in Victoria during the period after World War II, see Bob Stewart, 'Boom-Time Football, 1946–1975', in Rob Hess and Bob Stewart (eds), *More Than a Game: An Unauthorised History of Australian Rules Football* (Carlton: Melbourne University Press, 1998), 165–99.
37. Chris McConville, 'Camberwell', in Andrew Brown-May and Shurlee Swain (eds), *The Encyclopedia of Melbourne* (Port Melbourne: Cambridge University Press, 2005), 108; Janet McCalman, *Journeyings: The Biography of a Middle-Class Generation, 1920–1990*

(Carlton: Melbourne University Press, 1993), 67; and Barry Humphries, 'Foreword', in Bruce Raworth (ed.), *Our Inter-War Houses: How to Recognise, Restore and Extend Houses of the 1920s and 1930s* (Melbourne: National Trust of Australia, 1991), 5.
38. Bob Maybury, interview by Melissa Walsh, 14 August 2014, transcript, 5.
39. McCalman, *Journeyings*, 68.
40. Geoffrey Blainey, *A History of Camberwell*, rev. ed. (Melbourne: Lothian, 1980), 77.
41. Commonwealth Bureau of Census and Statistics, 'Analysis of Population in Local Government Areas, Etc', *Census of the Commonwealth of Australia, 1954*, 8 December 1955, vol. 2, par. 1.5, 92–3.
42. Blainey, *A History of Camberwell*, 81.
43. Ibid., 75–81; John Albanis, 'Liquor Licensing', in Andrew Brown-May and Shurlee Swain (eds), *The Encyclopedia of Melbourne* (Port Melbourne: Cambridge University Press, 2005), 420.
44. Mary Sheehan, *Victories in Camberwell: A History of Catholics in Camberwell* (Pakenham: Pakenham Gazette, 1989), 73.
45. Michael Hogan, *The Sectarian Strand: Religion in Australian History* (Ringwood: Penguin Books, 1987), 286.
46. Maybury, interview, 6.
47. Ibid., 18. See also Margaret Power's memory recounted in McCalman, *Journeyings*, 68. Note that in Australia, public schools are government schools.
48. Hogan, *The Sectarian Strand*, 147.
49. John Bodycomb, 'Sectarianism', in Andrew Brown-May and Shurlee Swain (eds), *The Encyclopedia of Melbourne* (Port Melbourne: Cambridge University Press, 2005), 650.
50. Leon Daphne, interview by Melissa Walsh, 29 September 2014, transcript, 14; Ross McMullin, *The Light on the Hill: The Australian Labor Party 1891–1991* (Melbourne: Oxford University Press, 1991), 276–80; and McCalman, *Journeyings*, 226–37.
51. Sheehan, *Victories in Camberwell*, 74.
52. Exodus 20: 8–11.
53. Decree of Emperors Leo and Arthemis 469 AD, cited in 'Ninety-Second Report of the Law Reform Committee of South Australia to the Attorney-General: Inherited Imperial Sunday Observance or Lord's Day Acts', 1987, 4.
54. Smith, 'Sabbatarianism (Sunday Observance)', 629.
55. 'Camberwell's Commonsense', 16 June 1959, YCW Archive Folder 24 'Newspaper Clippings: Sunday Sport, 1959', held at State Library of Victoria, Melbourne. For brevity, this folder is hereafter referred to as YCW Archive Folder 24.
56. Camberwell Tennis Clubs Inter-Club Committee, 'Vote Yes', c. May 1959, YCW Archive Folder 24.
57. 'Sunday Tennis Campaign Opened at Camberwell', c. May 1959, YCW Archive Folder 24.
58. 'Ratepayers Reject Sunday Sport', *Sun*, 28 February 1947, 1.
59. Leon Magree, interview with Melissa Walsh, 20 April 2015, transcript, 9.
60. Editorial, 'A Rational Approach to Sunday Sport', *Age*, 9 September 1947, 2.
61. 'Camberwell's Commonsense', 16 June 1959.
62. 'Sunday Tennis Campaign Opened at Camberwell', c. May 1959, YCW Archive Folder 24.
63. 'Council Will Hold a Sunday Sport Poll', c. April 1959, YCW Archive Folder 24; R.T. Cowling, 'Tennis Club Courts Idle', c. May 1959, YCW Archive Folder 24.
64. 'Council Will Hold a Sunday Sport Poll', c. April 1959.
65. 'Ratepayers Reject Sunday Sport', *Sun*, 28 February 1947, 1.
66. 'Council Will Hold a Sunday Sport Poll', c. April 1959.
67. 'Camberwell to Vote on Sport', c. May 1959, YCW Archive Folder 24; 'Camberwell for Sunday Sport' c. May 1959, YCW Archive Folder 24; 'Council Will Hold a Sunday Sport Poll', c. April 1959.

68. Donald Baker and Leslie I. Perkins, 'Referendum at Camberwell', c. May 1959, YCW Archive Folder 24.
69. Magree, interview, 9.
70. Parish Priest of Our Lady of Victories Church in Camberwell, 'Letter', 9 June 1959, YCW Archive Folder 24.
71. Cyril J. Brimblecombe, 'Lord's Day is for Rest', 21 May 1959, YCW Archive Folder 24.
72. Melbourne YCW, 'Camberwell Poll on Sunday Sports', 21 May 1959, YCW Archive Folder 24.
73. Ibid.
74. Ibid.
75. Joseph Pieper, *Leisure: The Basis of Culture* (South Bend: St Augustine's Press, 1998), 54.
76. Melbourne YCW, 'Camberwell Poll on Sunday Sport', 21 May 1959.
77. Kenneth Hince, 'Here's Another View on that Sunday Sport Poll', *Tribune*, June 4, 1959, YCW Archive Folder 24.
78. Ben Edwards, *WASPS, Tykes and Ecumaniacs: Aspects of Australian Sectarianism 1945–1981*, (Melbourne: Acorn Press, 2008), 231.
79. Baker and Leslie, 'Referendum at Camberwell', c. May 1959.
80. Hogan, *The Sectarian Strand*, 232.
81. Ibid.
82. Anti-Delinquency Council, '5 Reasons Why You Should Vote Yes', c. May 1959, YCW Archive Folder 24.
83. Melbourne YCW Report 'Sunday Sport Camberwell Referendum' c. May 1959, YCW Archive Folder 24; Ian Blair 'The Day of the Aimless', c. May 1959, YCW Archive Folder 24. Milk bars are corner shops.
84. J. Donegan, 'Delinquency on Sundays', c. May 1959, YCW Archive Folder 24.
85. W. H. Aughterson, 'Sport Before Bodgie Cult', c. May 1959, YCW Archive Folder 24. Bodgies (boys) and Widgies (girls) were names given to gangs of young, mostly working class people which emerged in the late 1940s. The first bodgie gangs in Sydney were inspired by American fashions, and during the 1950s the phrase bodgie and widgie became synonymous with 'the rejection of mainstream values'. Keith Moore, 'Bodgies, Widgies and Moral Panic in Australia 1955–1959' (paper presented at social change in the 21st century conference, University of Queensland, 2004) https://eprints.qut.edu.au/633/1/moore_keith.pdf (accessed 31 October 2017), 4; See also Jon Stratton, *The Young Ones* (Perth: Black Swan Press, 1992).
86. A. Parent, 'Sure Cure for Delinquncy', c. May 1959, YCW Archive Folder 24. See also R. Smyth, 'Sunday Sport', and F.P., 'Delinquency as a Reason', c. May 1959, YCW Archive Folder 24.
87. Blair 'The Day of the Aimless', c. May 1959.
88. Melbourne YCW, 'Camberwell Poll on Sunday Sports'.
89. W. A. Hespie 'Sunday a Day of Din'; Beryl Halinbourg, 'Noise From Motor Mowers'; E. G. Stewart, 'Sunday Roar of Mowers'; Bernard Barrett, 'Bell Ringers on Sundays', all c. May 1959, YCW Archive Folder 24.
90. Rick Winston, 'Melbourne's Sunday Gloom', c. May 1959, YCW Archive Folder 24.
91. Ibid.
92. Brimblecombe, 'Lord's Day is for Rest', 21 May 1959.
93. E. M. Halford, 'Our Best or Second Best?', c. May 1959, YCW Archive Folder 24.
94. McCalman, *Journeyings*, 102.
95. 'Church Men Praise Government Stand on Sunday Sport', *Age*, 19 June 1961, YCW Archive Folder 24.
96. 'Camberwell Votes for Sport on Sunday', c. June 1959, YCW Archive Folder 24.
97. 'Council says "Yes" on C'well Sunday Sport', c. June 1959, YCW Archive Folder 24.
98. The change in the by-law only permitted local sporting groups to apply to use sporting facilities on a Sunday. Camberwell City Council still held the right to deny any use of facilities that they felt were inappropriate or commercial in nature.

99. 'Big Fall Off in VFA Crowds', *Argus*, 27 June 1955, 18.
100. 'Win for Coburg in Sunday Game', *Age*, 26 April 1960, 16. Sunday matches became a regular fixture in the 1960 VFA season and they continued to attract large crowds. The *Age* also reported that the first VFL match to be played on ANZAC day took place on the same long weekend in 1960. A photograph in the *Age* depicts a near capacity crowd which watched Fitzroy versus Carlton, further evidence of the shift in attitudes away from conservative views on days of reflection and remembrance. 'First Anzac Day Football Games Brought Big Crowds', *Age*, 27 April 1960, 7.
101. 'New Move on Sunday Sport', *Sun*, 6 April 1963, YCW Archive Folder 24. See also Marc Fiddian, *The VFA: A History of the Victorian Football Association, 1877–1995* (Melbourne: Marc Fiddian, 2004), 9.
102. 'New Move on Sunday Sport', 6 April 1963.
103. Moore, 'Bodgies, Widgies and Moral Panic in Australia 1955–1959', 4.
104. Michelangelo Rucci, 'AFL Puts on its First Good Friday Game with Some Still Uneasy at Breaking the Taboo', *Advertiser*, 13 April 2017.

Disclosure Statement

No potential conflict of interest was reported by the authors.

ORCID

Nicholas Thomas Shaw Marshall http://orcid.org/0000-0001-9248-6244

'If God Be for Us, Who Can Be Against Us?': Religion and Religiousness in Polish Football, 2008–2017

Michał Mazurkiewicz

ABSTRACT
Relations between sport and religion constitute an intriguing field of research. The aim of this paper is to analyze the historical development of a religious face of Polish sport (mostly football). Religion – meaning here the Catholic Church, since Poland is an almost completely Catholic country – pervades sport in different ways. The teachings of Pope John Paul II, who appreciated the role of sport in developing the all-around integrated personality, are still often recalled in Poland. The paper includes several sections. First, the policy of the Church towards sport in the last decades is discussed; then, the question of sports chaplaincy in Poland is presented. Next, public manifestations of religious beliefs of football players, managers, and fans (for example, crossing oneself or fans' choreographies with religious overtones) are analyzed. The main focus of interest is, however, very popular religious pilgrimages organized (since 2008) by the fans of most Polish clubs. The main objective is to examine some selected cases, representative of Polish football fandom of the last decades, showing the phenomenon clearly. The study has largely been based on historical and statistical data. The information about this period (2008–2017) was garnered mainly from newspapers and fans' publications.

> Religion and sport have always sprung out of the same deep waters of the human soul. More than that, they have nourished and been nourished by, inspired and been inspired by, each other.
>
> Michael Novak.[1]

It is impossible not to notice the huge influence of sport on culture. It has visibly entered such spheres as literature, film, music, and the arts. Sport has influenced language (many sporting phrases have been assimilated into everyday speech; for example, 'play for time', 'get to first base', or, in Polish, *pokazać komuś żółtą kartkę* ['show somebody the yellow card']), literature (Hemingway's *The Old Man and the Sea* or Bernard Malamud's *The Natural*), film (*Chariots of Fire*, *Field of Dreams* and many others), and has been an artistic inspiration (notably in the output of George Bellows and other painters), just to mention some selected cases. Sport is also a part of the world of religion, and vice versa. Sports and religion have a long history of mutual interplay – in fact, they have had an interesting and interconnected relationship since antiquity.[2] As American philosopher Michael Novak states, 'sports requiring high skill and heroism have always generated electricity back and forth with religion, not only with Christianity'.[3]

In this context, Nick J. Watson and Andrew Parker note:

> Historians and anthropologists have mapped a relationship between religion and sport that spans approximately three thousand years ... Links between the sacred and sport have been identified in a number of historical epochs. These include primitive times when ritual-cultic ball games were played to appease the gods (for fertility); the athletic spectacles of ancient Greece and the Olympic games that were held in honor of mythological deities; the gladiatorial contests of Rome; the festivals and folk-games of the Middle Ages; the general Puritan suspicion and prohibitions against sports; and, lastly, Victorian muscular Christianity (1850–1910), a socio-theological movement, and some would argue ideology, that significantly shaped the character of modern sports.[4]

And the historian of religion Rebecca T. Alpert adds:

> ... religion and sports have a long and complex association in virtually every time and place. For some people, playing and watching sports have provided an outlet for meaning making, ritual celebration, and connection to ultimate reality that functions for them like religion. Others are fascinated by the many different ways sports were part and parcel of ritual in the ancient world and have been used in service of traditional religions' aspirations in modern societies.[5]

Obviously, the direct link between sport and religion – as it used to take place in the times of ancient Greece – does not exist anymore; sport became considerably secularized and, at first glance, it seems not to need religion on its way towards further expansion. Yet, these relations constitute not only an important segment of the history of sport, but they also function currently in different modified forms.

The fine interplay of religion with social, political, and economic forces had been a popular topic of study among sociologists and religion scholars, but the relationship between religion and sport received (until the last decades of the twentieth century) far less attention (although the situation is gradually changing for the better). This may be attributed in large part to the general neglect of sport as a topic of scholarly inquiry by those in the traditional disciplines.[6]

As for the beginnings, the field of study known as religion and sports started to emerge in the 1970s. A group of scholars such as Michael Novak, Shirl Hoffman, Charles Prebish, Andrew Cooper, and Joseph Price analyzed the ways sports resembled religion. Some of them, like Prebish, went so far as to define sports as a new form of religion. It employs, in Prebish's opinion, the same terms as each religion, namely: a formal series of public and private rituals, engagement, devotion, discipline, adoration, an experience of the ultimate (eternity), communion (one may use here the term *communitas*, introduced by anthropologist Victor Turner, which, in the case of sport, is collective euphoria), faith, temple, chants, coronation, and sacralization. Both sport and traditional religions have their legends and myths which provide them with a broader perspective – not really historical, but a little misty, in which the historical truth mixes with the alleged, not fully confirmed, pieces of information. As for legendary heroes, these are examples to be followed, heroes of culture, real archetypal models for the next generations of believers.[7]

Over the past 40 years there has been a noticeable steady growth in the academic literature concerning sport and religion. Within this genre authors have explored a variety of interesting topics and issues. There are publications on sport and faith, sport and spirituality, sport and religious ethics, and so on.[8]

It seems reasonable to start deliberations with an introductory reflection on the nature of the category of *sacrum*. Sport sociologist Zbigniew Krawczyk defines it in this way: 'it is a sphere of religious cult, meaning all behaviors aiming at expressing worship to the value of *sacrum*'.[9] Therefore, these are not only practices restricted to the church sphere. Religious behaviours appear in other realms as well – also in the world of sport, and not necessarily on sports arenas. In this vein, sports historian Wojciech Lipoński notes that

> what we today call 'sport' in its most primordial shapes provides evidence of the close relationship between *ludic* exercises and religion. This concerns both the early periods of paganism and the later epochs of the 'big' religious doctrines: Judaism, Christianity and Islam.[10]

Religions exist in all known societies. As for Poland, it remains one of the most religious countries of the world,[11] where religion is not only restricted to the private sphere – but it also quite often constitutes an important part of the public space. In the case of Poland, this discussion relates to one concrete denomination – Catholicism, which is the religion of the vast majority of Polish society (over 90%). Therefore, the relationship between sport and religious rituals in the Catholic environment (mostly its recent history) is the main focus. How football supporters live and enact their fandom has been explored widely in Europe. The aim is to try to show the unique changing face of Polish football fandom, which emerged in the first decades of the twentieth century.

The Catholic Church and Sport: Selected Historical Aspects

Sport may have a positive impact on many aspects of our lives. It can definitely help change the world for the better in many ways. The Catholic Church notices it as well and actively participates in the process. One can say that it has also embraced the broadly understood idea of muscular Christianity after centuries of being cut-off from the development of modern sport. Over time, several popes expressed their appreciation for the role of sport.

Building on the work of his predecessor (Pope Pius XII), Pope John Paul II, a passionate sportsman, who was generally considered the 'athlete pope', known to frequently summit mountains, alpine ski, bike, swim, play soccer, and volleyball (he even took part in an international kayaking competition in 1955), emphasized the educational and spiritual potential of sport, calling it God's gift to man.[12] Through the many years of his episcopate and papacy he made a lasting impression on the minds and hearts of sports enthusiasts all over the world as to what is the proper place and function of sports for humankind. The Polish Pope, in addressing Olympic

Committees, championed the role of sport as a vehicle that contributed to the harmonious and complete development of body and soul.[13]

He held two international sport gatherings in Rome's Olympic stadium, speaking about 120 times on the subject, and addressing both committees or associations and numerous athletes.[14] In 2004, a 'Church sport' office within the Pontifical Council for the Laity was established. Led by Father Kevin Lixey, it has held three international seminars. Safeguarding the legacy of his predecessor, Pope Benedict XVI launched 'The John Paul II Foundation for Sport' in 2008. Also Pope Francis states that sport helps lead young people forward and makes progress in their lives. He emphasizes that 'sports are a means to education'.[15]

Thus 'the Catholic Church recognizes and values the good of a healthy sense of competition as a stimulus for improvement and for bringing out the best in a person'.[16] As far as Poland is concerned, such organizations as the Young Men's Catholic Association (*Katolickie Stowarzyszenie Młodzieży Męskiej*, KSMM) and the Young Women's Catholic Association (KSMŻ) – both located in pre-war Poznań – should be mentioned. They conducted religious, cultural-educational (including sporting contests, camps, and trips), charitable, social, and patriotic activity with the aim of 'building Christlike Poland' and quickly attracted members in the 1930s. Just before the outbreak of World War II, both associations (being a part of the Catholic Youth Association since 1934) grouped altogether over 250,000 members.[17] Unfortunately, in the period between 1945 and 1989, in a country ruled by the communists, it was not possible to create Catholic sports associations.

As Grant Jarvie and James Thornton emphasize,

> Today, we find both religious organisations using sport and sports participants turning to religion in different ways. Despite the onward march of secularism in some Western communities, it is far from clear whether sport inhibits or promotes religious beliefs, and whether, in certain instances, such beliefs help to develop social cohesion, networking, or even psychological advantage in sport today.[18]

In this context, it also worth mentioning the activity of the Salesian Sports Organization of the Republic of Poland (SALOS RP), which was established in 1992 as an association of societies of physical culture. Its main aim has been development of educational, cultural, and social aspects of sport in the framework of the recognized ideal of man and society, inspired by the Christian vision and the richness of the Salesian educational tradition. Different kinds of SALOS RP activities include: promotion of sports and tourism among youth and children, organization of tournaments (which have a nationwide and international range), as well as summer and winter sports camps, especially for children coming from poor and pathological milieus. For its valuable activity, SALOS RP has received numerous diplomas from the Prime Ministers of Poland, as well as the Ministers of Education and of Sport. Another interesting issue is the SALOS RP annual academic symposia during which Polish sociologists and historians of sport meet and discuss the most important questions connected with sport. The fruits of the symposia are reviewed monographs.[19]

'I Am Not Ashamed of Jesus': Religiousness of Athletes

It goes without saying that 'religion has had a significant historical presence in sport'.[20] Surprising as it may seem at first glance, religion is frequently present at Polish sports arenas, mostly football stadiums. This process visibly gained in strength in the first decade of the twentieth century. It takes various forms, from consecrating newly opened facilities, through religious rituals of players and coaches, sports chaplaincy, colourful stadium choreographies, as well as Masses in the intentions of the clubs, to, finally, huge spectacles not connected directly with sport, such as, for example, the retreat 'Jesus at the Stadium', led by charismatic Ugandan priest John Baptist Bashobora (held for the first time in 2013), which attracts crowds of the faithful to the National Stadium in Warsaw.

Numerous athletes openly manifest their religious beliefs. This also includes public prayer, which has been a topic of discussion in many publications on sport and religion.[21] A good example is former professional American football player Tim Tebow. As Novak states, 'What makes him so beloved to the public ... is that he always goes down on one knee, his head in his hands, and communes with God. Win or lose, he thanks God'.[22]

Many Polish footballers cross themselves before a match. This gesture may sometimes have far-reaching consequences, like it did in the case of Polish goalkeeper Artur Boruc, who – being a player of Celtic Glasgow (traditionally Catholic club) in the years 2005–2010 – made this gesture more than once in front of the fans of Glasgow Rangers (traditionally a Protestant club), which brought him many problems, for he was accused of insulting the religious feelings of the Rangers' supporters.

Another example is goalkeeper, Jerzy Dudek (a former player of Feyenoord), who also emphasizes the importance of this ritual, and pays attention to a different perception of this gesture in the eyes of the much more secularized Dutch football fans:

> Like in Poland, both me and Tomek Rząsa, with whom I play in one team, always cross ourselves before entering the pitch. In Poland, the country of deeply religious people, this is normal, but in Holland it surprises many guys. We are not ashamed of our faith, though.[23]

Attachment to religion has also been demonstrated on the shirts of footballers, as in the case of Patryk Małecki, who is fascinated with John Paul II (An example from abroad is Columbian player Radamel Falcao, who has the slogan 'With Jesus you'll never be alone' on his shirt); moreover, attachment to religion very often manifests itself in the form of chains, medallions or pictures, and football coaches are no exception here. A pre-match ritual of coach Ryszard Tarasiewicz is kissing three holy pictures.

Some Polish footballers, openly declaring attachment to their faith and demonstrating it both inside and outside the stadium – together with numerous well-known people from the world of show business – joined the action 'I am Not Ashamed of Jesus'. It was initiated in 2011 by the members of the Youth Crusade and would constitute an answer to the allegedly aggressive attitudes of left-wing and lay milieus. The aim of this 'mass mobilization' has been a strengthening of the Catholic identity of Poland. The first words of the online description of the action are as follows: 'We live in the world, in which God is being put aside. Self-appointed "authorities", taking advantage of the power of the media, put themselves above the Truth, jeering at Good, humiliating Love, attacking the Catholic Church'.[24] It is worth noting as well that the stars recorded short films for the campaign, in which they bore witness to their faith.

Good examples coming from the world of football are: an ex-Poland national team player, Marek Citko, whose career was broken by a grave injury, as well as current stars of Polish football, such as midfielder Jakub Błaszczykowski and, most of all, the greatest representative of contemporary Polish football – Robert Lewandowski. Citko states: 'The Cross is very important in my life, [be]cause in fact I begin and end the day with the sign of the Cross ... My favorite book is the Book of Job, who – whatever happened – praised God'.[25] Błaszczykowski emphasizes that there are such moments in life when one cannot count on doctors and other people anymore – intimating it is only faith that remains then.[26] Similarly, the star of Bayern Munich, Lewandowski, has many times openly declared his religiousness and underlined how much he owes to God.

As priest Adam Podolski notices, sport found its place for good in the church reality, and because of it, also in chaplaincy.[27] Sports chaplains – present at stadiums and in locker rooms – have had a great (though immeasurable) influence on athletes' religiousness. Pope John Paul II emphasized that: 'The Church values and respects sports which are truly worthy of the human person. They are like this when they foster the orderly and harmonious development of the body at the service of the spirit'.[28] The Church undoubtedly notices a great educational potential in sport, for it can protect humans from losing themselves in the world of consumption and utilitarianism; yet it warns that one should, however, avoid the temptations of the idealization of sport.

A great enthusiast of sport, Kielce bishop Marian Florczyk, states: 'Where is life, there should also be a chaplain. John Paul II said that man is the way of the Church. Let us not leave another person to their own devices, even at sports arenas. This help is needed'.[29] It is worth analyzing for a moment what this help practically consists of. On the website of the National Sports Chaplaincy (of Poland), which was initiated in 1990, one finds out what chaplains' practical tasks are:

> Sports chaplaincy regards providing spiritual and pastoral care to sportspeople: players, coaches, workers of clubs and fans as its task. It organizes retreats, days of meditations and faith formation gatherings for them. It also animates all-Poland events, such as: Christmas gatherings of athletes, Easter meetings, pilgrimages, parish cultural and sporting events, scientific symposiums. The aim of these actions is to saturate the world of sport with evangelical and Christian values.[30]

To continue this presentation of religious practices of sportspeople, it is worth noting that another interesting phenomenon in Polish sport is Masses for the beloved team. Strengthening the bonds linking sportspeople and fans, they constitute a colourful ritual of great unifying power. Common prayers of the whole football milieus – a collective expression of religious feelings – are undoubtedly important local events. This ritual, which became fashionable at the turn of the twentieth century, takes place almost all over Poland. The websites of most clubs are full of invitations to Masses, both the ones before the inauguration of the season and thanksgiving Masses, being a form of manifesting gratitude to God for the finished struggle, especially for the laurels gained.[31] Dealt with here is a tangible connection of the sacred sphere with the world of sport. One could say that the light coming from the sacred sphere permeates through the reality of reality of football fandom in order to gain new lustre and vitality.

Religion in Polish Football Fandom: Choreographies and Pilgrimages

An important representative of Scottish football (as both a player and manager), Jock Stein, once stated: 'Football is nothing without fans'.[32] Avid supporters add colour to sports rivalry and their world is a complex phenomenon with a thousand faces. Sometimes, there are striking similarities between sports fandom and organized religion. Interestingly, religious manifestations have appeared at stadiums as well. Polish football fandom constitutes a good example of this.

Stadium choreographies (displays) have become an intriguing element of fan culture in most European countries, and also in Poland. The colourful and ingenious stadium spectacles meticulously prepared by Polish fans are frequently manifestations of patriotism as well as historical awareness (like the ones presented on anniversaries of national uprisings). It must be also noted that choreographies with religious overtones appeared at Polish stadiums over the last decades as well. References to religion (in particular, Catholicism, as there are no major clubs with a largely non-Catholic fan base) in the activity of supporters sometimes appeared in the form of choreographies prepared to commemorate anniversaries of the attempt on the life of John Paul II and his death. It should not surprise; journalist Piotr Lisiewicz is right when he remembers:

> ... when on 2 April, 2005 John Paul II passed away, it was the fans who first came out into the streets. It is around them that crowds of marching people assembled. It turned out that club scarves are the only symbols around which active groups of youth gather in the most important moments in history.[33]

Choreographies occasionally present God himself as well as the Mother of God. The famous display prepared by the fans of Legia for the match with the Dutch team Den Haag (10 October 2010) – depicting Jesus as well as the slogan 'God Protect the Fanatics' – made a huge impression and turned out to be the best one in the contest of the *ultras* in the autumn round of the 2010/2011 season. The stunning spectacle, supplemented with numerous flares and cardboard squares in 61 shades, gained admiration both in Poland and beyond the borders of the country.

Yet, it should be noted here that the religiousness of the fans does not seem to be above the average. According to Father Jerzy Wąsowicz, who has been actively engaged in the fans' movement:

> As for this religiousness, it is ... like with the religiousness of Polish society. There are no differences. It is rather tepid than hot, though there are exceptions. Like in the society, the same with the fans. 'Once in a blue moon' or holiday attitudes tend to dominate.[34]

Further, he emphasizes an important feature of Polish football fans – distinctiveness. He remarks:

Although the religiousness of the fans' environment can be described as 'the national average', they themselves rise above this average. They are recognizable against the background of general greyness ... well-organized, having clear views, which I would define as national-conservative.[35]

As Ludovic Lestrelin states, 'the collective practice of supporting is ... inseparable from the building of shared identities, representations, and a common world of meaning'.[36] The world of meaning can be provided – among other things – by religion. Another aspect of Polish fandom which is definitely worth discussing is the religious ritual of making pilgrimages to the Jasna Góra Shrine in Częstochowa – the most important place of the Marian cult in Poland. This annual patriotic event (initiated in 2008) has been organized by the football fans of many Polish clubs who are often accompanied by the fans of speedway racing, a sport which also enjoys great popularity in Poland. Undoubtedly, one of its aims has also been diminishing the aggression and animosities in the world of football fans, and consequently, challenging the 'fan-thug' stereotype. In front of the Miraculous Picture of the Mother of God numerous banners and flags are spread, and then they are consecrated during the Mass. Next, in the Kordecki Hall, well-known politicians, academics and columnists deliver speeches, usually on historical subjects. It is followed by a display of banners and flares and finished with communal singing of the national anthem. As Shaun Best notes more generally, 'Football fans are known to share a very strong "place identity"'.[37] The notion of 'place identity' is clearly evident in the case of the Jasna Góra Shrine, which has an obvious emotional meaning.

What the mix of fandom, religion, and patriotism means to the supporters one can read on the pages of the football fans' journal *To My Kibice!* ('It is us, the fans!'):

> The Pilgrimage of the Fans is a special event in the fans' calendar. And this is not only a question of faith, [be]cause even these fans who are not deeply religious, feel an unusual bond on that day. These are the moments which – like no others – hold our environment together. One can feel here a real patriotic spirit, the beating heart of Poland.[38]

As sociologist Radosław Kossakowski notes, 'this ideological turn has been observed in recent years, although anti-communist traditions have been characteristic of Polish fans since at least the 1980s'.[39] There are no clubs with different political agendas. Fan culture is mostly characterized by anti-modernist attitudes which result from a constant conflict with the neoliberal order.[40] The conservative character of Polish fandom is demonstrated by means of the pilgrimages to Częstochowa, which – as it has been mentioned – have been organized annually since 2008. It should be noted that it was not the first initiative of this kind. Gatherings of fans had taken place earlier in the Divine Mercy Sanctuary in Łagiewniki and the fans of Ruch Chorzów used to organize a walking pilgrimage to Piekary Śląskie. Yet the pilgrimages to Częstochowa turned out to be the most permanent initiative.

They were initiated by the milieu of the supporters of Lechia Gdańsk, mostly the legendary fan of Lechia Tadeusz Duffek and Rev. Jarosław Wąsowicz, a Salesian, theologian and author of numerous publications devoted to Polish football fandom.[41] The important political and social context – bad relations of fans with the liberal government of Donald Tusk (which would later lead him to a war against 'hooligans') as well as the ongoing secularization processes – could have triggered their idea. The first pilgrimage took place on 13 December 2008, on the anniversary of the introduction of martial law in Poland (1981). The beginnings were humble (200–300 pilgrims, mostly from Gdańsk), but the Biblical seed was sown. Priests and politicians, such as Jacek Kurski, took part in the discussions on sport and history. Importantly, the idea of the pilgrimage received support from several well-known people recognized by the fans, also authors and historians, such as Tadeusz Isakowicz-Zaleski – a Solidarity chaplain in Cracow's Nowa Huta district in the 1980s, an avid supporter of the lustration in the Polish Church, author, and activist. Media support from right-wing institutions such as *Gazeta Polska* (a conservative weekly news magazine) and *TV Trwam* (owned by the Warsaw Province of the Congregation of the Most Holy Redeemer) is also worth mentioning. They – in spite of some opposition from certain representatives of 'open' Catholicism such as the weekly magazine, *Tygodnik Powszechny* – definitely played an important part in trying to forge links between sport and Catholic conservatism, and also in the following years. The next pilgrimages would be organized in January.

The second pilgrimage attracted 300–400 people, who took part in the discussions led by journalist Paweł Lisiewicz (a great sports fan who enjoys immense popularity among the fans) and heard the lecture of the aforementioned legendary chaplain of Solidarity, Isakowicz-Zaleski, talking about the former Polish Eastern borderlands, mostly Lwów/Lviv as the birthplace of Polish football (the first Polish football match was played in 1894, between the teams of Lviv and Cracow). During the 2012 pilgrimage, which took place at the apogee of the conflict with the then government of Donald Tusk, fighting with might and main with the 'hooligans', historian and journalist Sławomir Cenckiewicz lectured about Russian threats. The event, which attracted 1,000 fans, received more media coverage than before.[42]

In 2013, the official motto of the pilgrimage was the words of Pope John Paul II: 'Here we have always been free'. And indeed, free demonstration of one's views (especially of those people who cultivate patriotism and Catholicism) – had always taken place at the Jasna Góra Shrine, even on the darkest days of communism. Over 2,000 supporters strongly protested against their freedom being limited, and against the sneering at patriotic attitudes. One of the fans of Lechia Gdańsk who took part in that event described that mixture of patriotism and religion in the following way:

> It is a very important event to us ... Our arrival here shows what does not exist in the media. We want to demonstrate that there are certain values which unify the fans, not divide them. These are: faith, tradition, the Church, and of course the motherland.[43]

In 2014, 5,000 fans who filled the chapel in Częstochowa and the nearby yard – raising up the clubs' scarves – entrusted themselves to the Mother of God and then listened to lectures on the Cursed Soldiers (members of the anti-communist Polish underground movement who continued their struggle against the pro-Soviet government of Poland after World War II) and on the patriotic activities of the fans of Śląsk Wrocław. Finally, there was a display of a great anniversary choreography devoted to the Warsaw Uprising (a major World War II operation in 1944 by the Polish underground resistance to liberate Warsaw from the German occupation), prepared by the fans of Legia Warsaw, which was followed by a concert of patriotic rap music.

In 2015, the pilgrimage of 5,000 fans was organized with the intention of commemorating the regained Polish lands of 1945. A group of veterans of the post-war anti-communist resistance troops took part in the celebration, which was followed by a concert devoted to the memory of Polish hero Witold Pilecki, who had organized a resistance movement in the German Death Camp Auschwitz and written the first comprehensive report on the camp.[44]

The pilgrimage of 2016 was an international event, the main intention of which was the commemoration of two crucial events in the history of Poland:

> This year, over 5,000 fans decided to go to the city of medallions. Among many Polish stadium delegations of hood monks from all over the country, the fans of Diosgyor Miskolc (Hungary), Polonia Wilno (Lithuania) and FK Lida (Belarus) appeared as well. There were also lads who came to this event from emigration. The leitmotif of this year's meeting was the 60th anniversary of Poznań June (the Poznań 1956 protests) as well as [the] 1050th anniversary of the Baptism of Poland.[45]

The 2017 pilgrimage to the Jasna Góra Monastery attracted about 2,000 fans. Many people did not manage to arrive because of extremely heavy frosts. It commemorated the 75th anniversary of the establishment of the National Armed Forces (*Narodowe Siły Zbrojne*), which were part of the Polish resistance movement during World War II, and the 75th anniversary of the martyrdom of the five members of the Salesian oratory in Poznań, who were arrested by the Gestapo in September 1940, tortured and guillotined (after being found guilty of high treason in a fake show trial). Rev. Wąsowicz emphasized the unique character of the Jasna Góra as a place where hearts beat stronger, and the importance of the pilgrimage, which made the world of football fandom better.[46] During the Mass, Wąsowicz proclaimed a new initiative – 'the Rosary of the Fans'. He announced:

> I would like that we – by means of this year's pilgrimage – undertook a new initiative: 'The Living Rosary of the Fans', keeping a prayer for Poland, for our milieu, for our families so that we would be better and better.[47]

Wąsowicz underlined in his sermon that aggression could be diminished, that hooligans could be converted and that the fans' initiatives could be an antidote for hooliganism.[48] As for the hooligan dimension of the fan movement in Poland, it should be noted that recently it 'has become a niche in search of new ways of expression'.[49] Arranged fights (*ustawki*) outside the stadiums are still organized but the political and religious background does not matter in this case as there are no groups that would be politically or religiously hostile towards each other.

Jarosław Szarek, the current chairman of the Institute of National Remembrance, who specializes in the recent communist-era history of Poland, also met with the pilgrims who prayed for the fans, the clubs, the motherland, and the (current, right-wing) government.[50] The fusion of Catholicism with right-wing politics should not surprise, taking into consideration Polish history (noting that the Church in Poland has always opposed communist or liberal ideologies).

Although the nationalism of the fans is rather limited to a domestic political agenda, it should be emphasized that during the last years the pilgrimage has become more international – more foreign guests arrived, for example, including Hungarians or Poles living abroad. Articles about the pilgrimage have been published in Germany and in Italy. As far as foreign policy objectives are concerned, the organizers declare that there are plans to extend their activity and to invite more fans from European clubs in future.

Pilgrimages of football fans are not restricted only to Częstochowa – they are also made to other holy places, for example to the aforementioned Divine Mercy Sanctuary in Cracow Łagiewniki, around the time of the anniversary of the death of John Paul II, as well as – every summer – to a hugely important place to Poles, which is The Gate of Dawn (*Ostra Brama*) in Wilno/Vilnius (via Suwałki-Wilno). In this second case, most of the pilgrimage route runs through the territory of Lithuania and the pilgrims stop in many places important for Polish history. In the case of the pilgrimages, but also the described earlier choreographies and Masses, the love of the fans is visibly linked with religious feelings, and the whole – together with patriotic attitudes – creates a unique reality.

Summary

As Jarvie and Thornton rightly note, 'the influence of religion on sport may have declined but it has not disappeared'.[51] In some particular cases, surprising as it might seem, it rises. Many times an apparently hidden *sacrum* in the *profanum* sphere (also in the domain of sport) can be noticed. Sometimes, perhaps, one can state that religion-inspired behaviours in sport, including the ones presented above, are only a substitute for the experience of *sacrum*, for nothing indicates that religiousness of the athletes or the fans rises above the average on a national scale. Such forms of fandom are a simple reflection of the current state of affairs in a given society.

In this paper – focusing attention on the first decades of the twentieth century – the historical development of some specific phenomena which create a religious face of Polish football has been analyzed. One can certainly find certain similarities in sport of other – not only Christian – countries (which will, hopefully, provide interesting research fields in the future). Religion-based rituals, however, can be found mostly where faith is still vivid. This is the case especially in the countries which have efficiently resisted the growing process of atheizing, and Poland definitely belongs to this group.

Football fandom has been the subject of much historical enquiry, and there has been a significant amount of research looking into its different aspects, but its connections with religion have been largely overlooked by historians of sport. This paper, which is based on original archival and press exploration, has examined a phenomenon which has developed and seems to be gaining in strength.

On the basis of the evidence presented above, it can be stated that in recent decades the influence of religion on Polish football fandom has become unprecedented. Why has a process which permeates religion (through different channels) into the world of football fandom, and therefore, broadening (in a way) the sphere of *sacrum*, taken place? A shown above, one of the reasons might be the fact that nowadays, in times of political correctness, as well as in peculiar battles frequently fought with religion, stadiums still appear to be a sphere of freedom. In this context, Polish sport constitutes – as the findings hopefully demonstrate – a fascinating field of research and without doubt many aspects of the correlation between sport and religion are certainly worth exploring further.

Notes

1. Michael Novak, 'Foreword', in Nick J. Watson and Andrew Parker (eds), *Sports and Christianity: Historical and Contemporary Perspectives* (New York: Routledge, 2013), xi.
2. Rebecca T. Alpert, *Religion and Sports: An Introduction and Case Studies* (New York: Columbia University Press, 2015), 24.
3. Novak, 'Foreword', xi.
4. Nick J. Watson and Andrew Parker, 'Sports and Christianity: Mapping the Field', in Nick J. Watson and Andrew Parker (eds), *Sports and Christianity: Historical and Contemporary Perspectives* (New York: Routledge, 2013), 9–10.
5. Alpert, *Religion and Sports*, 34.
6. Shirl J. Hoffman, 'Preface', in Shirl J. Hoffman (ed.), *Sport and Religion* (Champaign, IL: Human Kinetics, 1992), vii.
7. Charles S. Prebish, '"Heavenly Father, Divine Goalie": Sport and Religion', in Shirl J. Hoffman (ed.), *Sport and Religion* (Champaign, IL: Human Kinetics, 1992), 43–53.
8. Andrew Parker and Nick J. Watson, 'Introduction', in Nick J. Watson and Andrew Parker (eds), *Sports and Christianity: Historical and Contemporary Perspectives* (New York: Routledge, 2013), 1.
9. Zbigniew Krawczyk, *Sport w zmieniającym się społeczeństwie* ['Sport in the changing society'] (Warszawa: Wydawnictwo AWF, 2000), 29.
10. Wojciech Lipoński, 'From Profound Religious Expression to Secular Ritual', in Wojciech Lipoński (ed.), *The Truth of Sport* (Szczecin: Uniwersytet Szczeciński, 2016), 41.
11. Numerous sources confirm this fact. See, for example, Raziye Akkoc, 'Mapped: These are the World's Most Religious Countries', *Telegraph*, 13 April 2015, http://www.telegraph.co.uk/news/worldnews/11530382/Mapped-These-are-the-worlds-most-religious-countries.html.
12. John Paul II, 'Even the Greatest Champions Need Christ: Homily and Angelus at the Jubilee for the World of Sport', *L'Osservatore Romano*, no. 44 (29 October 2000), 1.
13. Grant Jarvie and James Thornton, *Sport, Culture and Society: An Introduction* (London: Routledge, 2012), 326.
14. Norbert Müller and Cornelius Schäfer, 'The Pastoral Messages (Homilies, Angelus Messages, Speeches, Letters) of Pope John Paul II that Refer to Sport: 1978-2005', compiled by Norbert Müller and Cornelius Schäfer with the help of the Office of Church and Sport of the Pontifical Council of the Laity. Unpublished report, cited in Watson and Parker, 'Sports and Christianity', 14.
15. Hannah Brockhouse, 'Who Benefits from Sports? Everyone, Pope Francis Says', *Catholic News Agency*, 5 October 2016, https://www.catholicnewsagency.com/news/who-benefits-from-sports-everyone-pope-francis-says-29647.
16. Kevin Lixey, 'The Vatican's Game Plan for Maximizing Sport's Educational Potential', in Nick J. Watson and Andrew Parker (eds), *Sports and Christianity: Historical and Contemporary Perspectives* (New York: Routledge, 2013), 256.
17. Katolickie Stowarzyszenie Młodzieży ['Catholic Youth Association'], http://ksm.org.pl/o-nas/historia.
18. Jarvie and Thornton, *Sport, Culture and Society*, 337–8.
19. See Zbigniew Dziubiński, *Kościół rzymskokatolicki a kultura fizyczna* ['The Catholic church and physical culture'] (Warszawa: Wydawnictwo AWF, 2008).
20. Jarvie and Thornton, *Sport, Culture and Society*, 326.
21. Shirl J. Hoffman, 'Prayer Out of Bounds', in Jim Parry, Mark S. Nesti, and Nick J. Watson (eds), *Theology, Ethics and Transcendence in Sports* (London: Routledge, 2011), 35–63.

22. Novak, 'Foreword', xi.
23. 'Boży Doping' ['God's doping'], online version of the book: T. Balon-Mroczka (ed.), *Boży Doping* ['God's doping'] (Kraków: Dom Wydawniczy RAFAEL, 2000), http://www.katolik.pl/bozy-doping,1031,812,cz.html?idr =359.
24. *Nie wstydzę się Jezusa* ['I am not ashamed of Jesus'] (official website), http://www.mt1033.pl/akcja.html.
25. Jakub Fila, 'Oni nie wstydzą się Jezusa – o religijności polskich sportowców' ['They are not ashamed of Jesus – On the religiousness of Polish athletes'], 8 April 2012, http://natemat.pl/9305,oni-nie-wstydza-sie-jezusa-o-religijnosci-polskich-sportowcow.
26. Ibid.
27. Adam Podolski, *Duchowy wymiar cierpienia sportowców wyczynowych* ['The spiritual dimension of the suffering of professional sportspeople'] (Rzeszów: Wydawnictwo Uniwersytetu Rzeszowskiego, 2012), 168.
28. The quotation comes from the Pope's Address to the Participants of the Italian Masters Water-Skiing (14 September 1991).
29. Maciej Urban, 'I spraw Panie, by Korona wygrała ... Historia kieleckiego kapelana' ['And make, Lord, Korona win ... A history of a Kielce Chaplain']. The article comes from the weekly *Kielce Plus*, 29 December 2013, http://www.cksport.pl/pokazWiadomosc/8237_i_spraw_panie_by_korona_wygrala_historia_kieleckiego_kapelana.html.
30. *Krajowe Duszpasterstwo Sportowców* ['The National Sports Chaplaincy of Poland'], http://www.sport.episkopat.pl.
31. See, for example, 'Msza święta dla kibiców Legii' ['Holy Mass for the fans of Legia Warsaw'], 6 June 2017, https://legionisci.com/news/71136_Msza_swieta_dla_kibicow_Legii.html.
32. The Celtic Wiki, http://www.thecelticwiki.com/page/Jock+Stein+-+Quotes.
33. Piotr Lisiewicz, 'Od Janosika do rotmistrza Pileckiego' ['From Janosik to Rittmeister Pilecki'], *Fronda*, no. 68 (2013), 147.
34. Jarosław Wąsowicz, 'Boże, chroń fanatyków!' ['God save the fanatics!'], *Fronda*, no. 68 (2013), 151.
35. Ibid., 152.
36. Ludovic Lestrelin, 'Entering into, Staying, and Being Active in a Group of Football Supporters: A Procedural Analysis of Engagement. The Case of Supporters of a French Football Club', *International Review of Sociology* 22, no. 3 (2012), 505.
37. Shaun Best, 'Liquid Fandom: Neo-Tribes and Fandom in the Context of Liquid Modernity', *Soccer & Society* 14, no. 1 (2013), 86.
38. 'VI patriotyczna pielgrzymka kibiców na Jasną Górę – 4 stycznia 2014' ['VI Patriotic pilgrimage of the fans to Jasna Góra – 4 January 2014'], *To My Kibice!* 149, no. 2 (February 2014), 4–7.
39. Radosław Kossakowski, 'Where are the Hooligans? Dimensions of Football Fandom in Poland', *International Review for the Sociology of Sport* 52, no. 6 (September 2017), 12.
40. Ibid., 14.
41. For more on the history of pilgrimages, see Jarosław Wąsowicz, 'Kibicowskie patriotyczne pielgrzymki na Jasną Górę' ['The fans' patriotic pilgrimages to Jasna Góra'], *Myśl.pl*, no. 30 (January 2014), 12–16.
42. Ibid.
43. Bartłomiej Romanek, 'Patriotyczna Pielgrzymka Kibiców 2013 na Jasną Górę' ['Patriotic Pilgrimage of Fans 2013 to Jasna Góra'], *Dziennik Zachodni*, 5 January 2013, http://www.dziennikzachodni.pl/artykul/733259,patriotyczna-pielgrzymka-kibicow-2013-na-jasna-gore-zdjecia-wideo-relacja,id,t.html.
44. 'Relacja: VII Patriotyczna Pielgrzymka Kibiców na Jasną Górę' ['Report: VII patriotic pilgrimage of the fans to Jasna Góra'], 16 January 2015, http://skwk.pl/index.php/skwk/2-wydarzenia/6127-relacja-vii-patriotyczna-pielgrzymka-kibicow-na-jasna-gore.html.

45. 'VIII ogólnopolska patriotyczna pielgrzymka kibiców. Jasna Góra, 9 stycznia 2016' ['VIII All-Poland Patriotic Pilgrimage of the Fans. Jasna Góra, 9 January 2016'], *To My Kibice!* 173, no. 2 (February 2016), 5.
46. 'Pielgrzymka Kibiców na Jasnej Górze' ['The pilgrimage of the fans at Jasna Góra'], *Dziennik Zachodni*, 9 January 2017, http://www.dziennikzachodni.pl/wiadomosci/czestochowa/a/pielgrzymka-kibicow-na-jasnej-gorze-2017-zdjecia-kibice-to-prawdziwi-patrioci,11663088/.
47. *Różaniec kibiców* ['The rosary of the fans'] (official website), http://rozanieckibicow.pl/.
48. 'Ks. Wąsowicz: Wierzę, że chuligani też mogą się nawrócić' ['Rev. Wąsowicz: I believe that the hooligans can be converted too'], *Niezależna.pl* (26 December 2016), http://niezalezna.pl/91265-ks-wasowicz-wierze-ze-chuligani-tez-moga-sie-nawrocic.
49. Kossakowski, 'Where are the Hooligans?', 16.
50. 'Poświęcone szaliki i modlitwa za rząd. Kibice z pielgrzymką na Jasnej Górze' ['Consecrated scarves and a prayer for the government. The Fans on the pilgrimage to Jasna Góra'], 7 January 2017, https://www.tvn24.pl/wiadomosci-z-kraju,3/dziewiata-pielgrzymka-srodowiska-kibicow-pilkarskich-na-jasnagore,705284.html.
51. Jarvie and Thornton, *Sport, Culture and* Society, 338.

Disclosure Statement

No potential conflict of interest was reported by the author.

Index

Note: Page numbers in *italics* refer to figures.

Abrahams, H. 18
abstinence, sexual 12, 13
ADC (Anti-Delinquency Council) (YCW) 96, 97–8, 100
AFL (Australian Football League) 101–2
The Age (newspaper) 106n100
ALP (Australian Labor Party) 93, 98, 102n13
Alpert, R. T. 108
amateurism 61, 67
Anglicanism *see* Church of England
Anti-Christian Movement, China 48–9
Anti-Delinquency Council *see* ADC
Arbeitskreise Kirche und Sport ('Workshops on church and sport'), Germany 19
Argentina 60–79; *Club Atlético Los Mormones* (CALM) 69–78; muscular Mormonism 63–4; Young Men's Christian Association (YMCA) 62
Argentine Mission History 78
Argentine Softball League 61, 62, 68, 70
asceticism 11–13, 15, 20, 21
Augustinian monastic order 11, 12
Australia 86–102; Catholicism 89, 90, 92–3, 97; liquor licensing laws 92; masculinity 90; Mormon missionaries 63; Protestantism 87, 92–4, 97, 100
Australian Football League *see* AFL
Australian Labor Party *see* ALP
Azusa Street Revival, Los Angeles 36
Azzione Cattolica 89

Bad Boll (academy) 19
Bad Tutzing (academy) 19
Bairner, A. 48n42
Baker, W. J. 37
baptism, adult 36
Baptists 36
baseball 61, 62, 68, 69–70, 72–5
Bashobora, J. B. 111
basketball 5, 11, 61–3, 65, 67, 69, 76–8
Błaszczykowski, J. 112
Belgium 88, 89

Benedict XVI, Pope 110
Bergeson, D. 76–8
Berlin 9, 20, 63
Best, S. 114
Billing, E. 30
Bismarck, O. von 17
Björkquist, M. 26, 31
Blainey, G. 92
Bodgies, Australia 105n85
body, concepts of: Argentina 75; China 47, 55; Germany 10, 11–17, 19, 20; muscular Christianity 52; Poland 110, 112; Sweden 29, 31–3
book burning 16
Boruc, A. 111
Bournaud, A. A. 77, 78
boxing 31
Brants, J. 88
Brimblecombe, C. 96, 97, 99
Brown, C. 3
Buenos Aires Herald (newspaper) 69, 75

CALM (*Club Atlético Los Mormones*) 60–79; baseball 5, 61, 62, 68, 69–70, 72–5; basketball 76–8; softball 61, 62, 68, 69–70
Calvin, J. 13
Camberwell *see* Melbourne
Camberwell Football Club 100
Capital (basketball team, Argentina) 77–8
Cardijn, J. 88–9
Catholic Action 89, 90
Catholic Boys' Legion *see* CBL
Catholic Young Men's Society *see* CYMS
Catholic Youth Association 110
Catholicism: Argentina 64, 68, 78; Australia 88–93, 96, 97; Germany 9–10, 11, 12, 13, 16, 18; Poland 109–17; *see also* YCW (Young Christian Workers)
Cavalli, C. 62, 63
CBL (Catholic Boys' Legion) 90
Cedergren, H. 32

Cenckiewicz, S. 115
Chariots of Fire ('*Die Stunde des Siegers*') (film) 18
Chevallier Boutell, F. 78
Chiang Kai-shek 50
China 42–55; Christian missionaries 43, 44–5, 46–50, 51–4; Hundred Days' Reform 43, 54; indigenization of Western ideas 48–51; National Games 48, 50–1, 53; nationalism 48, 49–51, 53; Olympic Games 50–1; reform movements 43–4; Western physical education and sport 43–8; women and sport 46; YMCA (Young Men's Christian Association) 43, 44, 45–54
China National Amateur Athletic Federation *see* CNAAF
China National Athletic Union *see* CNAU
Christian Brothers 90, 93
Church of England 11, 92
Church of Jesus Christ of Latter-Day Saints (Mormonism), Argentina *see* CALM (*Club Atlético Los Mormones*)
Church of Sweden 26–7, 28, 29–37
Citko, M. 112
Cixi, Empress Dowager 43–4
Club Atlético Belgrano 62–3
Club Atlético Boca Juniors 60, 61, 68, 69, 70, 73
Club Atlético Lanús 76
Club Atletico Los Mormones see CALM
CMM (*Club Mejoramiento Mutuo*) ('Mutual Improvement Club') 64
CNAAF (China National Amateur Athletic Federation) 49
CNAU (China National Athletic Union) 49
communism 19, 110, 116
competitiveness: Australia and 86, 94, 98; China and 49, 50, 53, 54; Sweden and 30, 32
Confucianism 42, 46, 52
Coubertin, P. de 9, 10
Cranach, L. 12
cultural imperialism 5, 51–5
Curtius, E. 15
CYMS (Catholic Young Men's Society) 90–1

Daphne, L. 93
Daskal, R. 65
Daume, W. 19
Davis 67, 69
Davis, P. 60–1, 75, 83n75
Democratic Labor Party, Australia *see* DLP
Deutsche Jugendkraft see DJK
Deutsche Turnerschaft 17–18
Dickens, F. W. 68
Diesseitigkeit see 'Here and Now'
DJK (*Deutsche Jugendkraft*) 18, 19
DLP (Democratic Labor Party), Australia 93
DPES (Dual-Track Physical Education System) (*Shuanggui tiyu*), China 47
DSB (*Deutsche Sportbund*) (German Sports Federation) 10, 19

Dudek, J. 111
Duffek, L. T. 114

Edwards, B. 97
Eichenkreuz Clubs 18
Elias, N. 17
England 3, 11, 18, 94
Enlightenment, European 9, 11, 15, 20
Erdozain, D. 4
Etzioni, A. 10
Europe, religious pluralism 27
Evangelicalism 4, 37, 44, 45, 51, 55
Evangelischer Kirchentag ('Protestant Church-Convention') 20

FECG (Far Eastern Championship Games) 49, 53
feminization of religion 3, 28, 33–4
Finlayson, J. 100
First Sino-Japanese War 43
Florczyk, M. 112
Folk Church 30
football: Argentina 62; Australian Rules 86–102; Poland 111–17
Forrest, F. 68–9
France 3
Francis, Pope 110
Free Church movement 30
French-Belgian Catholic Action 89
Frydenberg, J 65

Garcet, P. 103n16
Gaucho Gazette (journal) 65
Gauck, J. 20
Gazeta Polska (magazine) 115
Gdańsk, L. 114
GDR (German Democratic Republic) 19–20
Georgii, T. 17
German Sports Federation *see* DSB
Germany 8–21; *Arbeitskreise Kirche und Sport* ('Workshops on church and sport') 19; Judaism 18; Mormon missionaries 63; nationalism 16, 17–18; Protestantism 8–10, 12–21; refugee policy 20; secularization 18; sports movement 14–18; *Turner* Movement 14–18, 19, 20; unification 19–20
glossolalia 36
El Gráfico (magazine) 65, 70, 73, 77
Great Britain 31
Grefberg, G. 31–2
Grupe, O. 9
GutsMuths, J. C. F. 15
gymnastics: China 44, 46, 48, 54; Europe 2; Germany 8–21; Sweden 29

Halldorf, J. 36, 37
Hellas *see* The Reverend's Lads
Hellström, A. W. 32–3
'Here and Now' (*Diesseitigkeit*) 14
Herms, E. 10, 14

Hince, K. 97
Hitler, A. 63
Hogan, M. 92, 97
Horowitz, J. 62
Huber, W. 14
hubris 14
Hundred Days' Reform, China 43, 54

The International Journal of the History of Sport 2
Internationales Deutsches Turnfest ('International German Gymnastics Festival') 20
Isakowicz-Zaleski, T. 115

Jäger, O. H. 17
Jahn, F. L. 15–16
Japan 43, 44, 51
Jarvie, G. 110, 117
Jasna Góra Shrine, Częstochowa 114, 115–16
Jesuits 13
JOC (Jeunesse Ouvrière Chrétienne) *see* YCW
John Paul II, Pope 109–10, 112, 113, 115
Judaism 17, 18, 93
Juvenal 32

kalokagathia 13, 14
Kehoe, D. 90
Killander, E. 31
Kimball, R. I. 63
Klefbeck, E. 29–30
Kossakowski, R. 114
Krawczyk, Z. 109
Kulturkampf 17
Kyrklig förnyelse ('Church Renewal') (book series) (Rosendal) 35

Ladies of the Grail *see* Women of Nazareth
Larson, R. 65–7, 76, 77–8
Leibfeindlichkeit 11–14
Leistungsfrömmigkeit 11
Leo X, Pope 11, 16
Lestrelin, L. 114
Levine, R. M. 61
Lewandowski. R. 112
Lexikon der Ethik im Sport 9, 14
Lidell, E. 18
Ling, P. H. 15, 29
Lipoński, W. 109
liquor licensing laws, Australia 92
Lisiewicz, P. 113, 115
Liu Changchun 51
Lixey, K. 110
Ljunggren, J. 29
Lombard, F. 89, 90
Luther, M. 8, 9, 11–13, 16, 17, 19–20
Lutheranism 8, 11–13, 15, 16, 27, 34
Lutz, J. G. 44n8

Magree, L. 94, 96
Makkabi clubs, Germany 18

Małecki, P. 111
Malmer, E. 32
Mangan, J. A. 61
Marshall, B. 91
martial arts, China 49
masculinity 29, 32–5, 90; *see also* 'muscular Christianity'
May Fourth Movement, China 48, 49
Maybury, B. 92–3
McCalman, J. 92
McLeod, H. 40n27
Melbourne 86–102; Sabbatarianism 87, 93–4, 96–7, 99, 101–2
El Mensajero (journal) 65–7, 68
Merkel, A. 20
Methodism 92, 95
Mieth, D. 9
Mission Covenant Church 27, 32, 36
Molony, J. 88
monasticism 11–12, 13
Moore, L. 87, 101
The Mormon Yankees 64
Mormonism (Church of Jesus Christ of Latter-Day Saints), Argentina *see* CALM (*Club Atlético Los Mormones*)
Morteo, J. L. 62
mortification of the body 13, 14
'muscular Christianity' 2–4, 11, 31–2, 37, 52, 99, 108–9

Naismith, J. 11
Napoleon Bonaparte 15
National Catholic Girls' Movement, Australia *see* NGCM
nationalism: China 48, 49–51, 53–54; Germany 16, 17–18
Nationalist Party, China 49–51
Nazism, Germany 9, 16, 18–19
NCGM (National Catholic Girls' Movement), Australia 89
New Culture Movement, China 48, 49
New Humanism 14
New Life Movement, China 50
Nöjesliv eller frälsningsfröjd ('Entertainment or the Joy of Salvation') (Pethrus) 36
Noodt, J. C. 69, 70, *72*
Norrby, S. 33–4
Novak, M. 107, 108, 111
Nya Dagligt Allehanda (newspaper) 27

Olympia, excavation of 15
Olympic Games 9–10, 19, 30, 50–1, 63, 91
Opium Wars 43

Parker, A. 1, 2, 8, 108
Paul, epistles of 13, 14, 17, 30, 32
PE (physical education) in schools 29
Pentecostalism 27, 36–7
Pethrus, L. 36

Pietism 17, 34
Pilecki, P. 116
pilgrimages, Poland 114–17
Pius XII, Pope 109
Podolski, A. 112
Poland 107–18; Catholicism 109–17; football 113–17; pilgrimages 114–17; WWII 116
Pontifical Council for the Laity 110
Poplutz, U. 14, 20
Prebish, C. 108
professionalism in sports 2, 34, 61, 67
Protestantism: Australia 87, 92–4, 97, 100; and the body 12–13, 15; Germany 8–10, 12–21; and muscular Christianity 11; and sport 3
Prussia 14–15, 17, 18, 19, 20
Puritanism 37, 95, 108

Der Querschnitt (journal) 9
Qing dynasty, China 43–4, 46, 52, 54, 55n2

Reggiani, A. H. 75
religio athletae 9
Republic of China, creation of 46
The Reverend's Lads, Sweden (later Hellas) 29–30
RGRS (Renzi-Guichou Regulation for Schooling), China 46, 48
Romanek, B. 115n43
Roosevelt, F. D., good neighbor policy 63
Roper, L. 11, 12
Rosendal, G. 35
Ross, E. A. 45–6
Rovira, R. 70
Rumbo, E. P. 62

Sabbatarianism: Australia 87, 91–102; Germany 14, 18; Sweden 26–8, 31, 32, 34–5
sacrum 109, 117
Santamaria, B. A. 102n13
Santiago (basketball team, Argentina) 77–8
Schartau, H. 34–5
Schartauanism 34–5
Schelling, F. W. J. 29
Schilling, H. 11, 13
SCOC (Sunday Christian Observance Council), Victoria 94, 95, 97
secularization 10, 18, 20, 87, 101, 108, 111
Seiffert, H. 9
Self-Strengthening Movement, China 43, 54
'September 18 Incident' 51
Söderblom, N. 30–1
softball 5, 60, 61, 62, 68–70
Spieß, A. 17
Sport for Life, Sweden 37
Sprigg, G. 97

St Kevin's College, Melbourne 90
Stadion (journal) 2
stadium choreographies 113
Stuart, J. L. 45
Sunday Christian Observance Council, Victoria *see* SCOC
Sunday Observance Act, Victoria 94, 100
Sweden 26–38; Civil Code 27; Dissenter Acts 27; Free Church movement 30; Labour movement 27, 28; masculinity 29, 32–5; Pentecostal movement 27, 36–7; physical education (PE) in schools 29; sports movement 15–18; urbanization 28; *Volksschule* 29
Swedish Social Democratic Workers Party 28
Szarek, J. 116

Tan Hua 42
Tarasiewicz, R. 111
Tebow, T. 111
temperance movement, Sweden 27
tennis 87, 94–6, 97, 100
Thornton, J. 110, 117
Tientsin, treaties of 55n2
Tjeder, D. 34
To My Kibice! (journal) 114
Tonnet, F. 103n16
Toomey, K. 90
Torres, C. R. 65
Tucker, E. 99
Turner, V. 108
Turner Movement, Germany 14–18, 19, 20
Turnfest 16, 20
Turnphilologen 17
Tusk, D. 114
TV Trwam (TV channel) 115
Tygodnik Powszechny (magazine) 115

United States: and Argentina 61, 63, 64; Evangelicalism 4; imperialism 52; 'muscular Christianity' 2, 31; Young Men's Christian Association (YMCA) 11

women and sport: Australia 89, 92; China 46, 52; Poland 110; Sweden 28, 34; USA 7n18

YCW (Young Christian Workers), Australia 86–102; ADC (Anti-Delinquency Council) 96, 97–8, 100
YMCA (Young Men's Christian Association) 4, 11, 18, 43, 44, 45–54, 68
YWCA (Young Women's Christian Association) 7n18

Zwingli, H. 13